S*the*troudwater
Navigation

S*the*troudwater Navigation

A SOCIAL HISTORY

Joan Tucker

TEMPUS

This book is dedicated to the Company of Proprietors of the Stroudwater Navigation, past, present and future.

The Company claims to be the oldest canal company in Great Britain in continuous private ownership. First set up in 1730, it has been active since 1774. Tenancy of the Navigation will be handed over to the Waterways Trust who will restore it, to take its part once more in the life of the Stroud Valleys.

Front cover: Ebley Cloth Mills, *c.*1825, by Daniel Newland Smith (1791-1839). (Courtesy of Stroud District (Cowle) Museum)

First published 2003

Tempus Publishing Ltd
The Mill, Brimscombe Port
Stroud, Gloucestershire GL5 2QG
www.tempus-publishing.com

British Library Cataloguing in Publication Data.
A catalogue record for this book is available from the British Library.

ISBN 0 7524 2806 3

Typesetting and origination by Tempus Publishing.
Printed and bound in Great Britain.

Contents

Foreword

What a name! The title of this book, so proudly defining its status, will give many something to think about.

Seen from the Junction at Saul with the Gloucester & Sharpness, it seems to be the epitome of lost canals. Falling away to secret Framilode, the slumbering shrouded lock is wrapped in reeds and tufty grass. Only a short walk remains in water above the Junction, and like so many connections and arms of navigations, it has fallen utterly into disuse.

But now the canal system resembles nothing so much as a vast form upon the land, twitching to life, recovering lost circulation to restore moribund limbs to life again. The Stroudwater Navigation is incorporated in such a scheme of regeneration and this book will lead many historians and canal enthusiasts to understand the significance of this *ultima thule* of the east–west crossing, the history of which Joan Tucker has so meticulously and devotedly brought before us.

I am honoured to be involved in this to the extent of providing a brief foreword to a book which will greatly extend recognition of the regeneration of the many parts of this great enterprise.

The Stroudwater Navigation can claim its part as a crucial link in the new life returning between two of our greatest rivers: the Severn and the Thames.

Sonia Rolt
Vice-President, Waterways Trust
October 2003

Acknowledgements

My grateful thanks for their help and encouragement are due to Isabel Armitage, Ben Ashworth, Ann Baylis, Howard Beard, British Waterways Trust, Druscilla Bruton, Jean Buchanan, Richard Chidlaw, Hugh Conway-Jones, Cotswold Canals Trust, Country Life Picture Library, Jim Dallett, David Drew (Environment Agency), Peter Ford, Gloucester Folk Museum, Gloucester City Library (Gloucestershire Collection), Philip Griffiths, Michael Handford, Dorothy Harrop, Mike Hemming, Geoffrey Hoare, Martin Hyde, Nick Jones, David McDougall, National Monuments Record, National Maritime Museum, Kerstin Paul, Allan Peacey, Peckhams of Stroud, Arthur Price, David Purcell, Hugh Read, Society of Merchant Venturers, Sonia Rolt, Stroud Library, Stroud District (Cowle) Museum, Mary Townley, William Tucker, David Viner, Brian Ward-Ellison, Ray Wilson.

Special thanks for all their patient help and consideration to the County Archivist and all his staff at Gloucestershire Record Office.

The list of references to the present book, with further information about the canal and its archive, will be placed online at a future date, with a link envisaged to the Digital Stroud site, currently in preparation for 2005 opening. In particular, there will be a brief study of circumstances of the 1954 Act which closed the canal to navigation.

Introduction

In 1779, the year the Stroudwater Navigation was opened, the American War of Independence was being fought. The French Revolution and the Napoleonic wars lay ahead: Napoleon and Wellington were both ten years old. This was the year in which Captain Cook was killed in the South Pacific. In the world of science, Joseph Priestley was working on his discovery of oxygen and Edward Jenner had begun the observations at Berkeley which led to his experiments on vaccination. In this 'Age of Enlightenment', industry was reshaping the landscape. In Gloucestershire, especially the Stroud Valleys, the woollen and clothing industry was flourishing. Sir George Onesiphorus Paul, a local clothier of Rodborough, campaigned for better prisons and in this year the Penitentiary Act was passed.

In the same year Samuel Rudder published *A New History of Gloucestershire* which gave his optimistic views on the success of the Stroudwater Navigation. He wrote that it would be forty-two feet wide and would reduce the journey from Framilode to Stroud by two and a quarter miles. Revd John Disney was born in 1799 at Flintham, Nottinghamshire. He was to become Chairman of the Stroudwater Navigation and of the Thames & Severn Canal. Paul Hawkins Fisher, born in the same year, became a Proprietor and the solicitor to the Company as well as the town's first historian with his *Notes and Recollections of Stroud* of 1871.

Coalbrookdale in Shropshire, reputed to be the 'cradle of the Industrial Revolution', is where Abraham Darby cast the parts for the world's first iron bridge raised over the Severn in 1779. Ebbw Vale in South Wales, where foundries had been set up, is also a contender for the title. The Harford family, financiers of Bristol, were partners in the Ebbw Vale Company and expanded into establishing blast furnaces,

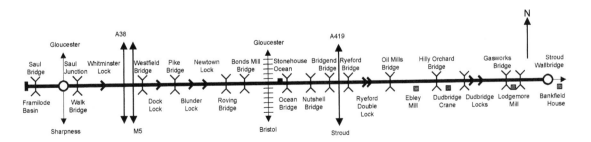

Stroudwater Navigation, from Framilode Basin to Wallbridge Basin (not to scale). (Courtesy of William Tucker, 2003)

EXPEDITIOUS WATER CONVEYANCE,
TO AND FROM
London to Glocester,
BY WAY OF ABINGDON, BRIMSCOMBE & STROUD.

GEORGE FRANKLIN'S FLY BOATS

Leave Brooks' Wharf, Thames Street, London.	DELIVER GOODS AT Swindon, Cricklade, & Cirencester	DELIVER GOODS AT Chalford, Brimscombe, Stroud, Cainscross, Ebley, & Stonehouse	ARRIVE AT GLOCESTER.
TUESDAYS	} SATURDAYS	Stroud, Cainscross, } MONDAYS	MONDAYS ...
THURSDAYS	Ditto .... TUESDAYS	Ditto	WEDNESDAYS *Wednesda*
SATURDAYS	Ditto .... THURSDAYS	Ditto	FRIDAYS ...

LEAVE GLOCESTER.	LEAVE BRIMSCOMBE.	Arrive at BROOKS' WHARF, THAMES ST. LONDON.	
...Monday. *Wednesday*	...Monday. ...Wednesday.	...Saturdays...	
...Friday Morning...	...Friday Evening...	Fridays...	

RATES FROM LONDON			To Cirencester, and Thames Head.	To Brimscombe, Stroud, and Stroud Canal.	To Glocester.
Tallows......	Fuller's Earth	Patent Bricks	35s. per Ton.	33s. per Ton.	35s. per Ton.
Raw Sugars...	Pipe Clay	Cements Plaister.	ditto	ditto	ditto
Barilla	Dye Woods, uncut.	Block Tin	ditto	ditto	ditto
Soap	Pig & Bar Iron ..	Pig & Sheet Lead.	ditto	ditto	ditto
Lead	Rags	Red & White do...	ditto	ditto	ditto
Pitch & Tar..	Deals & Timber ..	London Porter....	ditto	ditto	ditto
Woad	Pipe Staves	Oil & Vinegar....	ditto	ditto	ditto
Wool, Hops, & Tea			50s. per Ton.	60s. per Ton.	55s. per Ton.
Hemp, Flax, & Linen Drapery			45s. ditto	50s. ditto	45s. ditto
Household Furniture, 60 Cubit Feet to the Ton			35s. ditto	40s. ditto	40s. ditto
All other Articles			40s. ditto	45s. ditto	40s. ditto

RATES TO LONDON, ...		From Glocester.	From Brimscombe, Stroud, & Stroud Canal.	From Cirencester & Thames Head.
Stone		21s. per Ton.	16s. per Ton.	
Pig & Bar Iron, Gross Iron Castings,..		25s. ditto		
Tin & Tin Plates, Wire and Copper ..	Delivered	30s. ditto		
Cider, in casks		30s. ditto		
Castings	to any part	30s. ditto		
Cheese		35s. ditto	40s. per Ton.	35s. per Ton.
Cloth	of London.	35s. ditto	35s. ditto	35s. ditto
Paper & Leather......		40s. ditto	43s. ditto	40s. ditto

GOODS CONVEYED BY THESE FLY BOATS, TO ALL PLACES ON THE BANKS OF THE THAMES; ALSO EXPEDITIOUSLY FORWARDED TO OXFORD; OR AS DIRECTED TO ANY PART OF THE KINGDOM.

A tradecard of George Franklin. (Courtesy of The Waterways Trust, British Waterways Archive)

mining for iron ore and coal and quarrying limestone. A. Gray-Jones in *A History of Ebbw Vale* states, 'The year [1779] marks the beginning of the radical changes that were to transform the district and were to bring about what can truly be called its Industrial Revolution'. The same statement could be made of the Stroud Valley.

In January, four gentlemen of Stroud opened the Stroud Bank. They were Joseph Wathen, James Winchcombe, James Dallaway and John Hollings. On 21 July the same men were involved as Proprietors in the opening of the Stroudwater Navigation by the Company of Proprietors of the Stroudwater Navigation at Wallbridge, amid great rejoicing. The first share register book was opened on 8 December 1774 with an inscription and explanation that it was 'touching the raising of £20,000 divided into 200 shares. Value One Hundred pounds each.' Shareholders were Proprietors. Most of them came from the 'middling class', a phrase coined by Josiah Wedgwood. They were merchants, clothiers (some of whom were described as gentleman), lawyers, a few tradesmen and maltsters. Only one aristocrat, Lord Ducie of Tortworth and of Spring Park, Woodchester, was a Proprietor but sold his two shares before the canal opened. It is perceived that where Proprietors are recorded as living in places other than Stroud and its neighbourhood, they happen to have relations there, or were former inhabitants themselves. A little later, because of the political and economic situation, Bristol merchants and businessmen like the Harfords saw opportunities in a canal linking their city with London, other than by sea. Some of them were members of the Society of Merchant Venturers. It is also possible that some early Proprietors were Freemasons.

In his detailed book *The Stroudwater Canal* (1979), Michael Handford gives the account of the setting up of the Company and the background of it from Elizabethan times. Nine gentlemen known as 'Undertakers' obtained an Act in 1730 'for making navigable the River Stroudwater from the River Severn at or near Framilode to Wallbridge near the town of Stroud. If effected the Navigation would be of great advantage to the clothing trade and the public'. Cheaper coal was the greatest advantage. The Act stated the undertaking must be finished by June 1740. It was never started because there was too much opposition from mill-owners over the availability of water.

In the 1750s, the Dallaway family of Brimscombe revived interest in the canal and, to placate mill-owners, they proposed to build a cut and a lock round each mill. The proposal was beset by difficulties in obtaining finance and the weavers' unrest at the time. An alternative scheme, known as the 'Kemmett' scheme, was put forward. John Kemmett, who was later to be a Proprietor, planned with associates to erect cranes on platforms and to trans-ship goods in square chests at each millpond (the first container shipments!). Another Act was obtained in 1759 using powers granted under the first Act. Some constructional works were started and evidence of the straightening of the river Frome (or Stroudwater) can be seen near Eastington. However, lack of capital caused the partnership to be dissolved in 1763.

Gradually, as the economic outlook changed and mechanisation was brought into the clothing industry, cheaper coal became an absolute necessity. In 1774 a meeting was held in Stroud of those commissioners originally appointed for the 1730 Act. They agreed to begin a new cut, using powers given under that Act. Mill-owners at Framilode were incensed and sued the Company for trespass, leading to a case at Gloucester Assizes. However, they were encouraged by other mill-owners and business people to apply for a new Act. This was granted in 1776 and the Navigation was completed at an apparent cost of over £40,000. The extra money, spread over several years, was obtained by calls on shares not by further share issues.

Canal mania was not yet underway when the Stroudwater was being built. No major problems of levels or construction such as cuttings or tunnels were expected. Nor were they encountered, except for the trouble at Double Lock. The scarp edge of the Cotswolds was already broken at Stonehouse, and marls and alluvium of the valley to Stroud were easy to excavate. Puddling clay for the bed of the canal was

A useful card issued to traders on the Stroudwater and Thames & Severn Canals, early nineteenth century. (Courtesy of Gloucester Folk Museum, 2003)

used *in situ* or from the nearby river. No villages were passed through, the settlements beside the canal were all established later.

Deserted medieval villages are possibly near the canal at Whitminster and Stonehouse, because of the proximity of churches there, but no evidence has confirmed this. Signs of settlement, such as those of a Roman villa at Westend, are either on gravel banks above the river and canal, or the lower lias limestone near Eastington and Whitminster which shows as a small hill. Most of the land used for the canal was pasture or orchards.

Trade, as predicted, was largely in coal and came at first from the Midlands and Shropshire. Some trade came from South Wales in the form of coal and iron. Later, when the Forest of Dean ports were improved, coal also came from there. Previously, Gatcombe across the Severn was a chief place for export and trowmen had to be very skilful to navigate the river. Timber was brought from there and sometimes bark was used in tanning. The canal benefited trade on the Severn as it no longer had to get to Gloucester, a much longer way round. Salt, coming from Droitwich, was a most important commodity, as were chemicals mainly used in dyeing cloth. These were supplied by the firm of Samuel Skey of Bewdley who ran their own fleet of trows. Skey and his family were strong supporters of canals and owned shares in the Stroudwater and the Thames & Severn. He was also the brains behind the Gloucester & Berkeley. Gypsum was an unusual cargo, but perhaps the most poignant was the

Gatcombe. Looking across the Severn and sandbanks towards Gatcombe to the left, from Purton. Remains of a trow sunk as bank protection, 1955. (Courtesy of *Country Life* Picture Library)

Gatcombe, The Sloop inn, c.1913. It was also known as Drake's House, as Sir Francis Drake reputedly stayed here when purchasing timber for the navy. The Petheram family were salmon fishermen and also traded on the Severn: 'August 9th 1822. Giles Knight, master of trow *Nancy* landed 12 tons Forest perrin [bark] and 10cwts. timber from Gatcombe at Wallbridge.'

shipments of guns up the canal in first decade of the 1800s, presumably on their way to London during the Napoleonic Wars.

During its long and continued existence the Company has managed to withstand difficulties and to cope with competition from other canals, railways and roads, although turnpikes were an asset at the time. It was fortunate that the Company always had sound and dedicated management, often a family affair, like the Grazebrooks, Hawkers and, at the end, the Snapes. Proprietors were loyal and passed shares down through families, like the Clutterbucks, who bought shares at the beginning and kept them throughout the Company's existence as a trading organisation. There is little evidence of speculation on shares, which reached their peak value of about £550 in the 1830s and 1840s.

By the time of the Second World War it became obvious that the Navigation was not viable and Gloucestershire County Council (GCC) were very concerned about the state of the bridges, Walk Bridge and Bridgend in particular. A county survey of them was made in 1949 and led to the possibility of the Council taking them over, which could only be done if an Act of Abandonment for Navigation was obtained. The British Transport Commission, then owners of the Gloucester & Sharpness Canal, needed to safeguard their water supply at Whitminster. The solution grew like Topsy and the Act was passed in 1954. It seems a miracle the Company was allowed to continue, especially as opposers of the Act were disparaging of it. The opposers

Share No.119. One of two bought in 1774 by Edmund Clutterbuck of Hyde House, Chalford. It remained in the family until the death in 1924 of Madeline Charlotte Clutterbuck, widow of Edmund Henry Clutterbuck of Hardenhuish Park, near Chippenham. She and her brother Charles Fitzgerald Raikes were the children of Revd Charles Hall Raikes, vicar of Chittoe, Wiltshire. Both shares were sold in 1954 for £1.

themselves wanted to set up a trust to preserve the canal but were too late in starting activities, only giving themselves a few months to work on it.

Sir Robert Perkins MP became the majority shareholder and set up a trust to administer those shares 'for the benefit of the people of Stroud'. The Trustees and the Board of Directors and other shareholders are working towards restoration of the canal from the Junction to Wallbridge, inspired to do so by the Cotswold Canals Trust, which began in 1972 as the Stroudwater Canal Society. The Cotswold Canals Trust has done much maintenance and restoration work and raised a lot of money during the last thirty years. It now has over 4,000 members. At last the work is to be rewarded because the Company is to sign a 999-year lease with the Waterways Trust, which will re-open the canal in the next five years.

The reasons that originally led to the opening of the canal are relevant to today's reasons for re-opening this and the Thames & Severn Canal to create the 'Cotswold Canals'. They will change the pattern of the landscape again, this time adding a historical perspective. The quiet sanctuary for wildlife, otherwise in danger of being lost, will be maintained. There will be amenity for leisure activities and new commercial interests will present themselves. Brought back to life, the canals will again regenerate the areas they serve.

1

The Canal at Present
– A Perambulation

The Stroudwater Navigation in Gloucestershire in the summer of 2003 is discernible throughout its eight-mile length, apart from the short stretch between the main A38 road, marked Roman Road on the 1:25,000 scale Ordnance Survey map, and Junction 13 on the M5 motorway. Here the canal bed has been taken for the approach road. Walking on the towpath is convenient and easy and, as the canal follows the A419 quite closely all the way to Stroud, parking is not difficult. Although there are as yet few official footpath signs, the towpath is a dedicated right of way for pedestrians for most of its length. In the Stonehouse-Eastington area there is a purpose-built cycle track close to the canal.

Many stretches of the canal are in water but, until it is fully restored, the towpath provides the best access to a beautiful and historic waterway. Most of the original features still exist, as do the mills close by, which were the reason for the canal being built. Many country houses and parks border the canal and it is possible to walk the whole length by crossing only two main roads and two minor ones. A subway serves a public footpath under the motorway.

Starting just east of the church at Upper Framilode (SO755104) at the former swing bridge, the basin and lock out to the river Severn are on the left behind a hedge. The basin is filled in, now a garden for Lock House, a Grade II-listed building. It has a large lean-to on the right, probably an office, converted to a post office in the twentieth century. Behind it is the former warehouse, with outside stairs, kept as a feature when converted to a modern house. Beyond is the river lock with the walls built of large coursed limestone blocks and curved to the position of the former lock gates. It is an early example of such a river lock and is also listed. However, this little area is kept very private and is open to the public only on special occasions, such as the annual Heritage Weekend in September.

Eastwards from Framilode Bridge, the towpath is on the north side of the canal and passes behind some early nineteenth-century cottages, built of local bricks, called Canal Row. Despite the name, they were not connected with the canal company but were built by the Purnell family, who owned the tin mills nearby. There were fourteen of them originally, with long, large gardens facing the road, but in recent times some have been joined together to make desirable homes in this quiet backwater. Some of the residents paid 25s a year to the canal company for the privilege of having a window looking onto the canal. According to local memory, the sets of steps down to the canal from the towpath were for residents to draw water; however, no documentary evidence has been found to confirm this. Further on towards Moor Street, the larger detached houses, including The Ship inn, were also owned by the Purnells, as shown on the 1841 Inclosure Map and Awards for Fretherne with Saul. Dotted about the village are some substantial brick sheds which probably housed the horses, donkeys or mules, the motive power for the vessels.

Framilode Parish Council own the canal and towpath almost as far as Saul Junction. It becomes de-watered because of flood relief about 100 yards beyond Saul Bridge (Moor Street). The path follows the line of an embankment with the river Frome in a deep ditch on the left and the filled-in canal on the right. On the offside (opposite the towpath side) are some cottages which used to be The Junction inn, known locally as 'The Drum & Monkey'.

Junction Lock, just before the wide Gloucester & Sharpness Canal is reached, is listed Grade II because of its design, unusual for this area. Although it served the Stroudwater Navigation, it was actually built by the Gloucester Canal when they made the unique level crossing in 1826. British Waterways own Junction Lock, Saul Junction and the

Frank Cookley ran a coal merchant's business from Ash Villa near Saul Bridge, obtaining supplies from Cannock. He was also a sculptor and carver in around 1910. (Courtesy of M.A. Handford and Waterway Images Library)

Saul Junction, showing part of R.W. Davis' boatyard, and the swing bridge to it from Junction House, 31 August 2003.

half-mile stretch of the Stroudwater that leads to Walk Bridge and on to the other side of Whitminster Lock. They recently restored Junction Lock. They also own the dry dock which joins the two canals across the corner on the south side. A boat-building business has been at this spot for many years and still bears the name of R.W. Davis & Son, the former owner. The white Junction House, with its little office at the side, is the focus of this working/leisure conglomeration. Stroudwater Arm, as the short stretch is called, provides good moorings for boats as far as Walk Bridge but no further because the bridge is flattened, with about eighteen inches headroom.

Looking from the towpath across the meadow on the north side is Whitminster House, listed Grade II★, which plays a significant part in the history of the Stroudwater Navigation. The Victorian frontage belies its great antiquity, for a house has been on this site in continuous occupation since Saxon times to the present day. It is an interesting example of how a house has developed throughout the centuries, acquiring features and yet somehow avoiding 'restorers'. Richard Owen Cambridge, the minor poet who lived there in the eighteenth century, described St Andrew's Church behind the house thus: 'A loftie Tower rears its tremendous height'. Both the church and the house are open by appointment. The churchyard has a number of listed tombstones.

At Walk Bridge the towpath ends in a stile. There is no right of way along the towpath until Whitminster Bridge is reached. Instead, the road is followed to the left for about 100 yards to the footpath sign which directs the pedestrian across a

Whitminster House and Church. A barge is bow-hauled on the navigable river Frome. This engraving was published for C.O. Cambridge's edition of his father's works, *Miscellaneous Verses written at Whitminster from 1742-1750.*

low-lying field to the bridge and lock. Behind a hedge to the left is an interesting area with weir and settlement ponds. The water is taken from the Frome and culverted into the canal for supply to the Gloucester & Sharpness Canal at the Junction. This cannot be seen (or understood) too easily but actually it becomes one of the main supplies of water to the Bristol Water Company who have a large processing plant at Purton.

After crossing the farm bridge and its adjacent lock, the path is not the towpath, but a footpath leading to Fromebridge Mill. The canal, which now incorporates the river, is slightly higher, on the left. At Lockham Bridge, where the river separates again to follow its own course, a footpath from Frampton to Whitminster village uses the original towpath as far as Stonepitts Bridge, now a concrete plank structure, giving access to fields. Straight on, the towpath itself can be followed easily (except after heavy rain) to Bristol Road. For most of the way the towpath is on an embankment and not separated from the fields to the south by a hedge or fence. This stretch, owned by the Company of Proprietors, together with the eight-foot-wide towpath, is very tranquil and beautiful, especially when an original Company brick bridge called Occupation Bridge is reached. Fishing rights are let out to a local club, who also keep the canal reed-free when possible. Sometimes the Company has it cleared professionally.

From the towpath it is easy to see that Bristol Road Wharf was an important place, being next to the main road between Bristol and Gloucester. Originally, the wharf used the banks on both sides of the canal and the Company still owns the land on the south bank and, of course, what was the bed of the canal in front of the bridge. The wharf house and cottage opposite were sold for private houses in the 1950s. Although they have been renovated and extended, they can still be identified as canal structures. A wooden gate must be climbed with care to reach the main road. There is no sign whatsoever now of the canal which ran almost straight across the middle of the large roundabout.

In order to proceed further, it is necessary to consult the walking map to choose the most suitable of four possible routes: the river Frome; the busy new road; a footpath leading from the main road a little way up the hill to the left which crosses fields; Grove Lane which goes off to the right from the crossroads at the top of the hill. To join up with the canal again, aim for Westfield Bridge at Chippenham Platt, Eastington. The bridge itself stands forlornly in a field and carries a very old track which runs from Eastington Church to its outlying hamlets. There are groove marks on the edges of the bridge arch, cut by vessels making the difficult manoeuvre into the lock immediately to the east, being almost a part of the bridge. It is just a dried-up depression in the ground now, with a few bits of masonry scattered about. When the canal and surrounding land was acquired by the Ministry of Transport and drained to build the motorway, surplus land was sold off by them to neighbouring farmers. For some unknown reason the Company, although not owning the land, was still made responsible for the bed, which can be detected west of Westfield Bridge.

Whitminster Weir, looking north in 1948. The draw-off from the Frome (via Stroudwater Navigation) for the Gloucester & Sharpness Canal, showing outlet tanks. (Courtesy of Gloucestershire Record Office)

Westfield Bridge, 31 August 2003. Coping stones mark the site of Westfield Lock, showing signs of wear from tow-ropes.

Chippenham Platt, looking west in 1948, showing the overflow weir and drop-well outlet. (Courtesy of Gloucestershire Record Office)

Continuing east, the canal is in water and remains so until Ryeford. On the right a complicated weir, recently excavated and repaired by the Cotswold Canals Trust, takes the Oldbury Brook from the north, under the canal into a deep ditch and on to Meadow Mill. Across the canal to the left the large building with grounds sloping down to the water is William Morris House. It was built in 1835 as the workhouse for the Wheatenhurst Union. This is now a sheltered home and workshops for young people with special needs, run on Rudolf Steiner principles and not usually open to visitors.

The area known as Chippenham Platt forms a sort of island, with the canal on the south side. The Oldbury Brook curls around it on the north and it was here that the Company's maintenance yard was situated. Dock Lock in front of it is sometimes known as Court Orchard. Various working buildings can still be seen, although some have been demolished. The Cook family purchased the land from the Company in 1957 and run a smallholding. When the lock was restored in about 1998 under the auspices of the Cotswold Canals Trust, the dry dock was re-discovered with a rudder

Chippenham Platt, looking east, 31 August 2003. The restored spill weir taking water from Oldbury Brook and the canal.

propped up against the wall. This is understood to be now in the care of the National Waterways Museum at Gloucester. New safety ladders were replaced in the lock by the Company in 2003.

Still on the offside, the elegant white rendered house, formerly known as Dock House but now called The Leas, was that of the Resident Engineer. It has not been used by the Company since the nineteenth century, when it was let out and then sold for private occupation. In the 1960s it was a quiet guest house. Being close to the canal bank at the front, some strengthening of the bank was necessary a few years ago and this work was undertaken by the Company. Eastington Wharf occupied the strip of land at the corner leading up to Pike Bridge. On the other side is the start of Grove Lane leading back to Whitminster past the old workhouse. Wharf House was a simple four-roomed cottage, with lean-to, but has now been extended and the former wharf is a landscaped garden. It remained in use as a coal wharf in recent times, long after the canal had closed for navigation.

The towpath climbs a little slope to meet the Eastington Road at Pike Bridge. On the right is a small area where a row of cottages has been demolished. It then became a County Highways Depot and is now occupied by the Cotswold Canals Trust for

Chippenham Platt, 31 August 2003. Dock Lock, showing the top of a new safety ladder; The Leas is in the background.

storage of materials. Pike Bridge, so named because there had been a toll-house on its eastern flank, is at least the third structure to stand at this road junction. When GCC took over the bridge in 1954 it needed widening and its general condition was causing concern. Here the towpath switches to the north side over the bridge. The former lock-keeper's house was built in the 1880s but the present owner has added two extensions. There is a spill-weir running from the top of Pike Lock, under the towpath, the garden, the house and the bridge, and back out to the canal at the corner of the garden to the wharf.

Pike Lock, or Eastington Lock, is usually full of water and a close eye is kept on it in case too much water comes down. (The Stroudwater has never had any problem with shortage of water.) On the other side of Pike House garden is the former roadway of the A419, the Stroud–Eastington Road, before a new alignment was made to connect with the slip road to the motorway. This lay-by now serves as a convenient parking place and gives access to the picnic area which is the main focus for the Cotswold Canals Trust, the place where they first made an impact because, being so close to the road, the public could see what was going on as they drove past. From here the Trust run boat trips in summer months, going eastwards through Blunder Lock and Newtown Lock as far as Bond's Mill Bridge. In December Santa Claus travels on the boat at weekends, distributing presents. Private boats can be launched from a slipway provided by the Company and constructed by the Trust. In mid-September each year the Trust has an open day. The cycle trail can be followed from here, alongside, but is not part of the towpath.

Newtown Lock is a short distance upstream where another stretch of the old road provides a lay-by. There is a culvert with a complicated arrangement to take water from the top of the lock and round to outside the bottom gates. Although the brickwork has been restored, it is not operational now. The pound between the two locks is very pretty, being bordered on the north by an unfenced embankment and on the south by a narrow tree-lined strip of land forming the boundary of Eastington Park Farm. The Park itself is a listed classical Georgian house built slightly later than the canal. Its outstanding feature is a curved cantilevered staircase. Today the house is a private nursing home. Newtown Bridge gives access to the East Lodge of the park and a former drive to the house. It is also known as Roving Bridge because this is where the towpath crosses back to the south side of the canal and continues towards Bond's Mill Bridge.

Tradition states that the canalside hamlet of Newtown was built for the canal 'navvies' and that they first encamped in the nearby field. It certainly has the characteristics of such a development and was built around the same time as the canal. The size and southerly aspect of the cottages and the decorative dentils under the eaves are very similar to those at Upper Framilode. Researches have not uncovered any substantiation of Company involvement in these so far. In fact the Company was always parsimonious about ancillary buildings and tried their utmost to avoid spending money when someone else would do it.

After crossing Newtown Bridge the field on the offside presents a rural idyll and has been saved because it had a covenant on it. But this area on the outskirts of

The south front of Eastington Park, 1999. A former owner bought water extracted from Newtown Lock for supplying garden fountains.

Stonehouse is ideal for industrial development, having easy access to the motorway, and the covenant has been lifted by Stonehouse Parish Council. National awareness of the environmental and leisure elements of canals means that planning applications are now scrutinised carefully in case of detriment to the waterway corridor.

Bond's Mill Industrial Estate is shortly to the right, a large complex of buildings, some very new. The site has always been a prosperous one since the woollen mill was first established there in the seventeenth century. Its association with the canal company began when Thomas Bond became one of the nine undertakers of the first Navigation Act in 1730. The unique two-storey pill box beside the bridge has had windows put in to make it into an office. Close by it the seat looking over the canal and the countryside beyond was placed by the Company in memory of Miss Gwen Hooper, who served on the Board for many years, following in the footsteps of several generations of her family.

The bridge across the canal is the only access to the industrial estate and its upkeep causes much concern. The current structure is reputedly the first so-called plastic bridge in the world, being a prototype built by Maunsell Engineering, which approached the Cotswold Canals Trust with a package offer. The decking is made of lightweight GRP (glass-reinforced polymers), which is easy to lift and very durable close to water. Five tonnes of GRP will carry a forty-tonne lorry. A thousand spectators witnessed the opening of the bridge in July 1994. The historic abutments are still in place.

Beside the entrance to the industrial estate the towpath continues through a white gate and runs beside the canal on a high embankment which slopes down to the river below. This is perhaps the most vulnerable length of the canal and has to be watched for subsidence of the bank. A breach did occur about twenty years ago in the 1980s. On the opposite bank a depression indicates a place for cattle to drink. In the middle of the canal are remains of a dam. Messrs Hoffmans used to purchase cooling water from the Company for use in their ball-bearing factory. They no longer need it but instead pay the Company to allow them to discharge storm water into the canal via the concrete culvert.

Just before the railway bridge which carries the main line from Bristol to Gloucester is an area of scrubland divided in two by a fence and running steeply downhill. The piece furthest from the railway is owned by the Company, who used it as a mud-tip and may do so again, under licence, if access can be negotiated. In some ways mud clearance by a man with a horse and cart was easier than it is today by mechanical diggers.

British Rail replaced their railway bridge over the canal and the one over the road to the north in the 1960s, taking two weekends to complete the work. Armco concrete tubes – one for the canal, the other for the public footpath – are beneath the new bridge. Engineers suspect that the abutments to the bridge are still in place and it was merely filled in with rubble, especially as it took so little time to erect the new bridge. Investigations will soon take place.

On emerging from the darkness of the Armco tunnel, the towpath comes into the light at the Ocean. The origin of this beautiful stretch of water is obscure but it was probably one of three fishponds which served the ancient manor of Stonehouse at Stonehouse Court, now an hotel next to the church. The other two ponds were to the north. One has been filled in as part of a housing development but the presence of greater crested newts, a protected species, meant that the other remained, although in a diminished state. When the Company bought land for the Navigation it acquired the Ocean and still owns it, except for the estate farm, the buildings of which were converted in the mid-1980s into Court Farm Mews. This prestigious complex includes two former coachhouses, stables, cartshed, barn and farmhouse, all of them listed Grade II. The barn conversion was offered for sale in December 1999 for £225,000. Some of the twenty-nine willow trees which the Company planted in 1884 to mark its boundary are still growing. Tixall Wide, part of the Staffordshire & Worcestershire Canal (North), is also an open expanse of water with the canal going through it, but does not have the trees and tranquillity of Stonehouse Ocean. This tranquillity is only spoilt when the trains pass close by.

Plans are afoot to restore Ocean Bridge to make it swing again, which should be simple because the Company reserved the land on the offside for it to do so. Unfortunately, there were objections from residents because the bridge is not a right of way, although it can be used for pedestrians. The space for swinging has been used as a garden but it should be possible to find another solution when necessary. Natives of Stonehouse have been using the towpath and other paths for a circular Sunday walk for at least 100 years if not longer. They use the path which goes across the bridge, then runs alongside the wall of Stonehouse Court, through the churchyard with its fine pedestal tombs, twelve of which are listed Grade II*, and back onto Church Lane.

Stonehouse Court has associations with the Company, inasmuch as some of the Proprietors have lived there. The upstairs windows at the back have a clear view across the canal to the fields and hills towards the south. Most notably it was the venue for the meeting in July 2001 when the Waterways Trust announced plans to restore and re-open the Stroudwater and Thames & Severn Canals, and public bodies, the Company, Cotswold Canals Trust and private individuals pledged their support. It was a lovely day, in a perfect suitable setting and the atmosphere was so positive. The progress made as a result will be seen further on in this perambulation.

Back on the towpath, going east, St Cyr's Church, Stonehouse is on the offside. It still has a fourteenth-century tower but the rest of the church was rebuilt in Victorian times. Nevertheless, it forms the background to some lovely views of the canal, making it an ideal spot for calendar-makers. The bridge, Nutshell House and the cottage are listed Grade II, both as a group and individually. The bridge was restored with the help of English Heritage, who advised on the brickwork, but it needs attention again. After some years of neglect the house has been bought by a profes-sional carpenter who has known and loved the property since he was a boy, when he had riding lessons in the garden. With patience and a lot of hard work he is restoring the place to its former glory. When the cottage was offered for sale in October 1999 for £225,000 it was described as 'benefiting from an enviable location bordering a canal'. Canalside locations demand a premium now. The towpath passes under the bridge, but to cross the bridge the walker must take a public footpath which skirts three sides of the garden of Nutshell House. Vehicles must not traverse the bridge.

It is a short walk to the next bridge at Bridgend. On the right is a housing devel-opment and some industrial premises, whilst on the offside is the cemetery, with a new housing estate next to it. The principal road is Boakes Drive, named after a well-known local family. The late David Boakes was the full-time manager of the Canals Trust and it was he who instigated much of the restoration work which has been achieved, by organising volunteer groups, particularly the Manpower Services Commission before it was disbanded. Stonehouse Wharf was situated on the north bank, originally a canal wharf, but altered to have joint use by the Stonehouse & Nailsworth Railway. Eventually, the site was occupied by Hobbs Bros. who distributed oil. For many years the land was declared contaminated but is now cleared and houses are being built. The road junction on the main road has been enlarged and traffic lights installed. Perhaps the railway boundary wall, built of engineering bricks and separating the new devel-opment from the improved road, could be retained. As part of this regeneration GCC have rebuilt Bridgend Bridge which carries the Stonehouse–Stanley Downton Road across the canal, giving clearance for navigation and showing their commitment to canal restoration. The Ship inn which stood at the crossroads was demolished and discussions are ongoing about what should take its place.

After a few yards the bridge into Upper Mills is reached. Formerly a swing bridge, it is now fixed, with a concrete roadway, and is sometimes called Brush Works

Bridge, from when Messrs Vowles were the owners of the complex, which can be seen through the pillared gateway. The main building, with a tower dated 1875, is listed. On the offside is a gem of a boathouse belonging to Wycliffe College whose campus is across the road. It was erected early in the twentieth century. When the Stroudwater became impracticable for boating, activities were switched to a modern boathouse at Saul Junction. Then the old wooden boathouse became the Scout Hut. The Public School plans to use the narrow strip of land between the canal and former railway line as sports facilities. Hopefully, the scheme will incorporate the boathouse. It is worth preserving as a visible reminder of how the canal served the local community in a non-commercial way.

The railway bridge which carried the Nailsworth branch of the Midland Railway from Stonehouse crosses the canal on a skew and was adapted to take the first dedicated cycle track to be made in the Stroud Valleys. Fortunately, the bridge was kept intact when major roadworks took place to bring the new Ebley bypass to meet the A419 at the Horsetrough roundabout. The new concrete bridge across the canal is called Haywards Bridge and allows plenty of room for navigation, after prolonged negotiations involving the Cotswold Canals Trust and the Company in the planning stages. A row of cottages with their fronts to the towpath and backs to the river (the Frome bifurcates a little further to the east at Ryeford Bridge, so this part is actually a mill leat) appear to be linked to the canal and have interesting loading holes, possibly for coal deliveries. However, the cottages were owned by the Marling family and associated with Stanley Mill a short distance away. The nice stone gateposts may have come from the Marling quarry.

Apart from the noise of traffic from the old road on the north side and the Ebley bypass on the south, this part of the canal is peaceful and has always been in water, thus it gives a good indication of how the 'cut' enhanced rather than disturbed the natural beauty of the Stroud Valley. Soon this beauty will be restored along the whole length. Before Ryeford Bridge, on the offside, is a group of houses including Tankard House, which has a renowned garden and used to be The Anchor inn. This is where the Company's Ryeford Wharf was situated. The field just to the west of it, with an inlet into the canal, was the site of a boat-building and repair yard. Opposite, on the towpath side, is the large coal pen built for Messrs Marling to serve Stanley Mill which has deservedly been scheduled Grade II recently for its fine stonework and importance in the commercial aspect of the canals. No other canal coal pens of this quality are still in existence.

Ryeford Bridge used to carry the Stonehouse to King's Stanley Road over the canal but the road became a dead end when the bypass was made. It is worth peering over the parapet to see where the river emerges from under Spring Cottages, under the road, and then separates into two channels, with the canal a few yards to the right. The Cotswold Way long-distance footpath, which crosses the valley between Selsley Common and Randwick Woods, uses this listed bridge.

Through the bridge the canal is wider and has stone copings with iron mooring rings. This was the private wharf of one of the biggest traders on the canal, Messrs Ford Bros. of Ryeford Mill, who had their own fleet of trows and barges to carry

Above: One of several mooring rings at Ryeford Mill Wharf, 31 August 2003.

Left: Ryeford Sluices: the water level must not rise higher than the course of end-on bricks.

corn to and flour from their mill. Now a big brick wall separates the mill premises from the canal. Ryeford railway station and wharf were on the other side of their site. There is a door marked 'Stroudwater Navigation' in the brick wall. One of the main functions of the Company is to supply water to lower reaches of the canal by means of manual sluices which are behind this door. Regulating the flow between the canal and the river, and vice versa, is a difficult operation which requires patience, vigilance and foresight not easy to achieve. It can also be dangerous and the Company is grateful for the honorary services of Martin Hyde, the current resident of Double Lock Cottage. One day the process should be automated.

The white iron footbridge leads to a little close-knit hamlet of miscellaneous cottages, none of which appear to be canal-related. They were part of the Ford Bros. establishment and some, being a strange shape, were probably warehouses. Repair and restoration of the bridge was one of the first major projects undertaken by the Cotswold Canals Trust and did much to make the public aware of the advantages of re-opening the canal. The footpath over the bridge and across the car park of the garden centre is not a right of way.

Proceeding to the east, the towpath occupies a narrow strip of land between the canal and the mill leat for Ryeford Mills. The culverts which are controlled by the sluices run underneath the path at one point. About 300 yards further on the towpath opens out where the Double Lock and Lock Cottage are situated. As the crow flies, it is fairly close to the road and the bypass, and not too far from houses and work-places, but it seems a remote spot because the only access is by towpath, to right and left. Both lock and cottage are listed buildings.

Above and right: Paddle gear at
Double Lock, 3 September 2003.

Although not rare, double locks, where two locks share the middle gate, are unusual. There is another one on the Grand Union where the son of the owner of Ryeford Lock Cottage lives. Serious problems have sometimes occurred at Double Lock involving the north wall. Soon after the lock first became operational, the wall was bulging and the lock rebuilt at the builder's expense. From time to time after that water would build up behind the wall, which had a double skin, and the canal closed while repairs took place. The drainage holes incorporated at the top end of the wall were to relieve the pressure. The final straw came one Christmas in the 1980s when the water main in the main road burst and the huge amount of water cascading down the hillside demolished most of the wall. Of course it had to be rebuilt, being a listed building. No grants were obtained. Compensation was claimed with Severn Trent but the sum agreed was not enough to cover the eventual expenditure. The Company had to realise most of its assets and became almost bankrupt. The lock is not yet back in water because the south wall needs attention. Some of the paddle gear is still in place.

Lock Cottage is a perfect example of vernacular canal building, erected by a local builder in brick. It has been altered very little since it was first built in the first decade of the canal, except for modernisation – water, electricity and telephone. Gas was also laid on; the gas main travels under the towpath outside the front gate. Posted on the wall was a notice board with instructions to barge owners on how to operate the lock and, now that the precise wording has been discovered, the board may be re-instated. Martin Hyde is often in his lovely garden going down to the river at the back and will chat to interested visitors about the canal.

Holly Tree House. The spill weir is in the course of restoration by the owner of the property; the towpath is behind the fence.

Ebley Saw Mills opposite Holly Tree House, as seen from Oil Mills Bridge, *c.*1930. Messrs T. Mortimer were the proprietors in the early twentieth century, supplying timber in planks, boards or scantlings. Messrs Hooper have owned the premises since 1927.

In 1972-73 Stroud Urban District Council filled in the bed of the canal from just past Ryeford Double Lock to provide a roadway to the council tip in a field on the right. Fortunately, the tip was short-lived, being so close to houses, but the canal remains dry. The towpath still exists as a right of way but becomes rather overgrown. A weir taking water from a brook which is under the canal bed then via a brick culvert down to the river Frome can be seen over the garden hedge of Holly Tree House. It has recently been restored by the owner of the house. In the eighteenth century it was fashionable for gentlemen to build their house facing the canal. Although in this case the house (listed) does present a frontage, the more elaborate front is to the south, now facing a car park provided for the owners of flats.

On the offside, almost opposite Holly Tree House, the complex known as Ebley Saw Mills includes an early warehouse. Further along that side up to the bridge was a small wharf owned by the Company which still owns the derelict land at the point where the made-up roadway reaches the road over the bridge to Oil Mills. Here were some cottages, demolished not very long ago, including The Bell inn. Actually, it is understood that the bridge structure itself is still extant beneath the rubble with which the bridge-hole was filled. The crown was demolished and the surface flattened one weekend in 1973.

The Oil Mill at Ebley has acquired the more interesting name of The Snow Mill in the last few months. It produces artificial snow for use all over the world, mainly by the film industry. Bridge House, whose garden abuts Bridge Lane on the west and the towpath on the north, is a listed property which at one time was part of the Oil Mills Estate, together with Holly Tree House. It also has a classical Georgian frontage to the canal, although the back has fragments from the sixteenth century, suggesting that the owners took advantage of the prestigious location and turned the house around when the canal was built in 1779. The central doorway of rusticated pilasters and elaborate fanlight is an important feature. In the garden is another weir similar to Holly Tree but slightly later and not constructed by the canal company.

From here the canal is in water again after many years, a most encouraging sight! GCC bought the bed from the canal company when it was needed for the Ebley bypass. Eventually, another route was chosen, being further away from residential development and the site of the canal and towpath was sold back to the Company for £1 in 1984. The developer, Stroudwater Redevelopment Partnership Ltd, bought up a large area of land in the vicinity of Ebley Mill to build houses on the former football pitch in the field between the part of Ebley Mills which had become Greenaways Printing Works and Bridge House. Together with the Company, a 106 Planning Agreement was set up before planning permission was obtained. This required the developer to dig out the canal, restore the puddling clay where needed, especially where trees growing in the banks had damaged it, provide a new road bridge over the canal, more or less where an original swing bridge once existed, and

The front door of Bridge House, Ebley, 1996.

The canal being dug out for restoration at Ebley Mill, 31 August 2003.

tidy up the area generally. This is now happening, before the houses are built, because the restored canal will be an added incentive to buy a house, as in the eighteenth century. Work started in Spring 2003 at the Bridge House end and continued through a very wet season and undeterred by a JCB being stuck in the mud for five days.

Ebley House, seen across parkland on the offside, has a long association with the canal through its various owners dating from before it was rebuilt in Victorian times. Now bought by the developer, it was previously owned by the National Children's Home Organisation, who had treated the house most carefully during their occupation by protecting the unique decorative features, wainscots, ceilings and fireplaces with guardwork. The owner has just finished converting the house into prestigious office suites. The gardens surrounding the house, with a couple of fine cedar trees and an orangery, are to be retained, but the rest of the park running down to the canal will be a housing development by Persimmon Homes. A walkway will border the canal on the north of it. Stroudwater Partnership would also like to install a footbridge designed along the same lines as the original swing bridge.

Ebley Mill, formerly a cloth mill owned by the Marling family, was converted into offices by Stroud District Council in 1989, for which they received design awards. The first mill complex, on the north side of the canal, was demolished about 1820 and replaced by a block of four storeys and attics parallel to the canal. This is the one usually referred to as Greenaways, for which the developer has found a tenant who will turn it into a fitness centre. The main building is of five storeys and a tower, which replicates the tower of Selsley Church on the hill above. The Marling family paid for that too. Stroud District Council currently rent a strip of the filled-in canal from the Company as a visitor car park. That arrangement will cease when stage three of the Stroudwater redevelopment is ready to begin: digging out the canal in front of the buildings. In the area at the end where it opens out, the canal is already starting to fill with water, fed naturally from brooks.

Close beside the canal runs the river Frome which has been taking diverted canal water as well since 1956 when the Company allowed the Severn River Board to use the bed of the canal for a flood-prevention scheme. The Board were to erect fixed weirs at Ebley Mill and at the two locks at Dudbridge. The canal was then deemed 'main river' and so continues in water until the junction with the Thames & Severn at Wallbridge, although in a much narrower channel. The engineer was Fred Rowbotham, who later became Honorary Engineer to the canal company when he retired. The weir against the eastern wall of Ebley Mill is very impressive. There have been discussions about utilising the water to generate electricity by turbines to help supply the mill.

The downstream east side at Ebley Mill, with the weir taking river Frome and canal water. (Photograph by F.W. Rowbotham, 26 October 1956: courtesy of the Environment Agency)

Walkers can now follow the towpath's original course beside the canal on its south side. For several years the best way was across a grassy area known as Frome Gardens, from the name of the private estate at the bottom of the hillside. However, the dugout canal prevents this now. Stroud District Council owned the greensward but asked the Company to pay for the mowing of what was the canal, although filled in, and now almost indistinguishable from the rest of the land. That was in 2002; a year later we have nearly got the canal back! A small footbridge has been constructed where the canal is diverted to the river, then the towpath proceeds to Hilly Orchard.

There is no proper bridge over the canal at Hilly Orchard at the moment, as a result of the development being built on the north side between Westward Road (A419) and the canal. The previous bridge, which was low level and constructed of concrete slabs, has been removed and is to be reinstated at high level by the developers. If possible, they will use the previous bridge structure which was like a railway footbridge and was stored by the Company on the waste ground now owned by the developer, Chelbury Homes. There are problems protecting the bank and the width of the canal on that side but they can be solved. The bridge has always been important to the local community as it carries an old track leading across the valley from Randwick Hill to Selsley Common. Mill workers used these old tracks to get to work in the valley bottoms before the turnpikes were put in.

New developments are also taking place on either side of that track and will hopefully be sympathetic to the canal. Throughout its length the Stroudwater Navigation forms part of a Linear Heritage Conservation Area and this designation requires Stroud District Council to vet planning applications most carefully so that they do not cause detractions, not only to the canal but to the historic mills, the so-called 'string of pearls'. All applications which affect the canal in any way should by law be submitted to the Company and the Cotswold Canals Trust for comment.

On the latest Ordnance Survey map, Explorer 179, there is no path marked between Hilly Orchard and Dudbridge because no official towpath existed. This was because practically the whole stretch was Dudbridge Wharf, a very busy and important one, and security was essential. There were doors blocking the path at both ends. It is possible that vessels travelling to Wallbridge and not needing to stop at Dudbridge were required to cross over to the offside at Hilly Orchard (originally a swing bridge) and back again when they got to the bridge at Dudbridge. The space on that side between the canal and the boundary was wide and, until recently, the boundary was marked clearly with a mound and hedge. However, there is a path which serves as a towpath on the south side at present. It was cleared by Bruce Hall, Chairman of the Cotswold Canals Trust and some friends as a personal project, and metalled by GCC. The path is actually made in part of the canal bed, with the edge of the wharf discernible above.

Behind a fence on the right is a late eighteenth-century ashlar-faced listed house, Gladfield Gardens. Thomas Grazebrook, a member of the family who largely put the canal on its feet in the early days, built it for himself. The house, now divided into three, backs on to the wharf, the main part of which is owned by Messrs H. Wiggall & Son, Hauliers, who use it as a depot. At least one of the Company's wharf buildings

Dudbridge Wharf, 31 August 2003. The canal warehouse at the back of Gladfield Gardens, as seen from the towpath. The upper loading bay has been converted to a window.

Dudbridge Wharf, 31 August 2003. The crane rises above the towpath.

Dudbridge Bridge, 31 August 2003. The dressed stones were part of the Lower Lock.

is still extant, but the *pièce de résistance* is the crane. Gloucestershire Society for Industrial Archaeology (GSIA) did some research on the history of this canal crane and subsequently did some remedial work. Since then, Wiggall's have restored it to working order but it cannot swing properly until a special enclosure can be provided and some of the concrete block wall removed. Very few canal cranes of this simple construction remain *in situ*. The metal ring for the base remains in the ground at Ryeford Wharf, showing the position of the crane there.

The bridge over the canal at Dudbridge was altered and widened when the bypass was put in. The approach road was improved but the original canal bridge is still incorporated in the present structure. Beyond it, the distance to Stroud is one mile. Incidentally, no Stroudwater mileposts ever existed. Upper and Lower Dudbridge Locks were replaced by weirs, as part of the Flood Alleviation Scheme, but when they are restored as locks a bypass channel will be excavated to take the flood water.

Stroud was fortunate in having a gasworks early in Victorian times when the town was prospering and expanding. The canal company continued to benefit from the gas company for much of the time gas was being produced in Stroud, not only through carrying coal to the works and tar away from them, but from the rights given for gas pipes to be laid under the towpath to Stroud and Eastington. Latterly coal was supplied by the Stroud–Dudbridge branch of the Midland Railway which ran on the embankment away from the canal. Some parts of the coal shute which tipped the coal wagons down the bank can still be seen amongst the trees, from the cycle path which occupies the former railway line. There is no evidence of the gasworks left.

Gas Works Bridge takes a lot of heavy traffic, particularly lorries for Readymix Concrete who occupy the adjacent plot. Now known as Chestnut Lane, the road leading off Cainscross Road (A419) down to the bridge used to be called Gas House Lane. The Victorian house on the west corner before the bridge was the Gas Manager's House. The cottage on the east belonged to the Company while the grassed patch in front of it was the area where the former swing bridge swung and is still owned by them. The road continues as an unmetalled track towards Fromehall Mill, passing the site of a former millpond on the left. It is possible and permissible to explore the mill complex, through to Lodgemore Mill (listed) and back to the towpath further on. The mill leats, millpond and river are interesting and spectacular.

Like the towpath near the Ocean, this part of the towpath from the gasworks into Stroud is a favourite walk for local people and, judging from the large number of old postcard views, it has been for a very long time. Above the bank on the offside is a new housing development accessed from Chestnut Lane. In front of the houses is a strip of land with crack willow trees which the Company was given in exchange for a piece of land at the Dudbridge development. It may be useful one day for mooring or turning but it is unlikely to revert to a former use when the large millpond for Lodgemore Mill extended from around here as far as the north side of Lodgemore Bridge. In winter this often became a wonderful skating rink.

Lodgemore Bridge, although now fixed, still has the iron framework dated 1927, by Daniels of Stroud, which should not be too difficult to restore or replicate. The swinging space is still free. Known by Stroud folk as Murder Lane and by others as

Lodgemore Lane, the road which the bridge takes is a packhorse track which traverses the valley from the hills to the north, leading through the millyard, past the eighteenth-century mill-owner's house, over a fine listed Georgian river bridge, up a steep cobbled track onto the Bath Road on a corner by a former toll-house. It continues across the road, past the Clothier's Arms, an old hostelry, and up Rodborough Hill, high on to the Commons and on to Cirencester and London.

From Lodgemore Bridge the towpath is not a right of way, although it is a well-used path until the start of Wallbridge Wharf. The wall of the single-storey mill dyehouse skirts the towpath on the right. Some of the former mill-owners were shareholders of the Company. Indeed, it was to supply coal to these mills, when they wanted to expand in the late eighteenth century, that the Stroudwater Navigation was built. Sometimes there were difficulties between them but generally the enterprises helped each other. Messrs Millikens are the current owners of Lodgemore Mill and are carrying on the tradition of making very fine woollen cloth, famed all around the world. They still make the famous red Stroud cloth, some navy for naval officer's uniforms, billiard cloth and, at other premises, tennis-ball cloth, not forgetting the natural-colour cloth for the Pope's robes.

The Painswick Stream joins the canal on the north side, where there are indications that the banks have been strengthened. This was always one of the main feeders as allowed in the Act and still is. It is a fast-flowing little river in a deep cutting and was once used as a private branch navigation. The car park which it borders has just been sold by the owners, Stroud District Council, for a Homebase store. The

Lodgemore: the outfall of Painswick Stream, looking north. Work is in progress for the flood relief scheme. The site of the dammed-off syphon is on the right-hand side. (Photograph by F.W. Rowbotham, 9 May 1961: courtesy of the Environment Agency)

The exit from Wallbridge Wharf, with the canal on the right, 31 August 2003. Tow-rope marks are cut into the stone door jamb on the right, about two feet from the ground.

Company is to be given 8ft between the back wall of the store and the canal bank to do what they will. Suggestions so far include mooring and a canalside garden, incorporating an information board giving the historical importance of the site. Benjamin Grazebrook, the entrepreneur who largely controlled the canal in the early years, built his house, Far Hill, close to the wharf, the centre of operations. After serving in several guises, it was demolished in the 1970s and the ground has remained vacant ever since.

At the end of the towpath is a wall and archway which marked the entrance to Wallbridge Wharf. It once had a big strong door but now anyone may walk or cycle through, although with no rights and at their own risk. On the left, but not clearly defined because of the vegetation, is a pointed piece of land marked on the maps as The Point. It can be reached by an unmarked path and, if facing east, the ground on the right represents the Stroudwater running into the Basin and, on the left, into the beginning of the Thames & Severn Canal. As water belonging to each canal company was jealously guarded and they were mindful of which one owned a lockful of water, it can be said that the Thames & Severn began at the lower gate of the lock a few yards further on (Lower Wallbridge Lock). The unmarked path follows past the lock, now a weir, behind the Stroudwater Headquarters' building and on to Bath Road by a dangerous multi-roundabout.

Surprisingly, Wallbridge Basin has not been altered a great deal and could be revived as a marina. The Company sold most of the land in 1954 to the Severn River

Board who filled it in as a depot. The Company warehouse was used as a workshop and the ashlar house (listed) at the far end, built in 1795-96 as the Stroudwater Headquarters, became offices for the Water Board and is still a suite of offices. The garden and trees remain in front of it but where there was a little weighhouse and weighbridge on the wharf, is now a small office block. Nothing has been built on the actual filled-in basin except some temporary buildings and compounds for keeping machinery. The roadway alongside the river Frome is a main entrance to Lodgemore Mill.

When the number of obstacles that many canals have encountered – and surmounted – in the process of restoration is considered, the Stroudwater Navigation is extremely fortunate, having no great difficulties that modern technology cannot overcome. There is not even one building that would stand in the way of re-watering! The number of canal structures of any significance is large and the number of canal buildings of importance still existing is outstanding. Add to them other related places in the canal corridor, like Whitminster House, then we have a unique and rich heritage site, which will repay investment many times over.

Wallbridge Wharf: the eastern end of the Company warehouse, showing original barred apertures with stone surrounds, 31 August 2003. The upper window has holes for insertion of iron bars.

2

Structures: Basins and Wharves

Framilode Basin

No basin was planned at the entrance to the canal from the river Severn when the 1776 Act was obtained. There was just the lock out to the river, a short loading bay, a lock-keeper's house, a clerk's house and one or two cottages nearby which had possibly been taken over by the Company, but not built by them. However, it is presumed that a substantial piece of land between the road and the river had been acquired, as a plan of Framilode Pill (the tidal reach of the Stroudwater river), drawn probably in 1781, shows the area and is marked 'late Mr Kemmett's'. It was here that the basin was opened in Autumn 1795.

At their half-yearly General Meeting held on 8 April 1794, the Committee discussed ways in which the entrance could be made more convenient for Severn trows and accommodation of their cargoes if they found they needed to deposit them on or near the present wharf. As a weir may have existed from the canal into the Severn near Framilode, that would have added to the difficulties of navigating into the lock from the river, which is reputed to have the second highest tidal rise and fall in the world. Members suggested the remedy might be a new lock basin and a new wharf, and resolved to take advice from an able engineer. He was also to report on the present state of the canal and estimate the expense of repairing all locks and bridges where necessary. The Thames & Severn Company had already suggested raising the wharf at Framilode above the highest tides.

Josiah Clowes, the surveyor and engineer to the Thames & Severn Canal Company, was selected for the job. He gave his report dated 21 May 1794, after travelling along the canal in a boat accompanied by the chief carpenter, Mr Beard. In the report he advised widening the canal at the entrance to make a bason (*sic*) for turning vessels. He also suggested building a warehouse with a crane at each end and setting a capstone between the lock and the Pill to bring vessels into either the lock or the Pill where a dock could be made. The main problem he saw was to provide enough safe moorings away from the vagaries of the river Severn. Repairs were needed to some, but not all, locks and bridges; Blunder Lock was mentioned in particular. Mud banks and shoals, especially one just outside the lock in the river, needed to be addressed with urgency.

The next month the Committee accepted the report and decided to build the basin and the dock, although the latter was postponed to the next year, pending consultation with the Thames & Severn, because they were to pay half the cost of the project, obtaining free wharfage in return. In fact, the dock was probably never built. Work started on the warehouse straight away.

Detailed accounts exist for the building of the warehouse and wall of the basin. Thomas Greening charged for one man for four days at 7s – plus 2s 6d for one day for himself to dig out foundations for the warehouse on 30 August 1794. Dimensions of the carpenters' work include the length of floor 41ft 9ins; roof the same; breadth 19ft 6ins. Edward Keene did the woodwork for the three double doors for which he charged £2 3s 6d. This included 'a new oak sill to the front door 8ft long by 11ins wide and 4½ins thick.' The door itself was of deal boards and oak rails. Thomas Barnard reported on the tiler's work: 'The above tileing don in a Workman like manner except 6 feet in length on the North side which must be altered.' Unfortunately, part of a wall gave way and had to be rebuilt, but it was all finished by December and the accounts were paid out in March 1795.

Thomas Cook's account for building the wall gives the dimensions as 186ft long, 6ft 6ins high, 4ft 6ins thick, built of ashlar coping and steps. The total cost was £73 7s 2d. He must have extended the wall at a later date, because there is another draft account from him dated 19 October 1801. That includes 'To alling [hauling] five tun of stone from ye Quarry to ye Burne [the Bourne at Brimscombe] – 10s.' (This probably means per ton.) Limestone was burnt and also taken down to Framilode. John Pashley was the Company's surveyor on site, who, in October 1795, reported that the wall was completed except for 12ft adjoining the first lock where they were to put in a stop gate. This became unnecessary when the existing stop gate was mended. After the wall was completed in December it was decided to use the clay dug from the basin to make bricks 'when the Severn permits'. The Company was always economical.

Two clerks were employed by the Company, the first to keep the books and reside at Wallbridge. In September 1794 it was decreed that the second should be a working man who should live near the line of the canal, not higher than Stonehouse. The reason being that he needed to be on hand constantly to attend barge masters. In June 1797 William Smith of Newent offered his services to the Company as under-clerk, and was taken on at 8s per quarter, with occupation of the house at Framilode where John Pashley had lived. In November the following year he became indisposed and incapable of fulfilling his duties. Thomas Beard was to receive tonnage and to issue and collect tickets in his absence and act as under-clerk. This was a temporary situation and on 2 January 1799 Smith was given notice to leave by 1 March. Then William Pavey became under-clerk at the same salary with the tenement and garden. Two years later he applied for an advance in salary due to the increased price of provisions and was given an extra 8s per annum.

Further to Clowes' advice for the Company to build a dock, some responsible owners of vessels made a proposition in October 1807 to purchase or rent on a long lease a piece of land at Framilode for making a dock. The Committee replied they would consider this at the next half-year meeting. They duly examined the land and said that, in their opinion, there was not enough space for a dock without serious inconvenience to navigation. Eventually it was decided, thirteen years later, that a repairing dock should be built at Chippenham Platt.

When William Pavey died in 1809 the Company engaged Barnard Hole (*sic*) as lock-keeper and clerk at £40 per annum with house and garden, with the provision his whole time be devoted to the Company's service. Perhaps they guessed there would be trouble for, sure enough, in November 1811 it was reported that he was addicted to drinking and had neglected the Company's business. The Clerk was to give him a reprimand and advise him to be more circumspect in future or he would be dismissed. This was to no avail, for when he died early in 1813, papers found in his house showed that he had received tonnage to a very considerable amount for which he had never accounted. The listing of the discrepancies takes up one foolscap page, covering two years, 1811 and 1812, and amounts to £99 12s 6d.

Once again Thomas Beard stepped into the breach with a contract for a year at £70. He found a bond of £200 as surety. Straight away Beard asked for a supply of writing paper as being necessary for the efficient conduct of the Company's business. An unusual request, in view of the fact he was discharged a year later for fraudulently secreting money he had received for tonnage and ordered to quit the house.

William Purcell, aged twenty-eight, was appointed as clerk and lock-keeper on 10 June 1814 at a salary of £65 per annum, and rent for his house charged at £5 per annum. Nine days later he married Louisa Howell, daughter of Stephen Howell, Parish Clerk of Stroud, where his own family were innkeepers, latterly at the Chequers at the end of King Street. (The inn was demolished when Gloucester Street was put through.) Purcell's duties were onerous but he stayed with the Company for twenty-seven years. Apart from the normal duties of lock-keeper, he had to attend to putting in the flood gates at Whitminster Mill early every Sunday morning, so that the levels below Bristol Road were properly supplied with water. Conservation of water was a major concern on the cut but no vessels were allowed to proceed on a Sunday. It was his duty to walk up the levels as far as Stonehouse each day between tides to see no fraud was being committed 'by persons navigating'.

The duties of clerk also included attendance at the monthly committee meetings at Wallbridge to present his 'check book' in which he kept a record of the tickets issued to vessels entering or leaving the Framilode basin. On them details were entered as to the name of the boat, its owner, master, where from and to, cargo, weight of it, amount of tonnage to be paid, and to whom it was charged. No vessel was allowed to leave the basin until the tonnage was paid. Purcell had to pass the money to the chief clerk at Stroud at least once a fortnight. In 1816 he 'incurred the disapprobation of the Committee' by not keeping the check book regularly and the Clerk was told to inform him that 'unless a regular entry be made of every vessel coming into the canal, with necessary remarks, he will be dismissed.' As he had at that time one small child and another on the way, there was some excuse.

Purcell's salary was increased to £80 in 1821 and probably never went up very much after that, although from time to time he was given supplementary payments: £5 for discovering frauds and prosecuting offenders; £1 for saving a person from drowning. It is not clear why the Company did not bring the charges to the Petty Sessions themselves.

Following a 'shake-up' in the management of the Company in 1840-41, Purcell's services were dispensed with on 20 March 1841. He was paid £3 for the fruit trees he had planted and two months' salary. Eventually, he went to live with his unmarried sister Elizabeth at the Chequers and took it over on her death in 1861 but returned to Framilode the next year and 'went on Saul Parish'. He died in Stroud Union Workhouse on 11 February 1865 and was buried by his friends in Stroud Cemetery.

When Thomas Beard was still lock-keeper in 1814 the Committee were considering whether to repair the house he occupied or to have a new one built. Members William Stanton and Henry Eycott were sent to Framilode to view the situation. They decided a new house should be built in the most convenient place for the lock-keeper. Mr Upton, Clerk to the Gloucester & Berkeley Canal, was invited to give his opinion and an estimate of the cost of repairing the old one. Mr Greening, a builder, prepared an estimate and elevation for the new house, for which he was paid two guineas in November. Building began in June 1815.

As he was on the spot, the new clerk/lock-keeper William Purcell was charged with overseeing the building he was to occupy with his family and was given money to settle the tradesmen's accounts. These included £15 10s for 10,000 bricks; £2 10s 7d for paving stones; 12s 4d for sheet lead and painting work; also beer for the men. Purcell moved in during midsummer 1816 and immediately the tiles were taken off the old house and the sub-committee inspected it for repairs and alterations. They ordered repairs but the materials of the offices were to be taken care of until the Company should need or dispose of them. At Michaelmas, the old house was let to Samuel Lawrence at £8 per annum. (This is probably the part black and white house close to the Lock House.)

The Lock House, listed Grade II, is brick built with brick end-stacks. It has a single main range of two storeys and attics in the gable ends. The large lean-to on the right was the clerks' office. There is a brick dentil course at the eaves, reminiscent of similar buildings in the West Midlands. Also typical are two-light cambered head wood casements to the first floor and three-light to the ground floor. A nice feature is the central panelled door with a plain fanlight and semi-circular headed porch. The door opened into a hall and staircase straight up from the door and the main room with plenty of cupboard space to the right. To the left a passage led to the single-storey cat slide at a lower level to the rear where the kitchen and store room were, although that may have been put in at a later date. The lounge was added later in a single-storey cat slide to the front left, with shed at the back. There were two bedrooms and two attics. Architects Messrs Falconer Partnership prepared a survey drawing in 1980 and made subsequent renovations, including changing the shop/office into a kitchen.

Unfortunately, the warehouse proved an unnecessary expense, although the fact that it remains intact today, converted to a private house, shows it was a solid structure. Not long after it was built some sugar and tobacco brought up from Bristol

Lock House at Framilode. The large grassed area was the basin. The warehouse is to left, and Canal Row is in the distance on the right. (Photograph by C.H.A. Townley, c.1964: courtesy of J.A. Peden)

and stored there was stolen, and the Company had to pay compensation to the owner. The Company Minutes for 1 July 1811 note the warehouse discontinued for the reception of goods and merchandise; it was to be let at not less than £10 per annum. However, it was not until June 1814 that it was resolved to put in a fireplace and chimney, and glass in the windows, and to allow another lock-keeper, John Longney, to live there until his new lockhouse should be erected. At some stage it was used as a schoolroom.

A friendly society known as the Benefit Society of Water Men at Framilode proposed to the Company in May 1843 that they would take the warehouse, repair it and construct a room at an estimate of £4, and pay 10s per annum in rent. The Company was agreeable to this and would allow £10 in timber and other materials. The agreement was that, should the Company at any time take the warehouse into their own possession, they should recompense the Society £20 for immediate possession, provided the premises had been left and kept in complete repair. By 1847 the tenant seems to be James Nurse on behalf of the club. He was a boat owner himself.

Gloucestershire had the largest number of Friendly Societies in the West of England, there being 250 registered in 1873. The earliest listed in the files of the Clerk of the Peace for Gloucestershire is Fairford, which started in 1750, while the oldest for the Stroud area was the Society of Clothworkers which met at the Golden Hart in Stroud from 1764. Although an Act was passed requiring Societies to be registered, some smaller ones failed to do so, including Framilode. That was set up by Captain Charles Phillips Butler, a master mariner, and flourished with about 140 members until about July 1896, when notice was given to the Company that they wanted to relinquish the tenancy. Framilode had its own set of crockery and held an annual feast at Whitsun, lasting three days. Members had to march to church in Saul wearing red, white and blue rosettes, carrying a staff decorated with flowers, accompanied by a band. It is interesting to note that, in a pamphlet entitled *Rules and Regulations of the Friendly Institutions and Equitable Assurance Society for the Borough of Stroud and surrounding District*, 1833, the list of Honorary Members includes at least fourteen who were either Proprietors of the Stroudwater Navigation or adjacent landowners. Most gave a subscription of £1.

The Company owned six wharves, plus several others owned and run by adjacent landowners, usually mill-owners, timber and coal merchants. In English law all water-borne goods must be loaded and unloaded at specified places at particular hours and under supervision. Any such place, usually a platform of timber or stone alongside the bank of a navigable river or canal, is defined as a wharf. An owner or occupier of a wharf is styled a *wharfinger*.

Bristol Road Wharf

Bristol Road, or Whitminster Wharf, was one of the Company's secondary wharves and does not feature very much in the archive. It had the advantage of being situated next to a busy road, therefore both sides of the canal could be accessed from the bridge. As the stretch of canal from Framilode to this point presented no great difficulties in building, the opportunity was taken to make it the temporary head of navigation, and the first toll-paying cargo of coal was brought in on 17 December 1776. Thus the Company was provided with a steady income to meet everyday expenses until the canal opened fully in July 1779.

Coal was the main commodity discharged at the wharf, almost entirely for domestic consumption, as there was only one large mill nearby. The Purnells at Fromebridge Mill held the right to use the navigable Frome to serve that mill and Framilode Tin Mills, using their own vessels and carrying their own coal. Another commodity likely to be handled at the wharf was cheese, for which the Vale of Gloucester and Berkeley was renowned. One of the original shareholders in 1774 was the cheesemonger or factor Richard Bigland of Frocester Court. In November 1805 a London agent asked permission to erect an extra warehouse for housing cheese. It was to be 25ft long, 18ft wide and 6ft high on the side walls, covered with thatch and presumably ventilated with louvres. After paying for the erection, estimated at £60, he would take a fourteen-year lease and would pay rent after the sum expended was used. For an unknown reason the agreement was suspended two months later.

The Company already had a warehouse on the wharf, which was first commissioned at the end of 1799. It was not very big, the dimensions given were 16ft by 15ft, with side walls 8ft high. Coal was usually kept in the open, so this was probably meant for foodstuffs. There was no urgency over the building, which may not have been completed for a year. In fact it was not large enough for the goods landed at the wharf and enlargement was ordered in 1815. After seven years the warehouse was pointed and repaired, and the shoots of the gutters seen to and painted. Twenty years later part of it was converted to a dwelling house for a servant of the Company at a rent of £5 per annum. The work could be done for an outlay of £40 and still leave sufficient warehouse space. Wharf Cottage, much extended and with large gardens, was offered for sale at £350,000 in the year 2000.

On the other side of the road bridge was Bristol Road Lock and the Company's servants at this location are described as lock-keepers. James Barns was one of the first to be appointed at 8s a week, out of which he was to leave a deposit of 1s until it amounted to 40s (as surety), which was to be paid to him when he was discharged on his quitting the house without any trouble. He was still working for the Company in 1784 when he was required to make the annual stopping of the towpath between Bond's Mill and Bristol Road. John Critchley of King's Stanley proposed himself as a person to sell coal at Bristol Road Wharf and to act as the Company's warehouseman and lock-keeper there. The Company no longer sold coal themselves at this date. Critchley proposed William Yates of Stourport as surety for £500 but the agreement was rescinded the next month, in October 1816, when it was found that Critchley's character was not satisfactory. Members of the Critchley family did, however, serve the Company at Bristol Road and at Chippenham Platt for many years. In December 1843 Thomas Critchley of Whitminster Wharf died and his widow wanted to continue to occupy the house on the same terms as her husband but without occupying the warehouse. This was all right; the rent, to be £8 per annum, was paid quarterly. An oven was rebuilt by the Company for a Mr Critchley in 1853, if he did the labour. Local hearsay maintains that a window at the Wharf House on the canal side was used to dispense beer to the boat people but, in July 1866, notice was given to a Mrs Critchley to quit her house which she was using as a beer house because the Company 'think it is undesirable the house should be used for that purpose'. The notice was withdrawn in October 'on condition that she gives up beer-selling and pays attention to her several duties as lock-keeper and night passer'.

When Samuel Critchley left Bristol Road Wharf in September 1865, he sold the warehouse, stable and oak coal pen to the incoming tenant James Godsell King. The Company specified that those items were to be considered 'removable' but all else was not and remained the property of the Company. King also succeeded Samuel Critchley at Chippenham Platt, where Critchley was described as a coal merchant, aged forty-six, in the 1851 census.

An unusual happening occurred in the spring of 1858 when Mr Clutterbuck was allowed to launch a new boat he had built (most likely a pleasure boat), across the towpath near Bristol Road. He needed to temporarily take out one of the gates at Whitminster Lock to enable the vessel to pass into the Gloucester & Berkeley Canal. The Company stipulated that all the work was to be done at Mr Clutterbuck's expense and under the supervision of Mr Driver, the Company Surveyor, and the applicant was to be responsible for all consequent damage. It must have been successful as no more is recorded on the subject.

The Dock at Chippenham Platt

The canal was opened to Chippenham Platt just below Pike Bridge, Eastington, in January 1778, thus becoming the next head of navigation, and a coal wharf was established. An elongated piece of land from fifty yards east of Westfield Bridge to Pike Bridge was cut off by the Oldbury Brook to the north and the canal to the south, and it became known as The Island. When the brook had been diverted to run alongside the road and to a weir on the south side of the canal, the weir water was called the 'divers' (the divert).

Under the 1776 Act, the Company had powers to sell off surplus land and this they proceeded to do in the 1780s. Several pieces were offered for sale by auction at The Golden Cross inn, Cainscross, on 20 May 1785, but no purchasers attended. Instead, the lands were sold by private treaty, mostly to Proprietors themselves. Benjamin Grazebrook, the Company Surveyor, was able to buy two pieces at Eastington for 120 guineas. He had set up a family carrying business and made a deal where he had 'full liberty of conveying the produce of the lands during such time as they shall continue in his family free of charge on the canal'. Mr Bigland had occupation of The Island next to Eastington Workhouse and consented to let it to Thomas Banks for £1 10s in 1790. The Company was renting part of the land and establishing a dock, although it did not acquire the freehold until 1807.

A dry dock was made for boat repairs, opening at an angle from the canal just eastwards of Court Orchard Lock (renamed Dock Lock). When the new Eastington Baptist Chapel was being built in 1871 the dry dock was used for services. Once it was the venue for a tea party for 300 people. It had a high roof covered with wooden shingles and a clock-turret above the up-stream gable. J. Vick was paid £1 for mending the clock in 1848. The dock was filled with water from the canal and emptied into the 'divers' on the other side, both by gravity. Philip Woore, a boat-builder, took a lease of the dock at £30 per annum in 1833. However, the Company reserved the rights to put their boats in the dock at any time for repairs without paying for the use of it and to put their planks into the timber shed without payment. Obviously, it was a busy and convenient place for repairs as in 1845 the Company had to stipulate that all parties wishing to enter the dock should apply to the Surveyor first. He would then post up a list of vessels that were waiting and entry would be in the same order. Soon after, two new bars were to be provided for the use of the dock, the floor of it to be repaired and a new stepladder set at the upper end. After nearly ten years the floor was to be repaired again where needful, with bricks and stone taken from the old bridge at Saul. Charges for use of dry docks are still by the day and were 2s 6d then but reduced to 1s 6d in 1863. Good Friday and Sundays were not charged. James Nurse and other traders complained of not enough accommodation for their vessels to 'lie-by' while waiting to enter the dock, or after repairs are done but not completed. So it was ordered that vessels could lie in the brook for either purpose without charge but the Surveyor was to report any vessel 'lying bye' in any other part of the canal.

All the woodwork needed for the canal was constructed in the maintenance yard by the Company's own workforce. There was a timber shed to store the deal and other woods. Eight baulks, each 20ft long, needed for balance poles for one of the lower gates at Framilode and for one of the upper gates at the Five Locks, were bought at Gloucester in May 1836 for delivery to Chippenham Platt the same week.

Chippenham Platt: the western end of The Island, where the maintenance yard was situated. This photograph shows the Oldbury Brook joining the canal from behind the boathouse for the ice-breaker on the right. (Photograph by F. Restall, Stonehouse, *c.*1905)

At the same time the representative was to enquire the price of oak from John Dimock for a new breast for one of the upper gates. A saw pit was close to the public road but was a nuisance there and had to be moved elsewhere in 1792 and the old one filled in. The carpenter's shop near the dry dock burnt down in the 1920s.

A blacksmith's shop and forge supplied all the lock furniture and presumably the horse shoes after the towing path was adapted for horses. Job Blick applied to rent the dock with occasional use of the blacksmith's shop for one year in 1835 for £22 10s. A boathouse was at the end of The Island where the 'divers' joined the canal, for the ice-breaker. It was stoutly built and the width of the largest coal barge. It was towed by a rope on the bow and rocked by a rope on a short masthead by manpower from the towpath, so that the beam ends projected tooth-like at water level and moved up and down and tilting to break the ice. It was allegedly last used in the winter of 1895.

By an agreement signed 7 November 1777 with Thomas Stevens of Chavenage, the Company had taken The Island at a very low rent and subsequently erected a house for the carpenter, William Beard. Mr Hicks acquired the land in 1806 and wished to take over the house, paying the Company for the materials. A sub-committee was detailed to meet Mr Hicks and propose that the Company would concede the house and a sum of money to him in exchange for the freehold of the land. The Company offered 98*d* per acre and the land measured one acre, one rod and twenty-nine perches. Mr Hicks kept his coal wharf and paid £27 9s 0d for the materials of the house but could not take it over until a new house was built for Mr Beard.

The dimensions of the house were 28ft by 14ft, to contain a ground floor and a garret with a small lean-to behind for a brewhouse. It was begun in April 1807 and is likely to be the attractive double-fronted house with porch facing the canal and known as the former engineer's house. An addition of two rooms, one below and one above of 12ft square each, was made to a house at Chippenham Platt in 1824, then in the occupation of Mr Browning, with a rent of £8 per annum. The description of this was a 'cottage lately built' – probably different premises. When the Committee needed to discuss the plans for Pike Bridge on 18 April 1823, they met in the 'Company's house at Chippenham Platt', so it must have been fairly spacious.

Samuel Critchley was using the coal wharf at Chippenham Platt for selling coals in 1836 and applied to put a fence to separate the wharf from the highway for security. He was allowed to do so at his expense with the power for him to remove the fence when he should cease to use the wharf. It was stipulated that proper gates must be set up with a duplicate key for the use of the lock-keeper and wharfinger who lived there, and due access to and from the wharf be secured for the use of traders generally for landing and removing goods.

An advert appeared in the *Gloucester Journal* on 21 July 1843 for a junior clerk to keep the accounts. He would also 'be expected to make himself generally useful at a salary of £80 per annum'. Eventually, Mr Sherwood was appointed and took up residence at Chippenham Platt. He was to pay rates and taxes for the house. Soon he covered himself with glory as per his report to the Committee on 19 May 1845. Several times he had given information to Mr Walker, the Admiralty Engineer, and Captain Vidal about tides and currents in the Severn, and traffic and other matters with reference to the plan of crossing the river Severn by two bridges. One was to be at Hock Crib and the other at Framilode and both would tend very much to impede the free and open navigation of the Severn and therefore injure the Stroudwater Navigation. The Committee granted a gratuity of £20 to Mr Sherwood 'for the earnest zeal he has evinced in protecting the rights and interests of this Company'.

Not content with that, Mr Sherwood went on to give a further report, that of receiving annoyances from the family of his neighbour, Samuel Critchley. At the time Samuel's son Charles would have been twelve and his wife Hannah twenty-eight, the same age as her husband. The annoyances were not recorded, but the Committee ordered a letter be sent to Critchley saying if it did not stop he would be asked to quit his house. That was not the end, for sixteen months later the Committee received intimation of great neglect by Mr Sherwood in looking after the business of the Company. It was decided to give him notice and his services dispensed with. Critchley took lease of another piece of land in 1864.

Stonehouse Wharf

Stonehouse Wharf may not have been very big in the early days of the Navigation but increased in importance after 1866 when the Stonehouse & Nailsworth Railway opened, using the Company's land and constructing a siding. It is situated close to Stonehouse Cross (crossroads) where the road from Stonehouse to Bridgend crossed over the Stroud–Eastington turnpike road. The Ship inn occupied the south-west corner of the junction but faced the road not the canal.

There are very few references to the wharf in the Company Minutes, the first being an application by a Mr Elliott in 1794 to build a warehouse for putting in goods brought up the canal. It was agreed that it should be at the lower end. No rent is specified. Either the same man, or another from the same local family, one John Elliott, a professional land surveyor, drew a magnificent large map of Stonehouse parish and in 1804 added a new schedule giving numbers of parcels of land, owners, occupiers, areas and field names. Plot 132 was in the ownership of the Company of Proprietors and represents the area of the wharf.

In 1818 Thomas Clark of Stonehouse was chosen as the servant of the Company to sell coals at the wharf at Stonehouse and to reside in the house that had recently been erected there. He may have stayed a long time, because in August 1845 7s 6d was allowed to a Thomas Clark for his expense in putting up a door leading from the kitchen to the parlour at the house at Stonehouse Wharf. Actually, the payment must have been made after he left, as in May that year some people applied to rent the house in place of Thomas Clark. The person chosen was Robert Thompson of Nupend who wished to pay £10 for the house and to rent half the wharf for £4 10s per annum. Charles Hobbs followed in February 1847 at a rent of £12 10s. Five months later he was requesting a cellar but, when it was found that the costs to the Company would be more than £15, Hobbs offered to pay an extra £2 in rent. Mr Driver, the Surveyor, was only to buy materials that were not already in the Company's stores and was to use day work. Later the same year a portion of the wharf was let to Messrs Hughes and Keedwell and the area fenced off for £15 per annum. Samuel Critchley applied to take the house and the portion of the wharf which was usually let with it in September 1860. He asked for a stable to be built and a pump placed on the wharf. Thomas Spire of Eastington contracted to build the stable the next month.

By 1858 the Company was getting worried about the efficiency of wharves and some members of the Committee were assigned to three wharves as overseers. They were to direct wharfingers as to the use of the wharves by the several parties who were using them. Messrs Hooper and Marling, two influential gentleman clothiers, were given Stonehouse Wharf. Inspections took place and discussions held to determine how best to improve trade and allot space to traders. One solution was for Thomas Marling to take the house and garden with use of the wharf at £10 per annum when it fell vacant. However, when the Stonehouse & Nailsworth Railway was first mooted in 1862, the Company saw fit to oppose it.

In fact the Committee was so violently opposed, a petition was sent to Parliament and some members attended in London, incurring an expense of about £240. They concurred when the preamble of the Railway Act was proved and they resolved that arrangements would have to be made to avoid further opposition in Parliament. Mr Bruce, the engineer of the Stonehouse & Nailsworth Railway Co., presented plans of the Stonehouse Wharf alterations to a committee meeting on 25 April 1863. The basis of the plan was that the railway company would construct a lay-by and a new wharf for the canal as compensation for the passage of their lines through the existing wharf. The legal agreement between the two companies was signed and sealed on 28 November 1866. It incorporated the arrangements given above but added that the lay-by should be 12ft in width. While the canal company and traders were granted free and unrestricted use, the land remained vested in the railway company.

Ryeford Wharf

Although the canal was opened as far as Ryeford by 1778, negotiations for purchasing the land were prolonged and were not completed until August 1780. Then a sum of £224 19s was paid to the owners of the land called Rack Hill: these were Holliday Phillips of Ryeford and two others, being trustees under the will of Thomas Phillips, Holliday's uncle. The amount was determined by the commissioners who ordered it to be paid by the trustees into public funds, as per the law appertaining to trusts at that time. The description of the several parcels of land involved seem to indicate the area which became Ryeford Wharf. However, this cannot be properly verified because at about the same time the road from Stonehouse to King's Stanley was re-aligned. It had crossed the Frome by a ford roughly to the west of where the coal pen was made. After the new turnpike was put in, the ford was replaced by a high bridge which was a continuation of the canal bridge.

The wharf was quite small, being bounded on the east by the new road, on the south by the canal, and on the west by a boundary to the side of The Anchor inn. It contained open coal pens and possibly a crane. The row of houses on the side of the wharf included a workshop and warehouse. An iron ring in the ground indicates there was a crane. Some parts of the wharf were let out to tenants. In December 1824 Paul Beard requested a lease for fourteen years of a small piece of ground already being used by him as a landing place for coals for his own use. The Company stipulated that he must surround the wharf with a proper and durable fence. Five years later the Company paid a mason, Daniel Harrison, £5 for the considerable loss he had sustained for the materials and labour in building the wall. Messrs Charles Stephens of Stanley Mill missed paying their annual rent of 1s in 1835 for a small enclosed wharf, whilst for an undisclosed reason (presumably coal storage) Edwin Gyde, a dyer, applied to have a pen re-erected in 1848 and this was done.

Access to the bridge and wharf was difficult because of the gradient of the road. Counsel opinion was sought in 1866 when W.H. Marling applied to the Wheatenhurst Highway Board to raise the Stonehouse–King's Stanley road by three feet because of a declivity in the roadway. The Company objected because it would mean increased height at the wharf, necessitating compensation, though some of their other wharves were already as high. The counsel said the Highway Board were empowered to fill in the declivity and raise the road if the work was done with care and attention. Mr MacNamara advised the Company to come to an agreement and not to claim compensation until after damage had been done. So it was left to two stalwarts, Messrs Hooper and Beard on the part of the Company, to ascertain whether the work could be done without injury to the wharf. They decided it would be

Ryeford Wharf, looking east towards Ryeford Bridge. The former Anchor inn and ancillary buildings bordering the Company wharf can be seen here in 1979. The trees are now grown again. (Photograph by G.G. Hoare: courtesy of G.G. Hoare and M.A. Handford)

against the Company's interests to raise the wharf from the water's edge to the same extent as the rise of the road. However, the next year it was resolved to raise the wharf according to the plan submitted by the Surveyor at an estimated cost of £24 3s.

Coal was the principle commodity landed at Ryeford but the tonnage books do not record whether cargoes were landed at the Company's wharf on the north side, at Marling's pen opposite, or Ford's wharf the other side of Ryeford Bridge. Sometimes the cargo was to be landed at more than one wharf. For instance, the trow *Mercy* from Bristol carried 56 tons of roadstone in 1862, landing some at Ryeford, then Dudbridge and Wallbridge and other places. Earlier the same year *Harriet* had brought 56 tons of gravel to Ryeford.

Dudbridge Wharf

Dudbridge Wharf served the area to the west of Stroud and became the central depot for coal as far afield as Tetbury, Horsley, Kingscote, Avening and Nailsworth. After Wallbridge it was second in importance to the Company and was used by several traders at the same time. It was quite large, as can be seen by the amount of land still used as a wharf by a haulage contractor. Although it was in use as a wharf since about the time the canal was first fully opened, the land itself was not conveyed and paid for until September 1794. Perhaps it had been leased until then. The conveyance of that date cites some pieces of land owned by a trust set up by will of John Mosley, a woolstapler of Cainscross, in 1771. Included is a piece of land on the south side of the canal having the coal wharf at Dudbridge and being next to some land purchased in 1783 from William Chance, clothier of Dudbridge Mill. This mill was taken by Messrs Apperley Curtis and, in 1933, by Redler's who bought back a small triangle of land in 1950.

In May 1794 the Company allowed Thomas Grazebrook to fence off some part of the wharf near his new house, now called Gladfield Gardens, for himself until such time as the Company wished to take the ground into its own hands again. The rent was 10s per annum and the cost of the fence would be reimbursed if and when the Company did re-acquire. A reference has been found which suggests that Grazebrook did not give up the land until 1815. About that time he proposed to release his right of way across the wharf and to build a wall from his dwelling house

Dudbridge Wharf, taken from the bank on the north side looking towards Rodborough Fort, c.1888. Dudbridge Mill is on the far right. A crane can be seen on the wharf, before the gable end of the warehouse. (Courtesy of B. Wiggall)

near the wharf. This would be dependant on the Company granting him a right of way on the south side of the wharf. An agreement was to be drawn up. It seems he wanted a new access to the house, independent of the wharf, and this is evident today. Soon afterwards, he applied for a right of road across the wharf to and from his late warehouse, in order to use it as a warehouse again.

As usual with the Company, building works were not undertaken until it was expedient. To avoid too much congestion when vessels were loading and unloading at the wharf on the south side of the canal, it was decided in 1785 to widen the canal at that point by digging out the north side. This would facilitate the passage of boats not calling at Dudbridge to proceed. A wall would be needed there and one was built in 1793 but for which side of the canal is not stated. John Gubbins, a mason who owned Quarhouse quarry in Brimscombe, was given a contract in November 1792 to supply weather stone (for coping) with a water drip at each end for Dudbridge Wharf. The cost was 11d per foot for 300ft, measuring 2ft 6ins wide in the middle and 3ins less at each end. Aberthaw stone was specified, for burning into brown lime, because the mortar made from it sets well under water. Loading would be at the Bourne, for delivery on or before Christmas Eve, or else the cost would reduce by 1d per foot. The contract was completed by the last day of February.

It was not until May 1793 when the Committee made their annual inspection on board the Company's boat (as the present Board still do in May, although not on a boat) that the need for a wharfinger's house at Dudbridge was determined. Thomas Greening was contracted to do this and his bill ordered to be paid a year later, as soon as some paving was repaired. The house was probably built on the opposite side to the wharf on a building platform above some wet land. Edward Keene submitted a bill for carpenter's work in 1794. It included flooring, a new chimney piece at 7s 6d, thumb latches, new seat, window frames and bars, the whole amounting to £40 0s 9¼d.

William Playne, a very important clothier of Longfords Mill, near Avening, proposed to have a part of some land adjoining the wharf enclosed with a wall and secured by gates, for depositing coals, goods, wares and merchandise. Playne would do the work at his expense, provided no other person be allowed to use it as a wharf, nor would the Company be empowered to underlet it. For this he would pay £1 per annum for fourteen years from 1815. By the late 1830s his consignments were being handled by individual boat owners, including Fripp, Wakefield and Davies. In 1839 Brown's trow brought a chest of indigo, and James Nurse brought coals from Playne's pen. The Company agreed to the proposition and soon realised that the wharf needed enlarging. Then they remembered the land occupied by Thomas Grazebrook still belonged to them. If they took it back, the present carriage road could be moved and a new entrance nearer the centre of the wall could be made and be more commodious for carriages. Grazebrook duly made his claim for the cost of the fencing but it was referred to the next general meeting.

On 14 April 1818 a Mr Hawkins of Cainscross attended the Committee and offered to let to the Company the warehouse he intended to build near Dudbridge Wharf for £20 per annum. It was to be fitted-up at 137ft long and 11ft 6ins wide, with two floors. The Committee deferred to the general meeting. That was held the next day when it was decided the Company should build its own warehouse. Two weeks later William Blackwell gave his estimate for building the walls – 32ft long, 16ft wide and 10ft high – and the proposal was accepted.

The Company sold coal from the wharves on their own account until 1831, when it was discontinued from all except Wallbridge. From 1813 wharfingers had to render to the clerk at Wallbridge an account of sales once a week and these would be entered in a ledger. At one half-yearly meeting in January 1814 the balances of persons appointed to sell coal as agents at Dudbridge and Wallbridge amounted to £1,653 4s 10d. In February 1816 the price of coal at Dudbridge and Wallbridge wharves was altered and 'Handbills and cards to that effect [were to] be sent about the Country in every direction for the purpose of making the public acquainted with it as early as possible'. The new prices were: Bilston coal at £1 4s per ton and 1s 3½d per cwt; Newport at £1 2s per ton and 1s 2d per cwt; Shropshire at £1 1s 6d per ton and 1s 2d per cwt; Slack at 19s per ton and 1s 1d per cwt; Forest at 18s per ton and 1s per cwt. A directive went out in 1821 that in future bushels with iron rims should be used for measuring coal on all wharves instead of baskets. Also, 'wharfingers at each wharf do weigh the coals to all persons who are desirous of having them weighed at a price of sixpence a ton, and that all coals sold by hundredweight [cwt] be weighed to persons desirous of having them weighed without charge'. Notices of these regulations were to be affixed to boards at each wharf.

Mr Wilson, Clerk to the Thames & Severn Company, attended the committee meeting on 15 December 1843 and outlined the intention of his company to erect a machine for weighing vessels at Brimscombe Port to ascertain the tonnage. He explained it might be of mutual benefit to the Stroudwater Company and suggested the Proprietors ought to subscribe one third of the total cost of £1,100. With their usual caution the Company said they would consider it further, although the Committee were not in favour at present. Coincidentally, at the same meeting was John George to discuss his future tenancy of part of Dudbridge Wharf which was due to expire at Christmas. The Company would have liked to have kept him as tenant if the wharf could be made to accommodate both him and Frederick Nurse. However, it would mean that the weighing machine which George owned should become the property of the Company to prevent suspicion of incorrect weights. The Clerk met him to discuss it the next week when George intimated he was not willing to share the wharf, and that he wanted to dispose of the weighing machine and the wood fence and would accept £55. By the end of January he had settled with the Company for £37. When George had installed the weighing machine with a mound around it in July 1832, he had asked that, if the Company did not wish to acquire them at valuation when he left, then he could take them away with him. The Company had agreed to insert a clause into his agreement to that effect. He left to set up in business at Brimscombe.

James Nurse, the next tenant at Dudbridge Wharf, wanted the weighing bridge to be let to him in January 1856. The conditions were that the Company would retain use of it for their own purposes and he would receive payment from all other persons using it. Needless to say, the Company deferred consideration to the next meeting.

Their decision is not recorded, but the Company was responsible for the weigh-bridge in February 1859 when Mr Seys, the Inspector of Weights and Measures, asked for payment for attending to the adjustment of it. He was given £2 for his trouble. It was still in the Company's ownership in 1862 when Joseph Cottle, the lock-keeper at Dudbridge, was given a rise in wages to 18s per week because of the extra work given him for attending the weighbridge. It is marked on the first edition of the Ordnance Survey map (1884), situated just inside the wall bordering the road, close to a pump and some trees.

Very few complaints were inserted in the Minutes but, in October 1861, the Company became concerned about a communication they received from Mr Whiting of Nailsworth. He had incurred a loss of two casks of butter in the course of transmission from Bristol through Dudbridge. He stressed there was no implication of the loss having occurred from the wharf but he wanted assurance for himself and other traders as to the responsibility of the Company for goods left in the warehouse at Dudbridge. The Committee asked Mr Warman the solicitor and Mr Harris to see the wharfinger and form a plan for the safe keeping of foodstuffs for the future satisfaction of traders. Messrs Warman and Harris reported they could not 'recommend the Company to undertake direct responsibility for the custody of goods'. They suggested: 'the wharfinger should enter in a book at the time all goods deposited in the warehouse, and when and to whom they are delivered out, without giving any receipt to traders which shall implicate the Company in responsibility for the safe custody of them, but at the same time shall enable the Company to afford to traders precise information on the subject which has hitherto been wanting.' The resolution was carried.

The Company's practice of selling coal directly at the Wallbridge and Dudbridge wharves was not altogether satisfactory as they were so dependant on their agents. One of them was Bernard Hole, who gave notice, and was the clerk/lock-keeper from 1809 to 1813. Richard Croft of Cainscross was appointed in his stead and gave a security of £50. George Minchin and his wife Ann were guilty of 'malpractices' in the weight of coals sold at Dudbridge in 1799 and so were dismissed on the morning of 25 March. They were told to leave the dwelling house and premises by Monday 8 April. Robert Harper was recommended and appointed straight away. He did well because in 1813 he was given an increase of tuppence per ton on Newport coals and Shropshire slack which he sold. Unfortunately, years later, on 30 September 1831, Thomas Harper (Robert's son?) and his mother Sarah were declared insolvent and were dismissed from the situation. The Clerk was to inform all persons owing money to the Harpers to pay him direct; he was to appoint someone to enter the wharf to prevent further sales by the Harpers and to secure the Company's stocks. Counsel's opinion was sought as the case was complex. His advice was that the Company were not legally empowered to trade, the Harpers had been issuing invoices on credit to customers, therefore outstanding debts could not in law be claimed by the Company, although the money actually belonged to them. Basically, the Company was told not to 'lift its head above the parapet', and recover whatever it could quietly. Even the sureties could not be claimed; one had backed out some months earlier, and Joseph Grazebrook, who obviously had an inkling of what was going to happen, had

Dudbridge Wharf before the concrete block wall was built, looking west from Dudbridge Bridge. The house at Gladfield Gardens is in the distance, with the warehouse and crane before it. (Photograph by C.H.A. Townley, 1966: courtesy of J.A. Peden)

dramatically scored through the document and removed his signature and seal from it at a committee meeting.

Only one month later came the edict that the Company was not to trade in coals any more at Dudbridge. Independent traders then took over, prominent among them were the Nurse brothers. Two cottages, possibly the pair across the road from the wharf entrance, were occupied by Nurse and Grey when a sub-committee inspected them in 1834 with a view to establish whether brewhouses should be added, if necessary. James Nurse persuaded the Company to allow him to pay £5 per annum for landing coal on Dudbridge Wharf instead of paying wharfage in 1844. Perhaps he was 'pushing it' when, a few months later, the Company gave him notice that, when he had removed the coal lying beyond the boundary allotted to him, he was not to place any more there. A Mr Nurse was further admonished in 1865, along with a Mr Knee of Wallbridge Wharf, for depositing coal brought by rail, not canal, on the wharves, and were told to desist. James Nurse may have had some problems which were resolved because, after he applied in June 1861 to retake the houses and garden at Dudbridge and mentioned that he wanted to remove a shed he had put up, the Company reminded him that they had forgiven him 'a portion of the rent due from him at the time of his failure' and the claim ought not to be pressed. It was not.

Frederick Nurse, James's brother, was listed in the 1851 census as aged fifty-five and living at Cainscross with his sons, Charles, aged twenty-five, described as waterman, and Martin two years younger, a wharfinger. Fred was a coal merchant and they were all born at Saul. In August 1845 both brothers complained that too much of the wharf had been taken away as a result of alterations. Fred also said his rent was too high, and James asked for more frontage. A committee of inspection answered that the part of the wharf which was appropriated to the public was only enough for two barges unloading at the same time. However, some arrangement must have been made because the next year Fred was refusing to put up a garden wall, but capitulated when offered £5 towards its erection. It was to be 4½ft above ground, 2ft thick at the bottom and 18ins at the top, and built to the Surveyor's satisfaction. Another fence of larch poles was put up for him between his garden and the wharf in 1847. At the same time the Company made a deal with him, whereby if he landed 2,000 tons of coal each year at Dudbridge, he could have rent of his house for £10 per annum and, for every further 500 tons, the rent would be an extra £5. As he was already renting two houses connected with the wharf for £33 per annum, possibly for sub-letting, this seemed like a bargain. His house must have been reasonable, for it had a brewhouse, the floor of which was completed in 1848 and the roof pointed. A shed in the garden was to be pulled down and the materials preserved, but if Fred wished to use the pantiles to erect and cover a shed or stable (to belong to the Company once built) he could do so, but the Company did not sanction any more expense on the shed, unless recycled materials be used.

The Company continued to need a wharfinger and lock-keeper at Dudbridge and Joseph Cottle was appointed in place of William Hooper in April 1845. He was promoted with an extra 12s a week wages, from the position of just lock-keeper, and was given a better house. Always assiduous in his work, he reported to the Company in 1866 that J. Butt, master of the boat *Ann*, had placed road stone on part of the wharf, against his instructions. The Clerk informed the owner, G. Williams, that if it happened again then he and Butt would be fined.

On the wharf were various ancillary buildings, besides houses for tenants and workers. There were stables, one for four horses built in 1850 at the behest of Samuel Critchley for £42; a hayloft next to James Nurse's house; a warehouse which was stripped in 1848 and the roof covered on the front with Bangor Duchess slates and the back with old tiles; a new privy between the back of the warehouse and the agent's house with a fall into the canal and a spout at the back of the warehouse, to conduct water by a descending pipe into a vault and through it to the canal. As early as 1851 £5 per annum was paid to the Inspectors of Cainscross for lighting the canal bridge and entrance to the wharf with gas.

Initially there was not a crane at Dudbridge. Thomas Grazebrook had sold one of his to the Company in 1818 for only £5 but it was 1823 before consideration was given to an adequate one at Dudbridge, and estimates were invited. Charges for cranage were worked out before a crane was even ordered. They were to be 3d for

A close-up of the Stevenson crane, 31 August 2003. In 2001 it was scheduled Grade II by the Department for Culture, Media and Sport.

goods weighing less than two tons, then 6*d* per ton for upwards of two tons and proportionately for any part of a ton. The installation of it is not recorded but in August 1837 it was out of repair and the Company decided to employ a competent engineer to inspect it and advise whether it could be repaired and altered, 'so as to be adapted to servants of the wharf, and to be competent to raise at least five tons', or whether it was best to have a new one. At what price could a new or good second-hand iron crane be procured?

Joseph Small sent an estimate for supplying and putting up a new crane somewhat equal in strength to one belonging to Messrs Price & Co. (near the 'anti dry-rot co. wharf') in Gloucester for £125, provided he could use the cog wheels of the present crane. His tender was accepted, with the proviso that he include masonry and provide all materials and fixing. Adjustments were made for a longer chain and the question of masonry. Then a letter came from Messrs Isaac Marshall of Birmingham requiring a guarantee from the Company as Small was to obtain the crane from them. At a special meeting, which Small attended, the Clerk was instructed to write to Marshall's and ascertain the price and weight of castings needed for the crane before a guarantee could be issued. A reply by return suggested the crane be ordered direct from them. Small offered to withdraw his contract but still wished to put up the crane.

Therefore the Company ordered the crane from Birmingham, specifying best seasoned oak, for £140 and erection costs of £15. By 1846 the crane at Wallbridge was needing attention. Messrs Waring Bros. of Gloucester offered to make a new one for Dudbridge and to remove the present one to Wallbridge. The Company was not happy with the work and called in Captain Clegram, engineer to the Gloucester & Berkeley Canal, to supervise a trial at Dudbridge. Two pieces of timber, weighing 7 tons 18 cwt together, were attached. They had not been raised from the ground when one of the main wheels broke and the shaft had bent so much that it seemed to require strengthening before it would carry the weight. Clegram asked to see the contract. After protracted legal negotiations and after adaptations were made to the crane, the Company issued a cheque in payment to Messrs Waring for £126 10s on 4 January 1848, allowing Clegram's expenses of £7 17s 6d.

Special notices entitled 'Rules to be observed in working the crane at Dudbridge Wharf' were posted on the warehouse: it was not to be worked with less than three able-bodied men in loading timber, stone and iron; no person shall be allowed to lift a weight exceeding five tons at the inner sheaf of the jib and not more than two and a half tons at the outer wheel; no person shall at any time use the crane to haul or drag timber stone or iron lying more than 20ft from the base of the shaft of the crane; no person shall lower down a weight exceeding 1 ton 10 cwt upon the leverage wheel only; all persons doing any damage to the crane shall be liable to pay the expenses of repairing it and all owners of vessels will be responsible to pay for their servants. Further rules for preventing obstruction to the crane were added later. Nathan Driver, the Surveyor, purchased a pair of shears for use of the crane from Robert Osborne of Bristol for £5 14s 8d.

Pencil sketch by Alfred (Newland) Smith, 1838, looking west towards Dudbridge Lower Lock and Dudbridge Canal Bridge: beyond is Dudbridge Wharf. The trow is moored up to a private wharf where coal and possible timber are stacked. (Courtesy of F.J. Dallett)

Obviously the crane was going to break down and did so in 1854. It needed immediate attention, so the Company put out to tender for a new one in May. That submitted by Mr Stevenson of Preston, Lancashire, was selected, with Messrs Stothard & Co. as fall-back. The order was given to Stevenson in the middle of June and, by the middle of August, Mr Driver declared he was satisfied with the work and payment of £200 was made. The ground immediately round the crane and within the radius of it was paved with Bristol stone. In fact Driver and his men had done that work themselves because he had to take four extra hands to assist in mudding, as the ordinary hands were occupied in the erection of Saul Bridge and the crane at the same time. The old crane was to be advertised for sale and disposed of by the Surveyor.

Apart from repairs to the chain in 1889 after an accident with lifting a boiler, again in 1908 when it was sent to Cradley Heath, and an accident in 1913 when guards were fixed, no other work on the crane is recorded.

The Stevenson crane is still *in situ* today in the haulage yard owned by Wiggall & Son. It was taken over by Harry Wiggall, the grandfather of the present owner, when he bought the wharf from the Company, his former employers. A survey of the crane was made by the Gloucestershire Society for Industrial Archaeology and the history and detailed description were written by Dr Ray Wilson and published in their journals for 1994 and 1995. The Society then did some remedial work. In 2001 Barry Wiggall had the slurry dug out to enable the crane to slew.

Wallbridge Wharf

Wallbridge Basin, the terminus of the Stroudwater Navigation, was constructed at the optimum place in Stroud for such an undertaking, being close to the river and the main road to Bath, and at the confluence of Stroud's five valleys, allowing plentiful water supplies. A lot of mills requiring not just deliveries of coal but other necessary commodities like oil, soap, dye-stuffs, hay, timber and building materials were within fairly easy reach of the wharf. The town at the end of the eighteenth century was growing in prosperity and population, and trade increased in foodstuffs and luxury goods, mainly from Bristol.

A conveyance of the land on which the basin was built is not extant but most of it had been owned by the Webb family, clothiers of the Hill, a typical seventeenth-century two-gabled Cotswold house on the rise to the north. Their property stretched steeply down to the river Frome and an archway signifies a former approach in that direction. Before the Thames & Severn Canal was cut through in 1783 there was a lovely garden with gazebo on the site now occupied by the Stroudwater head-quarters. At the time the canal was first built the garden was owned by Peter Watts, dyer, and two of his sons became Proprietors in 1779. When the Stroud and Cainscross Turnpike went through in 1826 the gazebo was demolished.

A basin requires a strong wall. In January 1779 an advertisement was inserted in the *Gloucester Journal* for tenders for building the wall with ragstone, the price to include 'Halling' (hauling) and all materials. An agreement was made with William Franklin, an architect and builder, to undertake the work on those conditions using Aberthaw lime and Severn sand for the face of the work, at a cost of 13*s* a perch. Not wishing to waste anything, the Company ordered that clay dug up and thrown on the bank should be made into bricks immediately, so the quay may be levelled. But it was a year before that happened, after 20,500 bricks had been made, giving an income of £17 9*s* 03*d*. Gravelling was done by John Goodman over two months, September and October 1779, for which he was paid two guineas, then three guineas.

The improvement of the access was essential. In October 1779 Richard and Nathaniel Watts were paid £10 towards their expenses in widening and completing the bridge and road leading to the wharf, using their own land to do so. After that a quick mound (small bank planted with hawthorn or other hedging plant) was made between Mr Webb's land and the brickyard, while another hedge next to the quay was laid. By April 1780 trade was getting underway, for Joseph Grazebrook was given a lease for a year on the wharf on the north side of the canal extending from the crane to the lower end of the quay wall or as far as the coals were then laid, for 2*d* per ton.

It is surprising that the wharf was not enclosed until five years later, having been secured only by a palisade, for which William Marle was paid one guinea. The Clerk obtained proposals from Franklin and others for building a mortar wall 7ft high, 2ft thick at the bottom and 18ins at the top, to be coped with good weather stone and strong quoins at the gates and ends of the wall. Mr Gubbins also put in a tender but Franklin's was the most favourable and a completion date of 10 October was stipulated, otherwise a penalty of £5 would be enforced. At the same time, Mr Smith was to have notice in writing to remove the lime kilns and the building standing on the wharf. An agreement was made with Edward Keene, the carpenter, to make a pair of gates, with a good heart of oak, for 1*s* 3*d* per foot.

By far the most important event at Wallbridge in the first decade of the Company was the construction of the Thames & Severn Canal to connect with the Stroudwater and link the Severn with the Thames at Inglesham, a mile west of Lechlade at the limit of navigation of the Thames. On 30 July 1783 the Company of Proprietors of the Stroudwater Navigation signed and sealed the agreement with the Company of Proprietors of the Thames & Severn Canal Navigation in the presence of Henry Burgh, the Company's solicitor. They sold the piece of ground being part of the Stroudwater wharf, already marked out for the making of the Thames & Severn Canal, and gave all persons navigating vessels through the wharf free and unobstructed liberty to do so. The wall of the lock to be erected on the land at the entrance of the new canal was not to exceed a depth of 9ft, the spoil to be removed as soon as possible. This document, still in the Company's possession, makes it quite clear that the Thames & Severn Canal begins at the entrance to the lock, and *not* at the Point, as is sometimes assumed.

Cutting got started straight away and the first boat passed through the lock in January 1785 when the Thames & Severn was open as far as Chalford. In the summer of 1788 King George III spent five weeks at Cheltenham to take the waters for the good of his health. A visit to the Stroud area was planned for Thursday 14 August, which necessitated exact arrangements to be made beforehand. He was to have breakfast at 11.00 a.m. at Hill House, Rodborough (now Rodborough Manor), the

Wallbridge, facing east, with the Point in the centre, showing the leaky gates of the first Thames & Severn Lock to the left, and the entrance to Wallbridge Basin on the right. The Company warehouse can be seen in the middle distance, 1948. (Courtesy of Gloucestershire Record Office)

residence of Sir George Onesiphorus Paul, a clothier and philanthropist, who held Share No.3 in the Company. Dinner was to be at Spring Park (now Woodchester Park), a residence of the Rt Hon. Francis, Lord Ducie. Writing to Lord Ducie beforehand, Paul mentioned the difficulty of providing fresh horses for the king because his 'driving has killed and spoilt so many Horses on his Tour they are afraid of letting their horses go', speaking of post horses supplied by inns. Also people waiting by the road may become intoxicated if they waited on the same spot too long, so it would be best if the entourage returned by a different route.

> *Respecting the Navigation – the King seems so desirous of seeing everything that he would have embarked & gone down, but finding that the Queen would be alarmed with the Water it seems determined to be satisfied with passing the junction of the two navigations – & seeing the course of the Stroudwater from Selsly if agreeable to you.*

The party consisting of the king, the queen and the three eldest princesses did see a vessel passing through the lock, probably from a place overlooking it on Mr

Grazebrook's drive. Revd William Ellis recorded the event in the Stroud parish register but there is no record in the Stroudwater archive. The alternative way back over Selsley Hill would have given a good view of the canal, now obscured largely by trees.

Just after the canal was opened, the Committee ordered a warehouse to be built immediately, with an apartment at one end for the person attending. It was to be 9ft high 'under the beams', meaning the roof presumably. Samuel Hooper was to do the tiling, finding the pins and pointing it for 3s per square foot. Thomas Hitchcock was paid 19s for cutting the foundations, and James Wooley £1 for wheeling stone. Edward Edge wheeled bricks and built the new warehouse and William Franklin paved it for £3 18s 4d. Benjamin Grazebrook, who started life as a plumber, did the glazing for £8 3s 6d. The warehouse was ready at the beginning of 1780. Then it was to be let for one year at £10 per annum, after which time John King took it for two years at the same rent, when the Company agreed to erect a shed at the end for a brewhouse, which Mr Franklin was to build. King had a licence to live in the house which became a difficulty in June 1785 when he was dismissed, having 'abused the trust reposed in him'. He would be able to live in Richard Cam's house until Michaelmas and vice versa while Cam was to look after the two locks at Dudbridge. However, King left instead.

The same scene at Wallbridge from a 1930s booklet of Stroud scenes issued by Walter H. Collins of Stroud. The buildings by Lower Wallbridge Lock were part of Far Hill estate, the driveway of which can be seen through trees on the left.

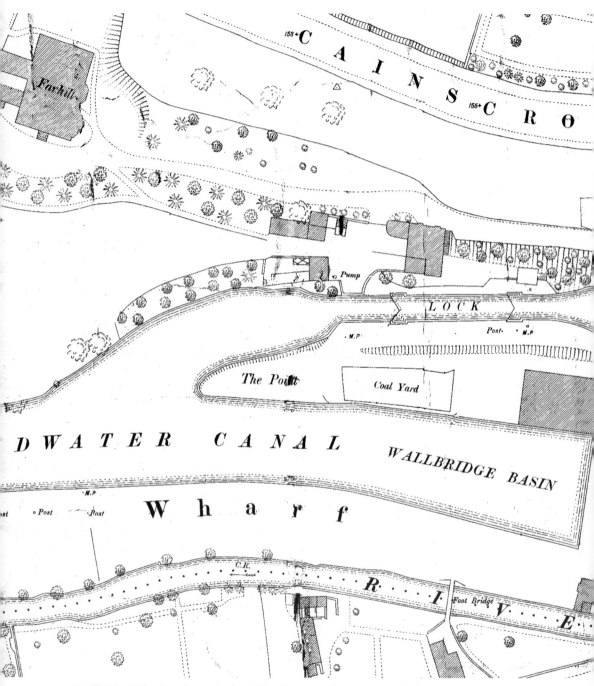

Wallbridge Wharf as shown in the 1884 Ordnance Survey map. Scale 1:500.

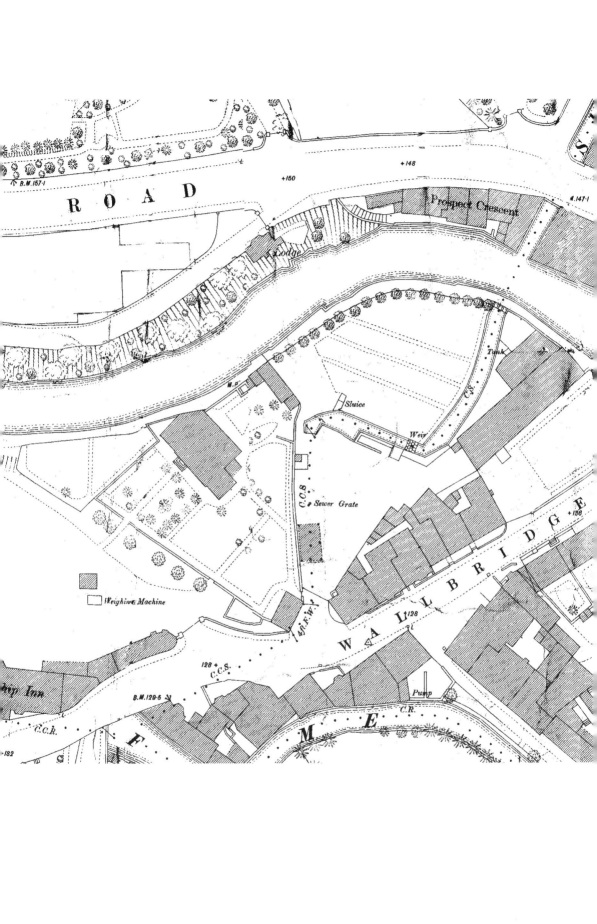

A shed was finished at the right-hand side of the gates to the wharf by Christmas 1793. It was for the benefit of the several teams (i.e. of bow haulers) to protect them from inclement weather. As it took over two months to build, it must have been fairly substantial. By 1795 the Company was feeling confident and looking to the future. They agreed a table of regulations for vessels passing on the canal should be put up on the wharf and set about planning for a company headquarters for the residence of the Clerk. It was to be at the eastern end of the wharf, and Mr Franklin was invited to produce plans and an estimate. At first his estimate was too expensive and another was submitted in December. This time it was agreed that the Company's men would dig the foundations, thus saving £7, and the Company carpenters would prepare the timber work under the direction of Franklin. All the rest – masonry, plasterwork and tiling – was to be done by the contractor, as per estimate, the whole to be completed by the following June. Subsequently additional requirements were made and the price adjusted accordingly. For instance, an office to the side was £56 4s 9d; the chimney piece and black slab in the best room was £3. Then there was a cellar of the same dimensions as the front room, a brewhouse, little house and wine vault. The Proprietors, at their half-yearly meeting in April, decided to add wings and they were quite right, as the house as it stands today looks large but is not. In fact the wing wall over the office nearest the road is a sham, with a blind window.

The sum total for the house, with all the extras plus a bow window made for Richard Cam's house, for which he agreed to pay increased rent, making it £2 10s per annum, was £763 11s 2d. The next year a wall of brick, with stone copings, was built to separate the Clerk's garden from the wharf. Steps led up to the front door to give lift from the cellar and makes the house almost identical to the Thames & Severn warehouses at Cirencester (now demolished), Cricklade and Kempsford, although the small oval window at the top is cut into the architrave on those and is above it in the middle of the pediment at Wallbridge, which has no wrap-around warehouse. There is no evidence to suggest that Franklin built those warehouses, although they seem to pre-date Wallbridge. Most likely the design is from an as yet unknown pattern book. The office is panelled with tongue and groove, with built-in shelves to take ledgers. These may be the iron ones that were ordered to be made in the middle walls of the office with two folding iron doors, secured by a lock with two keys for the safe keeping of the Company books. (It served the purpose, otherwise this book could not have been written 200 years later.) A fireproof chest was bought for £7 10s in 1848 and a new table chosen in 1859.

There is a pleasant prospect from the house, facing south-west, with plenty of light, especially upstairs. The hallway is cramped, with the stairs going straight up from the front door. They appear to be later than the house and could be a replacement for the original carpentry or an alteration in the position. On the left is the boardroom, with windows at the front. The side window overlooks the Thames & Severn Canal which runs across the back of the building with listed iron railings separating it from the towpath. The fireplace is now blocked and two doors give access to cupboards on either side of the back wall. The room on the right of the front door must have been the living room, because the office would have had a door to the outside for the benefit of callers. Outside walls are of rubble, rendered with stone quoins, and the chimneys were rebuilt.

Benjamin Grazebrook and his sons were doing well from the canal and enjoying many privileges. A piece of land on the wharf from the quoin of the brewhouse to the quoin of the stable was let to him in November 1784 for 10s per annum with power for him to fence it off. A concession given him in the next year was that his barges running to and from Gloucester and Bristol were to be allowed to pass and re-pass on the canal free of tonnage and wharfage if he should pay a flat £25 for six months. In consideration of this, his barges were not to be weighed. Grazebrook built Far Hill, a large house on the north bank overlooking the west end of the wharf probably in 1787. It was inherited by his son Joseph, the Company Treasurer, who died in 1843, leaving the estate to his only child, Hester Mansfield. During the First World War the house served as a war hospital depot, where bandages and dressings were made. In the mid-twenties it was the headquarters of Cotswold Stores, a local grocery concern. Stroud District Council bought it from the Stroud branch of the Labour Party and demolished it and the outbuildings in the 1980s.

A strange proposal was made in 1793 to the effect that the Thames & Severn Company should give up their wharf at Wallbridge to the Stroudwater on proper terms but, as the Company did not know what those terms were, nothing came of it. Their Wallbridge wharf was bigger than that of the Stroudwater and was situated to the north of their second lock behind The Bell inn, which also belonged to them.

The warehouse at Wallbridge Wharf was built between the basin and the Thames & Severn Canal to the north. (Photograph by C.H.A. Townley, January 1971: courtesy of J.A. Peden)

It was about 100 yards by a steep road from the Stroudwater wharf. Throughout the working life of both canals they were continually in consultation about tonnage charges, usually on coal and usually reducing them. It was of mutual benefit for them both to agree. About this time there was a 2s charge for tonnage and wharfage on all copper, brass and tin imported to Wallbridge, except what was brought by Messrs Grazebrook & Co. barges.

A succession of agents were contracted to sell coals (this is how the commodity was always referred to in the business documents) but not until 1804 was it recognised that at Wallbridge the agent was also the innkeeper. At that time William Hogg was appointed to succeed Richard Cam in the management of the coal trade and he gave £300 to be answerable for any deficiency in the coal account. On entering the house he was to take the fixtures, casks and stock of Mr Cam at the proper valuation and pay for it at a stipulated time. Hogg was given a licence to sell liquor at the Company's house on the wharf and it expired in 1807. John Sutton was then to take over and rent the house from month to month at £15 per annum, provided the magistrates would give him a licence. Sutton took over the house known by the sign of The Ship in Painswick Parish and engaged to sell coal for one year from 10 October 1807, on a bond from John Sims and James Hogg jointly of £300 each. Sadly, Sims appeared again two years later to apply on behalf of the widow of Sutton for her to continue to run The Ship; he would stand security for her and would find a suitable man to attend the coal trade. The Committee agreed.

In October 1813 John Lawrence was reported 'disabled by illness to conduct business at Wallbridge Wharf'. Samuel Adams was to take over, with the necessary securities, and a year later he was to be paid 6d a ton for selling Forest coal. Other traders were renting parts of the wharf, including Mr Tavey who in 1812 applied for part of the warehouse for laying in a stock of salt which previously had been landed at Upper Wallbridge Wharf (Thames & Severn). This was affirmed, provided Tavey paid for paving the warehouse. William Oakey was to rent the shed formerly occupied by Thomas Gardner, for £2 per annum.

Peter Smith, owner of land adjacent to the wharf and between the river and the Bath Turnpike (known as Anchor Road, between Wallbridge and the bottom of Rodborough Hill) wanted to rebuild the wall of his stable at the corner and to move the wall 3ft back on the corner to the mouth of the arch in 1810. The Committee had a look and said he may do so and he was to pay the value of the stone removed plus one guinea for the land. He applied again in 1816, this time he wanted to alter the turnpike, to take it through a part of the wharf, and had produced a plan. He proposed for the Company:

> to give up to Mr Smith a part of the wharf to enable him to make a road and the Company to receive as an equivalent, the garden ground of half an acre on the other side of the brook [Frome] near the wharf, Mr Smith reserving a proportion of the upper part of twelve feet. The fencing and the land to be made at the expense of the Company, as well as the repairing of the corner of the brewhouse.

It is not obvious why the Company agreed to this, but it is possibly the site where Wharf House was built later. Mr Smith appeared again in 1818 proposing to remove a small part of the Company's warehouse at the corner, not exceeding 4ft (probably next to The Ship). This was complied with on condition that he quit the portion of land at the back of the warehouse and exonerate the Company from any claim for repair of the arch on which the ground stood which was to be taken by the Company in lieu of the corner of the warehouse. A private wharf was made on land near The Anchor inn with a bridge across the brook. Many other drastic alterations were to take place to the road at the entrance to the wharf in future years.

Further building works took place in 1828. The walls of the main warehouse were raised to enlarge the upper room. The house occupied by Samuel Adams at the west end of the warehouse, which consisted of a room on the ground floor only, was raised to make another floor above.

A crane had been fixed on the Wallbridge wharf from when it first opened, although it may have been second-hand. By 1836 it was reported as 'insufficient' and one of the members of the Committee, John Holbrow, was to make enquiries at Gloucester for one capable of raising five tons. Mr Southam sold him a crane for £100. The Stroud Town Surveyor, Mr Mynett, damaged this crane in 1848 and the repair cost 30s. The Town Commissioners would pay only £1 towards it, alleging that one of the wheels was defective *before* it was broken and a piece of it was produced to confirm this statement. The Company climbed down but asked if Mr Mynett could be reprimanded for his carelessness. A lock and chain were ordered by the Clerk for the crane and left in the care of William Knee, the wharfinger.

Wallbridge Wharf, showing the Company headquarters, weigh-house, and the filled-in basin piled with bricks. Stroud Brewery's chimney is in background. (Photograph by N. Andrews, 1950s: courtesy of B. Ward-Ellison)

That particular crane was replaced in 1847 by the old one from Dudbridge. It was situated on the wharf at the square end of the basin and the base was still seen in about 1980. A weighing machine was further back in front of the Company House with a nice little square office alongside. This was still intact, with the desk, papers and inkwell in place until the early 1970s.

Apart from the Minutes in January 1844 when James Nurse was to be allowed to land his coals at Wallbridge free of charge, no reason given, most of the Wallbridge items in the Minutes for the mid-nineteenth century are concerned with The Ship inn and its licensee William Knee. In February 1845, Samuel Adams, who had taken over The Ship and was presumably retiring, applied for payment of the fixtures at the inn and compensation for the shed he had erected against the wall. The Committee ordered the fixtures to be valued and charged to the incoming tenant and £5 allowed for the shed. Four persons applied to rent The Ship and carry on the coal trade. They were: Bevan Smith, farmer and corn dealer of Harescombe; William Merrett, a person employed in pin manufacturing at Lightpill; Joseph Cottle, a shoemaker of Dudbridge; William Knee, a barge owner and coal dealer of Wallbridge, who was engaged. The latter took it on at £25 per annum and was to pay poor rates and all taxes, with six months notice on either side. Knee was not to land or sell coals, salt, timber or other merchandise on the Stroud wharves of the Thames & Severn Canal without permission. The shed and buildings erected by Adams and piece of garden

Wallbridge Wharf, looking towards Company offices, showing the new road alignment. (Photograph by C.H.A. Townley, January 1971: courtesy of J.A. Peden)

adjoining the wharfhouse garden were not included in his taking. His job included locking the wharf gates at night and opening them in the morning. A portion of the wharf was allotted to him for landing his coals; nevertheless, he was to pay the usual charge for wharfage. If he should sell more than 1,500 tons of coals in any one year, then the sum of £5 was to be deducted from his rent, or if more than 2,000 tons, the amount would be £10.

When John Biddle, a corn miller and important trader on the canal, requested more accommodation on the wharf in 1846, he was given the front part of the ground floor of the warehouse alongside The Ship, lately partitioned off from the cellar. The doorway communicating with the inn was to be walled up and the other door to the cellar and back kitchen widened. An open shed was to be erected between the back kitchen window to link with the existing shed and the old shed repaired. Other repairs had recently been made to The Ship in a manner typical of the Company when they transferred spouting (guttering) intended for Framilode warehouse to Wallbridge instead.

It seems that William Knee and the Company took some time to settle down together. At first there was some bother about credit. One Minute declared that he should have 'no more than three months credit on his tonnage account, on the agreement and understanding that the whole of the coals and other merchandise for the time being on the wharf at Wallbridge be subject and liable to be seized and sold for any deficiency that may happen in such account, in the same manner as under or distress for rent'. Soon after, Knee asked for permission to erect a stable on the wharf at his own expense. This was all right but the Surveyor was to supervise. Some repairs or alterations were authorised for The Ship inn in 1847 at the same time that the pavement in the hall and back kitchen were to be restored in the Clerk's house. The Company agreed that Knee could build a boat for himself on the wharf in 1855, provided it was finished within two months.

The Thames & Severn Company determined in 1847 that all wharfage charged on any goods, coals or merchandise put out on their wharf at Wallbridge or between there and Brimscombe Port should cease. Therefore, the Stroudwater had no choice but to do likewise.

In the summer months of 1853, coal landed at Wallbridge was 2,678 tons, only 600 more than in 1830. On top of that, John Biddle's trade in coal, wheat and flour at Lodgemore and Wallbridge was considerable. Most of the trade was at Eastington and Chippenham Platt, where over 2,000 tons were landed. By 1864, when there was pressure of competition on Bullo household coal and a reduction in tonnage at Downfield, the Company was looking to open a public wharf as reduction at Wallbridge was impossible, according to the Act. Mr Knee had a solution: he had bought a small property opposite the gasworks and offered it to the Company with all buildings for £280. The Company snapped it up but it is doubtful if a public wharf was opened. It is likely to be the corner on which the gasworks' manager's house was built later.

William Knee continued to work at Wallbridge for a long time. In 1864 his rent was increased to £25 for his house. Three years later he was listed in Slater's

Wallbridge Wharf. Taken from the garden of Company House in 1979, with the weighbridge and its office in front. When it was demolished soon afterwards, the desk, complete with ledgers and pen and ink, was still inside. (Photograph by G.G. Hoare: courtesy of G.G. Hoare and M.A. Handford)

The Ship inn at the entrance to Company Wharf at Wallbridge. There was also a private wharf off Anchor Road. The road alignments have now altered drastically, but some buildings remain. (Photograph by W.F. Lee, c.1910: courtesy of H. Beard)

Directory as brick, slate and coal merchant at The Ship inn. Stroud Brewery Co. took a lease but relinquished it in 1891 when the Committee arranged to inspect the property with a view to selling it. They decided against and inserted a 'To Let' notice in the Stroud papers. Solicitors Little & Mills reported that Messrs Holmes & Co. had made an offer of £35 per annum but had declined to take a lease for a term of years. Instead, Mr Chapman of Dursley had stepped in and offered £40 per annum for a term of seven, fourteen or twenty-one years, and so the Committee asked for an agreement to be drawn up. This was a case of gazumping, for then Holmes complained their offer had been superseded without good reason. The Company pointed out that their solicitor had acted according to instructions. However, to be fair, the Company accepted their claim for expenses of £5 in advertising for a tenant. A lease was signed with Mr Chapman, and Mr Gillman of the brewery had repairs made according to their agreement. The Company paid £12 for the exterior render and windows to be painted.

If the premises were to be connected to town water, the Stroud Local Board of Health, who had succeeded to the water company originally set up by Benjamin Grazebrook, required a cistern with a ball tap. This was agreed, so Mr Snape, the Clerk, wrote to the Board asking for connection. Two months later, in April 1893, they replied, declining to connect The Ship to the mains. The Clerk attended a meeting with the Board and the Company solicitor wrote a letter. However, the Board said 'they could not interfere further in the matter of the supply of water to

STROUDWATER NAVIGATION COMPANY.

NOTICE IS HEREBY GIVEN

THAT THE PORTION OF CANAL BETWEEN

Wallbridge Wharf, Stroud, and the Double Locks, near Ryeford,

WILL BE CLOSED FOR REPAIRS

From TWELVE O'CLOCK on SATURDAY NIGHT, the 17th day of AUGUST, to SIX O'CLOCK on MONDAY MORNING, the 26th AUGUST, 1901, or for such further time as may be required for the completion of the said Repairs.

The portion of Canal between the DOUBLE LOCKS and FRAMILODE will NOT be closed.

BY ORDER,

W. J. SNAPE,

A notice at Wallbridge Wharf, 1901.

The Ship'. After the tenancy had changed to John King and Frederick Worsey in 1895, Stroud Urban District Council, who had their own water supply, required the Company to connect with their mains. They decided the matter might stand until such time as the Council should *bring* the mains for connection.

Next came difficulty with tenants. The Clerk reported on 15 February 1898 that the inn had been closed for a week and sent them a letter. A notice to give up the tenancy came back, so the Company approached other breweries. Nailsworth Brewery offered £25 per annum, Cordwell & Bigg of Cainscross Brewery £20 and Smith & Son of Brimscombe Brewery £40. A lease for ten years was signed with Smith's who spent a considerable amount in improvements and the Company repaired the roof. John Lee was Smith's tenant in 1906. In 1915 the inn was refused a licence as 'the house has been ill conducted' and closed in March that year.

3

Structures: Locks

Framilode Lock

The position of the lock out to the river Severn at Upper Framilode caused some concern to the Company in the early stages of planning the Stroudwater Navigation. There was a question of using the mouth of the river Frome, called (in accordance with Severn estuary usage) Framilode Pill, about fifty yards to the north of the site finally chosen, but that would have meant upsetting the Purnell family who ran Framilode Tin Mill. The Pill is tidal but the mill was only partially powered by tide. Robert Whitworth (1737-99) of Calderdale was called to give an independent assessment for the Company. He had worked as Chief Surveyor and Draughtsman to James Brindley until Brindley's death in 1775. At the time of the report Whitworth was Surveyor to the Navigation Committee of the Corporation of London. The outlay involved in engaging Whitworth was considerable, but worth it because his report given at Gloucester Assizes in the case brought by the Purnells against the Company having no right to cut a new canal through Carter's Close at Framilode, was instrumental in a new Act being obtained.

Basically, Whitworth said that the place for the lock already chosen was the best one because the water of the Severn close to the shore was deep enough for vessels to pass into the canal almost at low water, which was not the case elsewhere in the vicinity. Most other places had a flat rocky shore, which would be costly to open a passage through and, if accomplished, would be difficult to keep clear, while 'it would be fighting against nature to attempt it'. He gave reasons for not using the Pill, and explained that if the Pill were deepened it would still get choked up and 'the Barge men would find great Difficulty in getting into it in Time of Land Floods'. Grazebrook's petty cash book shows £11 7s 0d spent in fetching Whitworth from London on 29 July 1775, and eleven guineas for his journey to attend the Assizes on 4 August, a further £3 10s 6d the next day, plus 7s 9d 'at the view' for Whitworth and Mr Wakefield (presumably for a meal). Whitworth was back in the area in December 1781 when he was invited to make a report for the Thames & Severn Company, and subsequently became their Surveyor.

In 1993 the walls at the entrance to the lock from the river were added to the list of scheduled buildings as Grade II. They were built, under the aegis of Thomas Yeoman (*c.*1700-1781), President of the Royal Society of Civil Engineers, of large coursed limestone blocks, curved to meet the position of the lock gates. Work on

Framilode Lock at the entrance to the canal from the river Severn.
Above: Looking west across to Crown Point.
Below: Looking east at the entrance to the basin.
(From a series taken by the Gloucestershire County Surveyor in 1948. Courtesy of Gloucestershire Record Office)

the Stroudwater was the last project undertaken by Yeoman. Edward Paget-Tomlinson has described the walls 'as an early example of a structure associated with a river lock'. There is very little evidence in the Minutes to suggest that maintenance work has been carried out on the walls or lock to any great extent. In 1999 the Environment Agency were permitted Listed Building Consent to place a block of limestone in the bed of the river to protect the walls from river erosion.

As the entrance was set at an angle to the river, to protect the walls and banks, it was never easy for vessels to negotiate the bend. In 1804 one of the beacons marking the entrance was broken by a Thames & Severn Canal boat, and that Company was asked to pay for repairs. William Purcell, the new clerk/lock-keeper, was allowed in 1815 to rent a piece of ground on the left bank of the lock at 30s per annum, on condition that should the Company want to land timber or stone for repairing the lock, it should be available for them to do so. The top gate was renewed in 1900, long after Purcell had finished gardening, and the bottom gates had a new frame for £12 in 1838.

Inevitably there was some earth movement in the ground, being close to such a forceful river. The curbstones on the left side of the lock had to be reset in 1845 as they were overhanging the wall. Piling was inserted in the brook (Frome) at the back of Mr Burbridge's house in 1854 to prevent the bank from giving way further. One major repair was undertaken later when a part of the wall abutting the Severn on the north side of the entrance gave way and immediate repair was estimated at £52.

Even after the Gloucester & Berkeley Canal opened in 1820, thus giving vessels a safer and perhaps quicker journey than negotiating the sandbanks and tides of the Severn, Framilode Lock and Basin continued to attract trade. Boat owners had been brought up to know the vagaries of the river for hundreds of years, so it was not a problem, and they could also avoid higher tolls. A list of boats entering the lock in 1890 is quite long, and includes some pleasure boats. *Economy* brought 2 tons of fruit from Bristol in August, and the same again a week later. *Betsy* had a cargo of 54 tons of coal from Bullo in June and August. Percy Snape, Clerk and Surveyor, copied out the dimensions of the two smallest locks, Newtown and Framilode, from statistics given to the Board of Trade for 1888. Fred Rowbotham, then of the Severn River Board, had requested the details in 1938. Framilode was given as tidal, measuring 71ft 9ins by 14ft 9ins and 5ft 6ins, with total rise or fall of 12ft 9ins.

How many lock-keepers can claim immortality in verse? James Harris took over the lock and care of the tides from Mrs Fanny Pocket, whose husband Richard had died on 25 November 1910. Ivor Gurney (1890-1937), whose increasing national reputation as poet and song-writer is forever associated with his native Gloucestershire, particularly with his beloved Cotswold hills and Framilode, wrote several versions of *The Lock Keeper* when recuperating at the Lock House from the onset of a nervous breakdown in 1913. Harris, although not named, is described thus: 'A tall lean man he was', and 'A tall lean man, proud of his gun'. His working day started with him 'by the lock gates, … Or busy in the warehouse on a multitude … Of boat fittings, net fittings; copper, iron, wood.' Then he was digging beneath the apple tree, with 'pipe between set teeth'. In the afternoon he 'trailed over four miles country tentaculous. … With coalmen, farmers, fishermen his friends, … And duties without beginnings, without ends.' At the end of the day he would enjoy talking with other men 'Outside the blue door facing the canal path'. Then after closing time he would sit in the chimney corner, quiet and thoughtful, not being a book man, but with knowledge of fish, watercress beds, tide running, badgers, stoats, snakes and foxes.

Gurney almost regarded Framilode as a panacea for all ills. He had known the place from an early age, as the destination for family walks. His friend Herbert Howells from Maisemore recounted that once, when they were both students, Gurney was playing the organ for morning service in Gloucester Cathedral, and the 'great east window was aflame with light, he cried, "God, I must go to Framilode!", walked out, a Scholar Gypsy, and stayed away for three whole days'. When staying at the Lock House, Gurney wrote to his friend Marion Scott urging her to come, telling her that as a lodger he paid 12s 6d a week, but 'lady friends of mine stay comfortably in a dear little cottage for eighteen shillings and sixpence'. In another letter he chronicles his day: 'Yesterday was spent in wheeling coal up a plank – barge loading. Today is eeling and haymaking. Tomorrow is boat mending and mullet fishing.' When his father was weak with cancer, he persuaded him to go to Framilode, which he did, for a week or two. Just before Gurney, after serving in the First World War, was certified insane in 1922, he wrote to W.H. Davies, another poet who lived in Gloucestershire, that 'Framilode was a place I read your poems most at'.

Framilode. A postcard posted in 1913 when Ivor Gurney was a lodger with James Harris, the lock-keeper. (Courtesy of H. Beard)

Poor Harris had his peace disturbed quite a lot in 1914 when there was a dispute between the Company, James John Harris, Frederick Wood (trow owner, stone merchant and general carrier of Westbury-on-Severn, on the west bank of the river), and Frank Brocher (a labourer of Framilode). It was about landing ferry passengers on Company land near the lock. Actually the proper ferry ran from the Darell Arms at Lower Framilode across to Crown Point. A handwritten note by W.J. Snape reads:

29.8.1914. 7 p.m. Brocher came across the River to fetch Fred. Wood. He landed on Company property and Harris [cautioned] him that it was not a landing ferry. He commenced to use abusive language, saying he would use it as he wished to do and should not take any notice of anyone or anything. Wood appeared on the scene and demanded entrance through the gate to the boat in question. This permission was not granted, he thereupon asked Brocher to fetch a hatchet and he would break the bloody lock off, which he did and threw it into the river. Our man left to obtain another lock and when he did return they had gone. The lock was removed during the same night and has not been found. The lock-keeper then put on another lock, which has remained. He has not seen Wood or Bocher since. Bocher was sober. Wood had had a little drink as could be seen by his manner.

The culprits were basing their actions on an Act passed in the time of Henry VIII when the King's subjects had the right to use paths that were one and a half foot broad on each side of the river.

This situation dragged on for six months, with Brocher putting up a fence alongside the Company's fence, destroying a notice board, and removing six locks from the gate, which he obstructed. PC Clutterbuck from Fretherne Police Station twice asked the Company to prosecute Brocher, but they failed to do so. Harris and his wife continued to write, giving accounts of further disturbances, and one letter in March refers to Snape having been ill. The police constable once pointed out to the Company that 'people are trespassing on Company land between the new fence at the lock gates, catching elvers. They do no damage, only do this through elver season to earn a few shillings. If I catch any of them, will you prosecute?'.

Brocher himself wrote in only once, but the signs are it was dictated to a school-child:

If your so-called lock-keeper would clean the dirt from the sills of the bridges instead of sweeping it into them so one man instead of three could open them, it would be better instead of troubling about footpaths on river banks and trying to cause myschief [sic] in the village it would be better for him we inhabitants of Framilode which or [are] nearly all watermen have always tried, and have done our best in the interests of the canal.

PC Clutterbuck did have some success. A newspaper cutting reveals that in December 1914, Frank Brocher and Joseph Nicholls were charged with poaching on the estate of Sir Lionel Darell. The constable had found them with a gun, two rabbits and a pheasant in a wood. Each was fined £1 with costs of 6s.

Many people remember Leonard Pockett, described as lock-keeper, lengthsman and tidesman. He bought the house, warehouse and basin from the Company for £1,000 in 1955.

Junction Lock

The schedule for listing Junction Lock and lock gates as Grade II describes it thus:

Squared stone walls with stone copings, modified by some later work on the bridges. Lock is approximately twenty metres long and five metres wide with two pairs of original timber lock gates, balance beams and paddle-gear, all of unusual design for the Stroudwater Canal lock system. This is a major historical survival, intact and in remarkably good condition.

In fact, although on the Stroudwater Navigation, the lock was built by the Gloucester & Berkeley Canal Co. and was always operated and maintained by them and their successors, the British Transport Commission and British Waterways, who restored it in the 1990s.

On 19 September 1796 a delegation from the Gloucester & Berkeley Company attended the Company meeting respecting the proposed deviation from the line marked out as per their original Act. They would now intersect the Stroudwater at a level created by means of an embankment, with a new lock below the junction in lieu of Whitminster Lock. The Stroudwater Committee suggested the embankment should be kept in repair in perpetuity at the expense of the Gloucester & Berkeley, and the Company indemnified from all consequences arising from it. This was agreed and a stipulation made that a culvert should be put under the embankment to drain adjacent fields. The Gloucester & Berkeley Canal would pay all Stroudwater expenses regarding the deviation. Thomas and Benjamin Baylis, contractors to the new Company, began on the lock for the new line in 1817. They had to raise the water level of the Stroudwater by about 4ft. Two huge pairs of stop gates were erected to safeguard water from being lost from the Stroudwater, and after some setbacks the levelling and linking of the two canals was finally achieved in Autumn 1825.

Whitminster Lock

Whitminster Lock, or Shallow Lock, was built just below the place where the original line of the canal used the river as a channel. This arrangement was soon found to be unsatisfactory because of the amount of mud brought down by the river, hampering navigation, and a separate cut was made. When the Gloucester & Berkeley Canal found a problem with water supply, they made an agreement with the owners of two mills on the Frome, Whitminster and Fromebridge, whereby any surplus river water could be passed into the Stroudwater Navigation, which would then act as a feeder as far as the Junction. The new level left Whitminster Lock with only a two-inch drop, thus acquiring its alternative name of Shallow, and the gates were normally left open. With so many interests being party to this system, difficulties were bound to arise.

One of the main problems was that of mud again. The Company had insisted the Gloucester & Berkeley Canal should be responsible for mud clearance. Unfortunately this task was not carried out with diligence and matters got to a head in 1831. Following a complaint by the Company, the Gloucester Canal engineer Captain Clegram replied to the Clerk on 16 September, 'I ordered boats up to commence dredging through this morning. The mud would have been removed when the boats were last through, but I was obliged to take the men away to stop some leaks.' This did not satisfy the Company, who pronounced at their next meeting that the lock was in future to be used as it was before the advent of the Gloucester & Berkeley Canal, so the lock gates were not to be left open, but to be used to keep up the water in the Bristol Road pound to its normal and proper height. In the best interest of the Company it was necessary for the Gloucester & Berkeley Company to find another method of obtaining their water. Before this could happen, the owner of Fromebridge and Framilode tin mills took the matter into his own hands. He was Purnell Bransby Purnell Esq., later to become Chairman of the Gloucestershire Quarter Sessions from 1842 to 1863, and he withdrew from his agreement with the Gloucester & Berkeley Company, resulting in a disastrous situation one morning when its canal was found drained overnight to a depth of nine inches. As the Gloucester & Berkeley Company were prevented from making their own decisions quickly, being hamstrung by the necessity of checking all developments through their 'backers', the Loan Commissioners, circumstances deteriorated. It ended in a fisticuffs at Whitminster after Charles Owen Cambridge, owner of Whitminster Mill, had intervened.

The Shallow Lock. (Photograph by C.H.A. Townley, April 1971: courtesy of J.A. Peden)

The outcome was that Gloucester & Berkeley obtained an Act in 1834 authorising them to obtain a further loan to rectify the problem of water supply, which included a new intake below Whitminster Lock, and four methods of transferring water were explored, the one chosen being a set of conduits leading from the river under the field to the Stroudwater Navigation. Settling ponds and a weir were constructed, on the site of Whitminster Mill and millpond which was bought from C.O. Cambridge. A keeper was appointed to control the flow and the Company contributed to his salary if he monitored and adjusted Stroudwater levels.

Clegram requested permission to fit stop boards into grooves in the wing walls at the upper end to enable a stank to be made there to keep back water when it may be necessary to draw down the Bristol Road level. The request was deemed by the Committee to be without prejudice to the Company's rights as secured by the Act, therefore they did not concede to the Gloucester & Berkeley Company any rights to interfere with any of the locks or other works without permission. That was in 1837, the year after the Stroudwater Company had issued the following edict: 'It is desirable that in future the locks should be opened by our own servants for the passage of vessels.'

Relations between the two companies improved over time concerning the lock. In 1848 Clegram signified he was willing to do what he could to enable the Company to repair the lock gates. At the beginning of 1854 it was realised the gates needed inspection but Mr Driver, the Surveyor, was unable to do it because of the

Lockham Aqueduct on a misty September morning in 1963. 'Iron posts and chains to be erected on the side of the brook where it runs under the canal' (Minutes of May 1844).

continued frost. In the summer a site meeting was held, attended by George Nurse representing the boatmen. He explained the difficulty of getting through the pound above the lock owing to shortness of water. Realising the solution would be to install two new pairs of gates, the Company held the matter over.

Troubles with lack of water, of maintenance of lock gates and with mud were not over. In the 1890s the Company had to contend with delays to vessels with consequent claims as well as loss of revenue. In a note from Henry Thomas of the Canal House, Wallbridge, dated 11 November 1895, the plight of the *Exelsior* running from Dudbridge to Bristol was recorded. She had a cargo of gravel and was drawing 4ft 10ins, and took seven and half hours to travel from Bristol Road Lock to Shallow Lock. A horse, six donkeys and a rope on a pole windlass were needed to get her out of the tail of the lock, and this stopped four loaded barges from proceeding the other way up to Stroud. By 1899 matters were exceedingly bad, and the trow most affected was *Reliance* which belonged to the Stroud Gas Light & Coke Co. and regularly carried Newport coal up to Stroud. Her overall measurements were 67ft 3ins from stem to stern, breadth 15½ft and drew 5ft when fully loaded with 70 tons. She arrived at Shallow Lock on 23 October and stuck there fast until Tuesday 24 October, the canal being very low. Previous to this, she had been detained in August when a letter was sent to W.J. Snape, the Company Clerk from the Sharpness New Docks & Gloucester & Birmingham Navigation Co., the new name for the Gloucester & Berkeley and known as the Dock Co., giving an explanation: 'We are short of water, and I regret the only real remedy will be to put your gates in working order. It is a rare occurrence.' Another letter dated 4 November stated:

> *Our canal was nine inches down. It would be wise for the Company of Proprietors to re-instate the top gates of this shallow lock, which I believe are in a fairly good state of preservation. Then it would be possible after the passage of one vessel to impound the water in Bristol Road reach and would merely involve a slight delay of a couple of hours whilst drawing down the pound and allowing it to fill up.*
> [...]
> *Our man at Whitminster could look after the gate and see to its being closed when necessary or desirable.*

The reference to 'our man' was rather strange because only two years earlier the Dock Co. had offered to dredge the Bristol Road pound if the Company would pay half the cost of £75, with the specific proviso that the Company would relieve them of the obligation to keep a man to attend the Shallow Lock gates. What the Company said to the Dock Co. in reply is not known, but can be guessed by the answer dated 7 December 1899: 'I entirely fail to see what safeguards our Act provides for the present contingency. You should keep the lock in good order. It's only rarely you are inconvenienced by lack of water.' In fact, the real reason for the lack of water seems to have been identified by Fredericks, the man at the Junction who served both companies. In October 1897 he noted the height of the Gloucester & Berkeley at the Junction, over three days, when it barely deviated from its normal height of 18½ft:

'The stop gates here work the wrong way to maintain the Stroudwater level. They are for keeping the Gloucester & Berkeley level up. The only remedy is for the Shallow Lock gates to be made good, and for the small weir above them to be repaired.'

This was written just after the *Reliance* had had one of its detentions, and the Gas Co. had sent in a bill for £1 5s to make up for the 1s per ton extra for the 25 tons unloaded to another barge.

All was resolved eventually, as shown in a letter of March 1904. The Dock Co. were responsible for keeping the Shallow Lock gates and works in order, and the Stroudwater the Bristol Road Lock. However, it was not always lack of water which caused delays, as witnessed by William Staddon of Chalford who told his tale to the *Stroud News* in 1948 (reprinted in the *Trow*, the magazine of the Cotswold Canals Trust, in Winter 1986/7). In around 1893, when he was a young man of about twenty, he worked on one of Jesse Smart's boats, and one winter they had two loads of birch timber brought to Stroud. The ice-breaker was working on the Gloucester & Berkeley Canal, but they got stuck in the Shallow Lock and were there fourteen weeks without moving an inch. They used to go home, but had to visit the boat to check it periodically (because if left, the ice can cut into the hull, and needs to be loosened sometimes several times a day). During all this time the horse was stabled. At last, when all was ready, the horse was fetched, but it stumbled and fell into the canal, only a quarter of a mile from the boat. It was impossible to save it from drowning; it had to be pulled from the water with the help of another horse and a noose.

At the time of writing, Whitminster Lock is in a form of limbo. Cotswold Canals Trust started excavating it and Mrs Teesdale, the local landowner, turned the first sod in a JCB in the summer of 1995. The bed was found to be unusual, made of large stone blocks each 18ins by 9ins, and in very good order. A guillotine lock gate is now ready to put in place.

Bristol Road Lock

Due to foresight and good planning, all locks on the Stroudwater Navigation are situated close to a roadway, with one exception. This led to ease of delivery of materials, carts and workers to the site during initial building operations, as well as for later repairs and maintenance. Bristol Road Lock was a case in point, being on the east, or Stroud side of the road bridge, with the wharf on the west.

This was a busy lock, and records show that lock gates were renewed often. In June 1820 a new pair of gates were ordered, and again in 1825. There must have been others too between then and 1872 when the top gates were renewed, followed by the bottom ones in 1891.

Staffing the lock was not usually a problem as, being so close to the wharf, the wharfinger could fulfil a dual role. Critchley was given remuneration in 1834 for his trouble in locking and opening 'lashers' (a local word meaning the water which lashes from an opening or weir, or the pool into which it passes, or alternatively another word for 'weir' (*OED*)) and attending to the lock over and above his normal line of duty. Also, books were provided for lock-keepers to enter the date, the under-level of the water, times of opening and closing, when they take their water supply, and any other observation which may occur to the state of the streams, complaints or otherwise, and in the case of Five Locks and Bristol Road, to enter the time when and for how long water in the canal may be brimming over the weirs there. These ledgers were to be shown to the Clerk once a fortnight, and brought to the Committee's monthly meeting.

At the same time it was decreed that lashers of Foundry Lock, Double Lock and Bristol Road should be kept locked during the night by the lock-keepers, except they may be opened to let barges navigate by night. Normally no vessel was allowed to pass through any lock after sunset or before sunrise. Permission to do so could be granted by the Clerk or Surveyor, who would issue a night pass each time for 1s. There should be a good light at the head of the vessel, and the lock-keeper of every lock passed through should be in attendance.

Considering their obligations to keep the canal in a safe and acceptable condition following the 1954 Act, which closed it to navigation, the Company proposed in 1958 to build a dam to replace the derelict lock gates at Bristol Road. As part of this scheme, a weed-control firm was called in to advise on clearing the bed between Eastington and Bristol Road, with a view to putting it back in water, possibly to derive an income from fishing, and to demarcate land boundaries. The firm could not guarantee cattle would not be harmed, and the landowners, Mr Wight of Grove Farm and Macpherson Grant of Whitminster Court, were not co-operative, and the scheme was dropped. Three years later it surfaced again, this time without the weed-killing.

Estimates were invited to 'construct a Concrete Dam in place of the existing Lock Gates at the Stroud end of the Lock. The height to be equal to the Lock Gates; Seal the Sluice Gate on the Whitminster side of the lock; Repair the Sluice gate on the Bristol Side of the Lock. … The Concrete Dam to be similar to the one constructed at Newtown.' Before a decision was made the Surveyor amended the measurements to a height of 9ft, and the width to be two 9ins hollow concrete block walls, 5ft apart from outside to outside, and the middle filled in with mass concrete. The Directors reported the work completed at the end of 1963, the water restored and fishing rights let. They added that the length was to be acquired by the Ministry of Transport and restored for agricultural purposes. Subsequently it was sold to adjacent landowners, and the lock was demolished for the large roundabout on the A38.

Eastington: The Five Locks

Westfield Lock

The five locks, comprising Westfield, Dock, Pike, Blunder and Newtown, constitute a flight, but are too far apart to be a staircase. Westfield is immediately beside Westfield Bridge, which carried a bridleway from the hamlet of Westend to Eastington. In the Minutes it was usually referred to as Bottom Lock of Five, and apart from when first building, the earliest reference is for 5 July 1825, when the north wall was to be taken down and rebuilt, the south wall cased and a new pair of lower lock gates put up. They were replaced again in 1896. The lock was built of brick, but some of the coping stones are still lying in what was the lock chamber.

As the lock was a bit isolated, the boatmen would take the opportunity to cut a few corners, and not adhere to rules governing passing through locks. G. Bird, owner of *Faith*, was reported for entering Westfield Lock on 3 June 1865 without drawing the paddles and shutting the lock gate, and was fined £1. On 3 March the next year J. Tanner, captain of *Sarah*, passed out of the lock without opening the gates properly and with only two hands aboard, thus contravening one of the strictest rules. He was let off with a fine of 5s. After some unfortunate accidents, including drowning, the Company had issued a regulation that 'lock-keepers must enforce to the utmost of their power the Company's regulations re. the employment of three men to navigate boats'. William Adams had disobeyed this rule early in 1855, when an accident to his barge caused him and his crew to be drowned. The Company gave £3 back to his widow out of the fines he had recently paid for breaches of other byelaws by him and Mr Allen, his captain.

When the Ministry of Transport was making plans to transform the area by filling in the canal and constructing an approach road to the M5 motorway, Alan Payne the Company Secretary in 1969 consulted F.W. Rowbotham about the best way to treat the canal. Without being specific about the plans, Rowbotham describes them as grotesque and 'straight out of an engineer's text book'. He suggested the most natural thing would be to return the waterway as near as possible to nature, by treating the canal as a tributary of the Frome, which it almost was, and 'giving a river as "sweet" a flow as possible.'

Dock Lock

Court Orchard was the original name for the lock at Chippenham Platt, but after the dock was made for repairing boats and housing the mudding machine in 1821, Dock Lock was more specific, being alongside the maintenance yard. One lock-keeper was responsible for all five locks, and had a house on The Island, until the new house was built on the site of the Pike Gate. So the affairs of the lock-keeper in the Minutes are tied up with the dock, and sometimes the keeper was also the coal merchant.

When the Committee made their annual inspection in August 1835, they noted a new wing wall was needed for the north side of the tail of the lock, but it could be put off until next year. Some repairs were ordered for June 1859, but complaints broached two months later were serious. Boatmen were in the habit of flushing locks, especially on the Eastington flight, to enable heavily laden boats to pass up the pound, causing loss of water to mill-owners. Any offenders would be warned by the Surveyor, and if repeated, penalties would be enforced. New gates were put in, and the canal stopped for a week in May 1861 for the work to take place. The top gates were further replaced in 1873, and the bottom in 1889. During the purge of malevolent boatmen in 1866, the *Jane's* (owner E. Webb) master, Amos Workman, navigated through Dock Lock without opening both top gates; he was fined 5s.

Pike Lock

Pike Lock is immediately east of the bridge carrying the road from Stonehouse to Eastington where it makes a ninety-degree turn from the A419. It was a busy lock, and in 1816, when new gates were required, the Company resolved that plates of iron instead of wood planking be used. However, the next meeting was informed that the wood for the planking was already prepared, so the iron plates were held over until new ones were required elsewhere. Perhaps they should have been put at Pike because only six years later a new pair of upper gates was needed. In 1838 the Company was still thinking in terms of iron to protect lock gates. They ordered twelve pairs of blocks of cast iron, a pair for the lower gates of each lock to prevent 'injury or damage by the violent striking of boats or barges against them'. New bottom gates were installed again in 1885.

A small wharf was used beside the turnpike road just upstream from the lock. This was where hard 'foreign' stone was discharged: blue limestone, black basalt and pink granite. Thomas Beard reported William Yates for taking onboard a load of hay here in 1811, paying tonnage on only four tons. The Committee wanted to ascertain how much hay had been bought from the farmer. It brought home to them that a super-intendent should be appointed 'for the better conduct of the Navigation '. Beard was to have the post at 18s a week, but his career was stopped at Framilode shortly after.

Alice Brinkworth (left) and Alice White with four-year-old Harold Brinkworth, outside Pike House in 1928. On the right are Pike Lock gates, and the leaking gates of Blunder Lock can be seen in the distance. (Courtesy of M.A. Handford)

Fewer defaults are recorded for this lock, it being in public view from several angles. C. Cox, master of *Trader* (owner G. Hazle), passed through without opening both gates and was towing the vessel with two donkeys *abreast* on 10 April 1866. This incurred a 5*s* fine.

Detailed records are held concerning the sale of land and subsequent building of the Lock House on the corner site. It was formerly owned by the Cainscross Division of the Turnpike Trust who had a toll house, garden and two gates across the roads. The sale to the Company of Proprietors was made on behalf of the Trust in 1877 by Samuel Stephens Marling, William Henry Marling and Frederick Eycott, all of whom were Proprietors themselves. An agreement was made with Harper Bros., builders of Stroud, to erect the new lock house for £180 in 1878. The brickwork specified was four courses of blue bricks and finish with a plinth, the bricks being 9ins thick; a slate course to be put in the foundation for prevention of damp. There was to be a lobby, back kitchen, two front rooms, three bedrooms, a wash-house and closets, and a fanlight over the front door. The rooms to be all 11ft square, 8ft 5ins high, except the back kitchen and bedroom over, which were to be 14ft by 10ft. All chimneypieces were of stone. The lobby was 6½ft wide, 11ft long; the wash-house 6ft square and 10ft high at the back, dropping to 8ft at the front. Then there was a closet and ashpit. The fittings were: two sideboards in the parlour, with double doors panelled; one sideboard and one cupboard in the front kitchen with double doors panelled; one cupboard in the back kitchen; one shelf in the wash-house. The grates and locks were to be chosen and supplied by the Company. John White was the lock-keeper in the first decade of

Excavating the canal bed in the pound between Pike and Blunder Locks in the 1970s. (Photograph courtesy of *Stroud News & Journal*)

the twentieth century, and lived in Lock House with his family. He also acted as the clerk. The Company sold the property to the sitting tenant, Walter Cecil Miles, in 1955 for £850. The present owner has added two extensions in the last decade, both of them using materials in keeping with the original house.

Blunder Lock

This lock, properly Lower Nassfield Lock, got its nickname during the building when it was alleged one of the non-resident engineers made a mistake in calculation, suspected to be deliberate because of a previous dispute he had had with the Company. Blunder has been its official name ever since. It is about 200 yards east of Pike Lock. A path which led from the hamlet of Nastend was diverted over the lock when the canal was cut through and obliterated when The Leaze (Eastington Park) was built.

Blunder was the scene of an horrifying accident in April 1834 as reported in the *Gloucester Chronicle*. The canal was impeded for a fortnight, though not recorded in the Minutes.

> *A boat, heavily laden with stone, belonging to a man named Twine, and steered by a woman* [which was perhaps unusual]*, entered the fourth lock without sufficient care having been taken to check the speed at which it was proceeding. It consequently struck with considerable force against the further gates – the weight and the impetus of the vessel instantly burst them open, and the pressures of the immense body of water from behind flung it, with the fury of a cataract completely out of the lock through the forced gates, head foremost into the whirlpool formed beneath by the escaping element. The woman at the helm was fortunately saved.*

New gates were fitted to the lower gates in 1822, and again in 1880. J. Wakeman was guilty of pushing the gates open by using his vessel in August 1864, and paid 2s 6d as a fine.

David Boakes, Manager of the Cotswold Canals Trust, submitted a report on Blunder Lock to the Company in 1988, outlining its recent history and the problems encountered since the disastrous water mains failure and damage to Double Lock at Christmas 1987. The main lock structure is of stone blocks, with the upper gate recesses and upper wing walls of brick construction. Following the Act of 1954 the upper gates were removed and a mass concrete dam built to contain water in the pound for fishing, around 1960. The ground paddles were removed too, and culverts sealed with concrete. Boakes then logged all the work in the previous ten years to restore the lock, sometimes using labour from the Manpower Services Commission, whereby long-term unemployed were retrained in building skills. Most of the labour problems were caused by silt, vandals and piling until, in Autumn 1987, the dam started to be demolished. On Boxing Day Newtown Lock was found flooded, and equipment ruined, whilst Blunder Lock chamber, 400 yards below, was filled with silt above the water level of the lower pound. The upper pound had a deep channel scoured out of the silt over the whole length. An estimate for over £12,000 was given to clear the silt from the chamber, but no compensation was forthcoming from Severn Trent Water Authority whose alleged neglect had caused the mishap.

Newtown Lock

Only in recent times has this lock been known as Newtown. Intended to be named Upper Nassfield, in the records it was Eastington Top, or Top Lock of Five. Its dimensions in 1888 were 72½ft by 16ft by 5ft 4ins, with a total rise/fall of 7½ft. It is built in brick throughout, with stone quoins and coping stones, and was repaired and repointed in 1825. The top gates were renewed in 1876, and the bottom in 1864 and 1907. Messrs Ford of Ryeford, who were major traders on the Navigation, asked to have Eastington Lock widened and enlarged for their benefit in 1858 as they had difficulty getting their steam vessel *Queen Esther* through. The Company were wont to accede to their demands, but on this occasion it was a No!

Stonehouse & District Angling Club instigated a dam being built at the lock in Autumn 1957 of concrete blocks approximately 3ft wide. They did the work, but the Company paid for materials. Before it was finished a horse fell into the shallow water just east of the dam and construction of it was held up when the pound was drained. Another horse fell into the actual lock chamber in 1976 and was rescued by the Fire Service, who broke down the hedge to bring in heavy equipment. Someone suggested the firemen would not mend the hedge because they were on industrial action, but in fact they pointed out it was not their responsibility. Cattle were unable to reach low water for drinking when the sluice gate beside the dam was broken in 1964. The Company were obliged to provide free watering places under the provisions of the Act.

In his report of 1988, David Boakes refers to Newtown Lock under the section on water flow. He describes the next pound, up to Ryeford Double Lock, as having a continuous water channel for the whole 2 miles 370 yards. Newtown Lock then had stop planks fitted to the upper wing walls to hold the water to a nominal 6½ft depth for fishing. A spill at the head of the lock maintains the level back to the Double Lock, and excess water flows over it through a culvert to below the tail of Newtown Lock and into Blunder pound. This spill weir has now been restored, showing fine workmanship, but is no longer active.

Double Lock

This is an unusual structure, particularly for the south of England. It is two locks sharing a middle gate, and the primary advantage was cost. A double lock was used at St Helens, Lancashire, on the Sankey Navigation, the first British canal of the industrial age, which opened in 1757. To dig out a pit deeper and longer for a double lock is not much more expensive than two separate locks, when the amount of time, labour and carting away spoil is considered. Added to which, the volume of water used is the same, and the lock-keeper would save time. Surprisingly, no lock was

Looking south-east at Double Lock in the early twentieth century. Note the separate door to what was probably the stable to the left of house, and the ladder against the wall on the right. Is the mast for wireless? (Courtesy of M.A. Handford)

indicated here on the first plan of the Navigation produced for potential subscribers in preparation for the 1776 Act. No surveyor's plans still exist for this canal, unlike the Thames & Severn, but this lock may have been an afterthought as several surveyors had come and gone, and the Company had to fall back on the services of an architect from King's Stanley, Anthony Keck.

The land on which Double Lock was built was bought in March 1778 from John Andrews, a clothier who had a large house at Stonehouse Cross. Joseph Grazebrook acted for the Company in Trust, and paid Andrews £200 19s for over three acres, part of pasture land from Haywardsfield Leazes, besides granting him a good acre from the Marle Pitt in Randwick parish. The Company did not know until years later that this land was unstable. Geology was still in its infancy. William Smith, known as the father of geology, was born in the Cotswolds in 1769. He started his career at the age of eighteen, too late to benefit the Stroudwater, though he did advise on Sapperton Tunnel and canals around Bath.

Listed Grade II, the lock walls are of red brick, with widening entrances at both ends, large ashlar limestone coping stones and granite dressings at the gate positions with iron restraining straps formerly attached to timber gate-posts. All timber work is missing, according to the schedule of listed buildings. Some of the ironwork is still present. A nice set of steps on the south side lead from the lower to the middle level. By the time he contracted to build the lock, Keck was in his fifties, a well-known provincial architect/contractor and follower of Wyatt and Adam. He was already engaged on his finest work, Moccas Park in Herefordshire, and Longworth with its wonderful lodges, on the Ledbury to Hereford road at Lugwardine. Fifty of his buildings still exist, but no other canal architecture is recorded. His estimate to the Company was for £760 and this was adhered to, paid by instalments.

Benjamin Grazebrook reported on 16 December 1779, five months after the canal officially opened, that he was 'very apprehensive that the right-hand wall below the gate of Double Lock will sloff [sic] down if not immediately repaired'. The Committee, of which Keck was a member, asked the Clerk to inform him to do whatever was needful to prevent the wall from falling and obstructing the canal. Keck replied that he was not expecting the locks to fall, but at the proper season he intended to rebuild that part which had given way. He considered himself account-able for any consequence which may attend it. Three weeks later another letter was sent to Keck asking for his immediate attention. His second reply reiterated the first. By the middle of April, as nothing was happening, the Clerk was to inform him that the lock was ruinous, it obstructed navigation and was dangerous to the passage of vessels. The Committee further specified that if Keck continued to refuse to repair the lock, they would apply to Lane & Jepson, their Gloucester solicitors, to warn him they would sue for damages if it was not speedily repaired.

A Minute of 25 May 1780 indicates that work was expected to start, because the Old Mill pond at Whitminster was to be deepened at the same time as the Navigation was stopped for repairs to Double Lock. However, by the next meeting a month later, all there was to report was that three letters had been sent by Keck, and the Company had replied to two of them. Therefore the Clerk was to take the contract and all correspondence to the solicitors and to 'desire them to take lawful methods of obliging Mr Keck to fulfil the said contract, provided they do not hear further by Tuesday week'. They did not hear further, obviously Keck was still busy in Herefordshire on more important work, *and* he had a teenage daughter! The General Meeting held on 7 July resolved unanimously that the solicitors should commence action against Keck for non-performance in building Double Lock. Realising that some money was still held on account for Keck, he was paid quickly, and Lane & (now) Stock drew up an agreement 'to prevent reparation from quashing, or otherwise destroying any part of the original agreement until it can be brought to an issue at the next Lent Assizes'.

At the end of September a letter came from Keck recommending that no vessels must pass Double Lock for at least a month. Then at the next half-yearly meeting in October another letter was produced, together with a bill for £132 17s 8½d for repair of the failure of Double Lock. The meeting voted to reject this bill and abide by their previous resolution.

Anthony Keck remained Proprietor of one share until his death in 1797, but must have been on reasonable terms with the Company who gave him first refusal on a piece of land on the lower side of Ryeford Bridge which they wanted to rent out in April 1781. That was exactly the same time as the General Meeting, the Minute of which is as follows. 'In consequence of the late Tryal [sic] at Gloucester with Anthony Keck relative to Double Lock, it has appeared that the said lock is not built agreeable to Plan and Module'. It was ordered that William Franklin and Edward Keene should make a survey and prepare an estimate of rebuilding the lock. Franklin's report, submitted a year later, stated the lock was not falling, and suggested Keck should repoint it. Nothing seems to have happened until April 1789 when an agreement was made that gained the consent and approbation of Keck, that he should repair such parts of the lock that belonged to him under the direction of Mr Clewes, so that it would stand with safety for many years to come, at Keck's expense, who should then be exonerated from any further expense or trouble. This inferred that Keck had not transferred ownership to the Company of the defective wall. Repairs were reported as completed in October 1789. The payment of £58 5s 9½d was not made by Keck until 1791, and he died six years later.

A remedy was found by rebuilding the wall and inserting circular drainage holes with culverts into the hill side. At some point an inner lining wall was constructed on the north side. The problem was that between the marl and the clay at the lower part of the hill was a layer of fuller's earth. This substance retains water, which it then throws off at the spring line, but it tends to slip. Thus the water builds up behind the lock and wing walls, causing them to bulge. This happened again in August 1845, when it was noted that 'water runs in a considerable stream behind it and the wall appears bulged in consequence'. There was also a leakage from the wall at the foot of the lower lock which had to be seen to immediately, but it was not clear if that was due to the same cause.

Installing new top gates at Double Lock, Ryeford, by Gloucestershire County Council, possibly in 1907. The double board-bolted girder on the top could be taken apart and moved. (Courtesy of M.A. Handford)

New gates were put in during Spring 1823. The top gates had been renewed in 1812; the middle gates were then renewed in 1874 and 1922, and the bottom ones in 1894. In 1950, Ryeford Saw Mills below Double Lock were complaining about the state of the gates, but were assured by the Company that even if they did collapse, it would only be a plank at a time, which would result in an insignificant extra flow of water, not enough to flood their premises. If they wanted to take out their own insurance against this, they were at liberty to do so.

Just after the canal was opened in 1779, owing to the isolated location of the lock, the Company realised they must have a man on site. This is the only place on the Navigation which is not adjacent to a roadway. The Cainscross–Eastington road is only a small field away up the bank to the north, but to reach it on foot means a third of a mile walk in either direction, east to Oil Mills Bridge, or west to Ryeford foot-bridge. There is no vehicular access, and it is said the locals call Double Lock 'nowhere'. The man was to be paid wages not exceeding 6s a week and a sentinel box provided for him immediately. This was only a stop-gap until proper houses could be built 'for the security of locks' at three places: between the first and second locks at Dudbridge; Double Lock; near the lock at Nassfield. Each house was to have two rooms below, and two above, about the same size as that at Easton (Eastington) Lock. Inevitably, the Company got cold feet from the expense involved, and the plan was postponed two weeks later, until further orders.

Actually it was nearly five years before further orders came, in May 1784, when estimates and plans were invited from Mr Franklin the Contractor, and John Davis. The latter was the one chosen, and his estimate dated 18 August 1784 reads as follows:

Proposals for building a Lock House with good sound bricks near the Double Lock agreeable to the Plan herewith shewn [not present now], *with such additions & alter-ations as are herein particularly specified. – The front wall to be a brick & half thick – all the rest of the Building to be a brick & half up to the Chamber Floor & one brick thick from thence to the top – The Walls to be raised two feet above the Garret Floor by means of kneeling blades – The Garrett Floor & Chamber Floor to be good elm or oak either – deep joists of sufficient strength, or Beam & Joists & to be boarded with the same kind of Timber – the two staircases one from the Ground floor to the Chamber Floor & one from thence to the Garrett to be Ash or Elm – two windows in the Garrett, one in each Pine End – All the window frames & the outside Door frame to be good sound Oak – The Roof to be of sufficient strength with good sound Ash or Elm & covered with Througham Slate – Two iron casements, one above & one below & Iron cross bars in the lower windows – The Ground Floor to be paved with Stone – The lower Rooms & Chambers & all the rest part of the House to be plais-tered. A piece of bond Timber to be fixed in the Wall at each floor, for the Joists to rest on.*

Davis was contracted to do the work, finding all materials and workmanship and to complete by the end of November for £65.

1 Framilode entrance lock and site of basin from across the Severn at Crown Point, 6 September 2003.

2 Stones in bank acting as protection for lock walls. The former warehouse is now residential.

3 Framilode Lock looking downstream, showing walls listed Grade II.

4 The interior of the office at Junction House, June 1990.

5 The Junction with Junction Lock, dated 1826, in foreground. The stop gates at the entrance to Stroudwater Arm can be seen.

6 Moorings on the Stroudwater Navigation, looking towards Walk Bridge, 31 August 2003.

7 Looking back to Dock Lock, Eastington, from where the canal is stanked off.

8 Westfield Bridge, a few yards from the site of the previous photograph, 31 August 2003.

9 Pike Lock, showing the position of the upper lock gates.

10 Pike Lock, showing the bracket which used to hold the lower lock gate fixed to coping stones.

11 Bond's Mill Bridge from the towpath, 4 September 2003.

12 Bond's Mill Bridge: the deck lifts hydraulically.

13 National Heritage Weekend, 1999. Juliet Shipman and the author staff an information point at the wartime pill box at Bond's Mill for the Stroudwater Open Day.

14 Ryeford Footbridge: its restoration was one of the first projects of the Cotswold Canals Trust.

15 Framilode Friendly Society of Watermen. This crockery is on display at Gloucester Folk Museum. (Courtesy of Gloucester Folk Museum, 2003)

16 The view up the canal to Bridgend Bridge from the upper window of Nutshell House.

17 Nutshell House, 2 September 2003: the east front may originally have been shuttered, and bricked in later. The position of other openings can be seen.

18 Double Lock House, 4 September 2003, showing the extension for the kitchen at the rear, and the shed or stable on the eastern side.

19 Double Lock House, with the possible original sentinel box shelter close to it.

20 Stonehouse Court, 3 July 2001. The gathering for the Waterways Trust presentation to announce their plans for the restoration of the Cotswold canals.

21 Fishing at Stonehouse Ocean. Armco tubes take the canal and towpath through the railway embankment, seen in the distance on the left.

22 Ryeford Double Lock, the lower lock, with the rebuilt wall on the north side, 4 September 2003.

23 Detail of trow from a painting by Daniel Newland Smith.

24 Ebley Mill seen from Oil Mills Bridge, with the canal back in water, facing east, 31 August 2003.

25 Drawing in crayon of the scene from the top of Lodgemore Lane to the canal and gasworks, by R.C. Perry, who taught at Stroud High School. The water in the foreground before the canal is part of a reservoir for Lodgemore Mill, 1925.

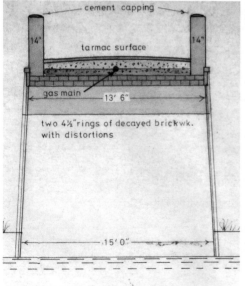

cement capping

14"   14"

tarmac surface

gas main

13' 6"

two 4½"rings of decayed brickwk. with distortions

15' 0"

HALF SECTION

NORTH SIDE

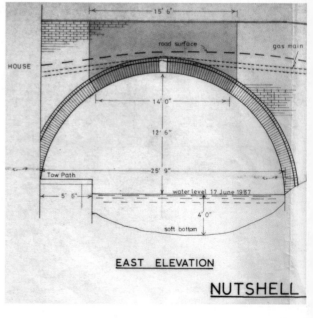

15' 6"

road surface   gas main

HOUSE

14' 0"

12' 6"

25' 9"

Tow Path

5' 6"

water level 17 June 1987

4' 0"

soft bottom

EAST ELEVATION

NUTSHELL

26 Plans drawn by F.W. Rowbotham in preparation for repairs to Nutshell Bridge, June 1987. Scale: 4ft to 1in.

27 Lodgemoor Bridge, c.1905. The entrance to the mill is on the left, and the reservoir is behind the trees bordering the canal on the north side.

28 Painting by unknown artist, of Wallbridge, c.1789, showing the Thames & Severn Canal cut through land formerly owned by the Stroudwater Company, whose wharf is to the right. Company House was not yet built. (Courtesy of Stroud District (Cowle) Museum)

29 The Company House at Wallbridge, 31 August 2003. The façade was not altered from when it was first built.

30 Ebley, looking towards Cainscross Church, showing the dug-out section of the canal with piling in August 2003.

Basically the house remains as described in the estimate, with the date 1784 inscribed above the central front window, and is listed Grade II. The porch over the front door is of later date, and the chimney at the east gable end has been raised using blue engineering bricks for about four courses. The windows have segmental arched lintels in brick and some of the original ones with three lights each of four panes still exist, although some have lost the glazing bars. In an upstairs window the casement latch is one of the iron ones as fixed in the beginning. Initially the two rooms downstairs and those above were divided by a wooden board partition and part of the downstairs one is still in place, whilst the upper is intact. The boxed-in wooden stair which goes up in the middle of the house against the back wall, before the later extension, is very steep and has the original door and fittings. The ground floor is still stone-flagged.

In April 1798 a 'shed' was ordered to be built on the eastern end of the Lock House. It was to be 8ft wide, but despite prodding it was not finished until November. There is a single-storey extension at that point now, and it is 8ft wide, and built of the same bricks (probably made on site, or very close) as the extension at the back of the house. The north end did have a wide doorway, now bricked in, and it had a flagstone floor, but not good quality. When the present owners, Mr and Mrs Hyde, came in 1965, there was a stable-type door from the living room beside the fireplace into this narrow extension. The lock-keeper may have had a horse; the Surveyor had a stable at Chippenham Platt.

There is another single-storey extension lean-to across the back of the house, accessed down three steep steps through the original 2ft-thick back wall of the house, facing south. This now houses the kitchen and bathroom, which was converted from a coal store in recent times. A few feet away, across a path, is an interesting small building almost 13ft square, built of old bricks, formerly lime-washed, gabled with a pan-tiled roof. The south gable has a brick chimney stack, and the fireplace is

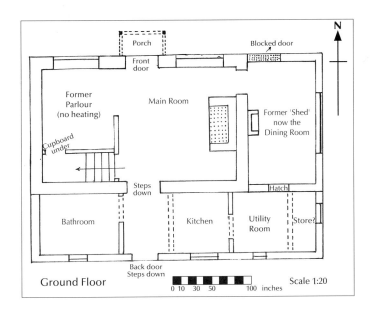

Double Lock Cottage. It was surveyed on behalf of the Gloucestershire Buildings Recording Group in 2001.

original, similar to that in the house. The stone-flagged floor is of good-quality sandstone, possibly from the Forest of Dean. The plank outside door is very old, and one of the small windows retains fixtures for an outside shutter. As this is a substantial building, too comfortable for a wash-house or brewhouse, it is suggested it is the sentinel box, which was not demolished when the house was built but used as shelter for boatmen or lengthsmen, who had difficulty getting home from this remote spot.

Thomas Lewis was the first lock-keeper, being appointed on 25 April 1780. He had some status in the locality, the *Gloucester Journal* reported the marriage of his eldest daughter to William Hevan of Ebley on Monday 9 August 1803. In 1813 his wages had been raised by 2s a week in summer months, but remained the same for winter. By 1815 the Company seem to be dissatisfied with him; his wages were reduced by 5s a week because he was to be employed only in looking after Double Lock and taking care of the water in Ebley level and the one below. The Clerk was to inform him 'that unless he discharges his duty with the greatest care and attention, he will be dismissed'.

Other lock-keepers at Double Lock were: William Hairs, who succeeded his father in November 1831 at 17s a week plus the house; Thomas Barnfield, who died in 1841 and was replaced by William Musty, who was unsatisfactory and stayed only three years. William Daniels took over at the age of forty-seven and in 1851 was living in the house with his wife, one teenage son, two teenage daughters and one daughter aged seven. He remained until his death in 1890. William George Bullock was lock-keeper in the early years of the twentieth century, and in 1916 was paying £5 per annum for his house. He is still remembered by older residents as a bully, being a small man, stockily built. Lionel Minett was likely the last keeper for the working life of the canal, taking over in 1930. After the canal was closed to navigation, the house was sold to Geoffrey Parrot who worked at Ransome, Hoffman, Pollard (RHP) at Stonehouse.

Martin Hyde has found George III coins in the garden, also a horse bell, large iron bolts and animal bones, which suggest there was cooking over a brazier.

RULES FOR PASSING THE LOCKS
of the Stroudwater Navigation, as ordered by Act of Parliament

---

A Vessel going up the Canal, if within sight of one at a distance not exceeding three hundred yards below a Lock shall pass through said Lock before the Vessel coming down. and then the next vessel shall come down; and if there are more Vessels than One below and above any Lock at the same Time with by the distance aforesaid, such Vessel shall go up and come down at such Lock by turn as aforesaid, till all the said vessels going up or coming down shall have passed; and every Person offending in any of these particulars, and being convicted thereof before any Justice of the Peace, shall for every such offence forfeit the sum of forty shillings.

W.J. Snape

Clerk to the Proprietors

A sign found by Martin Hyde at Double Lock Cottage.

The Spirit of Double Locks
by Martin Hyde

Often we heard the ghostly ring
of harness passing by us in the night.
The lock pawls clatter and the children bring
news of strange faces at the windows seen.
Always this presence of some unknown thing.

By night he came and sat upon my bed.
Round as the watchglass on his waistcoat chain,
his cheeks puffed out in anger. Said
we had no business on the premises
and should be gone, and wagged his head.

With buttoned boot he tapped the floor,
short legs encased in tailored trews,
straightened the beaver hat he wore.
The Company would bid us be gone,
we might not stay here any more.

And so it was I clearly saw
today is yesterday in time, and we
but part of everything that went before.
We shall not forget the past, I said.
He nodded and was there no more.

(This poem describes a true event which took place after we [Mr and Mrs Hyde] went to live at Double Lock Cottage.)

Dudbridge Locks

There are two locks at Dudbridge, 100 yards apart, called the Top and Bottom Locks. The Top Lock used to be referred to as Foundry Lock, being next to a foundry. Dudbridge was an important industrial area from earliest times to the present day, with few private houses until very recently. Both locks are built of stone, the bottom one is right next to the stone bridge which carried the turnpike from Cainscross to Nailsworth over the canal.

An agreement was made with William Franklin of Stroud on 30 July 1778 to build the Bottom Lock, but he must have built both. The dimensions were to be

Lower Dudbridge Lock, looking east, towards Foundry Lock, 1950. (Courtesy of M.A. Handford)

given by the Surveyors, but the rise was not to exceed 10ft, and thickness of walls was to be the same as the brick locks already built. The specification stated he must:

> *Face walls with square quoins, the coping to be of good weather stone from the quarry on Hampton Common – stones to be well hewn and set in good ranged courses and no stones less than nine inches in the bed to be used in face walls, and no stones be used in the back of walls except as approved by the Company Surveyor* [in which case Franklin was to remove them at his own expense].
>
> [...]
>
> *Large parpin or Band Stones to be at a proper distance in the walls of lock. Hollow quoins from Hanham Quarry* [near Bristol] *to be well worked, close jointed and set in Barrow Lime and none to be used of less size in the bed of two feet. Stone for backing the lock to be from Selsley and Rodborough Hill quarries, Sand for face mortar from the Severn. Franklin to agree to find the stone and all freight, workmanship, scaffolding and every kind of material (excluding lime). The upper part to be finished by November 1st, the remainder by May 1st 1779.*

The cost was to be £465, paid in instalments; the Company was to dig out the foundations ready to begin, and deliver the lime.

A lock-keeper was appointed, but a house was not provided until 1786. Besides attending to the locks, a keeper was expected to keep the paths gravelled, banks mowed in summer, and the quickthorn in the fences kept trim and weeded. John

Davis made an agreement with the Company to build the lock house near the bridge at Dudbridge. The exact position of it has not been verified yet. It was to be:

> *on the same plan and with as good materials as at Double Lock, with some specified alterations. They were: floors to be well-seasoned boards to prevent shrinking in the manner those have shrunk at Double Lock; all rooms except garrets to be ceiled; doors to be made with one inch stuff instead of half inch; brewhouse and oven to be under one roof the whole length of the house* [which suggests the lean-to at the back of Double Lock Cottage was a brewhouse] *and a necessary house under one end of same.*

It was to be complete by Christmas 1786 at a cost of £86 13*s*. Job Guy was one of the early lock-keepers and on his death in May 1836 the Company paid tribute to him: he had 'been a faithful servant of this Company for more than twenty years'. His widow was given £5 towards funeral expenses. and she and her son were allowed 5*s* a week jointly for looking after the wharf and the water, from his death till the next committee meeting (about five weeks) when and if they quit the house.

Mr Chance was an important mill-owner who owned a lot of land in the area. In 1784 it is reported he had given leave for Mr White to land his wool on a bit of land adjoining the lock at Dudbridge, but it is not clear whose wool it was or why it could not have been landed at the wharf nearby. Three years later an exchange of land was

Foundry Lock, showing the syphon culvert of Randwick stream opened up and being cleared. The spike in the wall on the left (in the man's hand) is the invert level of outfall. (Photograph by F.W. Rowbotham, 20 November 1956: courtesy of the Environment Agency)

The scene at Foundry Lock in 1979, when lock gates had been replaced by dams as part of the River Frome Improvement Scheme (flood relief). (Photograph by G.G. Hoare: courtesy of G.G. Hoare and M.A. Handford)

agreed with Mr Chance. It was a small strip on the side of the footpath leading from the stone lock to Dudbridge, for an equal quantity of his land in order to make the fence straight, and the said road to be turned up into the turnpike at the wing wall of the bridge.

Most of the entries in the Minutes for Dudbridge Locks concern damage done by careless boatmen. On 10 September 1805 John Hunt had run his vessel against the lower gate of the first lock, breaking it so much that a new one was needed. The Clerk was ordered to detain the vessel next time it was in the canal until compensation was obtained. The same thing happened in January 1835 when the *Defiance* damaged a gate, and damage was estimated at £15. A more serious happening occurred on 25 August 1854 when boatmen of the *Bourne Lass*, owned by Richard Webb, broke the lower gates of the bottom lock. As a result, trade above Dudbridge Wharf was stopped until 11 September. Mr Webb paid £15 fine, but must have died soon afterwards, for in October 1861, the barge *Conway* steerer Robert Gardiner, for Mrs Webb of the Bourne, was summonsed for banging against the lock gate without a fender, *and* he had only one other crewman on board. The Company were not caught out for so long this time as they had previously arranged for two pairs of lock gates to fit the highest locks be prepared in readiness for these mishaps.

The locks were so well built by William Franklin that they rarely had any other repairs done to them. On their annual inspection by Company boat in August 1845, the Committee noticed the state of the embankment at the foot of Foundry Lock which needed attention. They took up the Surveyor's suggestion of a dry ragstone wall instead of piling.

Before the Stroud sewage works were set up a couple of hundred yards from Dudbridge on the south of the canal, the Company had become concerned about drains and sewers emptying into the canal, and commissioned the Surveyor in 1865 to prepare a report. His recommendations were 'to put in vaults to all privies belonging to the Company's property which now empty into the canal.' It was resolved that all other parties whose privies emptied into the canal be asked to put in vaults forthwith, and that all parties taking water from the canal be requested to stop or enter into an agreement as to the quantity taken and pay a yearly rate.

Prior to the 1954 Act, the retired GCC Surveyor, W.F.A. Alderton, who was then Honorary Surveyor to the Company, did a walking survey of the canal. He found the top gates of both locks shut and holding water, but in a bad way. When the Severn River Board implemented the Flood Alleviation Scheme in 1956 the locks were replaced by dams.

4

Structures: Bridges

Bridges over the Stroudwater Navigation, as built in the beginning, were of two types: swivel (now called swing) and hump-backed, which were usually of local brick. Responsibility for them did not always rest with the Company, and to this day there is controversy about upkeep of some. Nevertheless they have been of major concern throughout the Navigation's history, and indeed contributed the prime factor in the decision to close for navigation in the 1950s.

Swivel bridges were prone to accident or misuse. When the canal first became operational an order went out that stays be put to prevent them from being opened too wide. Byelaw VI 'Swivel Bridges' passed in 1808 was as follows, 'Serious inconvenience has been experienced by sundry persons on account of persons navigating barges on the Navigation leaving them open. It is resolved that any person wilfully or negligently leaving open any bridge shall pay a fine of £5'. Byelaw XX states, 'Any person who opens a swivel bridge without lawful cause or reason, or who shall unnecessarily swing any bridge or damage it, shall pay a penalty of £5.' In the 1870s the Company asked their solicitor, William Woodruffe Kearsey, to investigate the liability with respect to swing bridges, possibly in the aftermath of Daniel Kilmister being drowned near the gasworks, where he was employed, in January 1869. Kearsey wrote:

> When the highway traverses a canal by a swing bridge, and the bridge is opened for the passage of boats, the Company is bound to provide sufficient lights or persons to watch and warn passengers [pedestrians?], or have some apparatus to protect passengers when the bridge is open and prevent them falling in the water.

He cited a case on the Sankey Navigation where someone had drowned at the very time boatmen had opened the bridge to take their boat through. There was no apparatus and no light to prevent accidents, and as the Company had not taken sufficient precautions, they were liable. But if the boatmen had wrongfully left the bridge open, then they or the owner was responsible.

Brick or stone bridges, being of sound structure, rarely caused maintenance problems and only required repointing now and again. However, some restricted visibility on roads and some were difficult for boatmen to negotiate. It was said all bridges were made to carry the traffic for which they were first built, that is, a loaded wagon at most. Therefore the Company are empowered to put weight restrictions on their bridges. In 1890 there was concern about steam rollers, and it was resolved that they 'would not be responsible for any weight beyond the ordinary traffic of the district'. Notices to that effect were placed on each of the bridges likely to be used by steam rollers.

In 1822 the Committee minuted that roads over bridges generally be put and kept in good repair, so as to protect the crowns of the arches. Mr Basham, the Contractor, extended his contract to do this work for a further three years in 1835, his payment being £115, further extended in 1839. Wharves were also included in the contract.

Framilode Bridge

This bridge did not need much maintenance. It served only a few cottages and a warehouse near the river Severn and the track beside it to the Passage at Lower Framilode. Later it was used to gain access to the church and school. Always a swivel bridge, it was repaired in June 1787, and repainting was ordered in January 1856.

Mr Hadley, a timber merchant from Cambridge, Gloucestershire, wrote to the Company regarding some elm trees he had purchased from the Vicar of Framilode. He intended taking them over the swing bridge, but considered it not strong enough, so he would hold the Company responsible for any damage that may occur. The Clerk was detailed to meet him, and come to any arrangement as to the packing of the bridge and the safety of it. That was in November 1881, and the bridge seems to have survived without mishap.

Pencil sketch of Framilode Bridge (1872) by John Walton, a customs officer based at Purton. In 1865 B. Gardner of Saul was fined £10 for carrying, dragging or floating timber on the canal without permission. (Courtesy of D. Harrop)

The same buildings at Framilode Bridge as in the sketch, but viewed from the side. The warehouse in the middle served as a boxing ring.

Mr Alderton in 1953 described the bridge as timber, in fair order, but a concrete wall had been placed under it at mid-span on the edge of the canal wall, therefore it was impossible to swing. Only a few months later, the Chairman of Fretherne with Saul Parish Council wrote to the Company's solicitors expressing concern over the bridge, and requesting a site meeting. Whether he was told that was not necessary because GCC would soon take it on, is not known.

Saul Bridge

Saul Bridge, or Moor Street Bridge after the road it carries bearing that name, was first erected as a brick hump-backed bridge. Little attention to it was needed, except in February 1811 when a wing wall had fallen down. Repairs were ordered to be done as soon as the season permitted, and 'stone should be procured as soon as possible for preparing lime for the repairs of the Navigation'. Bricks would have been made close to the site; a piece of land is marked as 'Brick Pit Piece' on the tithe map, near the Tin Mills, but that belonged to the Purnells.

In January 1846 the Surveyors of Highways for Saul and Frampton expressed concern about fences bounding the canal bridges. Mr Sherwood, the Company Surveyor, attended a parish meeting at Saul, and reported back that the Company was liable to repair the road over Saul Bridge only as far as their masonry extends, and Walk Bridge likewise.

After some boatmen complained about problems navigating Saul and Gallows Bridges in 1854, a solution was determined that they should be replaced with swing bridges. George Perry offered to contract for the work of removing the brick bridge, and erecting a swing. If he could use Company men for one day, he would charge £15 for the work, but if he was allowed to take away the old materials, the cost would be £10. The Company agreed, and arranged to post notices at the roads over Saul Bridge and advertise in the Gloucester papers about the stoppage of the canal for works. Three months later, in August, the new swing bridge was completed satisfactorily, but the Company wanted an iron handrail with proper supports to be added on either side of the approach on the north side.

The 1953 report stated that Saul Bridge was of timber, in poor order. There was a five-ton restriction, and a brick wall at mid-span meant it could not be swung. After the 1954 Act, it came under the care of GCC.

Gallows Bridge

Gallows Bridge is an enigma, the name a mystery. Its whereabouts in Saul was unmarked until the 1841 Tithe Map revealed a two-acre piece of ground called Gallows Bridge Orchard, a bridge shown at the western corner. A footpath ran along the southern bank of the canal, then veered north across the bridge, which seems to have continued over the river Frome. Whether the name came from the shape of the bridge, or local folklore, is unknown. Saul is unlikely to have had a gallows: maybe it was a nickname. The bridge connected two open fields, Saul's Meadow and Pool Field, which had been in arable strips in multiple occupation, to the south.

Saul Bridge shown in 1948 when its condition caused great concern to Gloucestershire County Council. The bridge was replaced soon after the 1954 Act of Abandonment for Navigation was passed. (Courtesy of Gloucestershire Record Office)

The first mention of the bridge in the Minutes was in 1795 when the Company were selling off land. Thomas Grazebrook bought at auction several pieces of land in Saul, including one long strip in Pool Field extending to the bridge, and one triangular piece above it. Thomas Baylis also bought a piece next to the bridge adjoining the withy bed. The cottages at the eastern end of the orchard next to the canal on the offside are mentioned in a Minute of 23 April 1822, when the south bank of the canal near them needed to be raised and repaired. Apparently the Company did not own these cottages.

Repairs were made to the bridge in May 1846, when a Mr Poole was to find timber and the Company provide workmanship. From then on, the bridge gave problems. They started with the Clerk's disclosure at the meeting on 14 December 1853 that many vessels entering the canal at Framilode and passing to the Junction were experiencing difficulty because of Saul and Gallows Bridges being fixed. Mr Driver, the Surveyor, added he knew many instances of loss from these vessels, which would be prevented if swing bridges were put in. The Committee instructed him to find out the cost, and to ask the owner of most of Pool Field, Mr Cambridge, if he still wished his offer of paying for the cost of changing Gallows Bridge to stand. The answer was no.

Saul Parish were expected to contribute £25 towards the cost of altering the bridge. However, when Mr Croome, a lawyer, inspected it, he found that the paths leading to it had been stopped. So the Company determined to remove the bridge completely. Henry Brinkworth, owner of the orchard, claimed a right of way, but this was quashed. Amazingly the bridge was blown down in October 1854! Mr Kearsey, acting for Brinkworth, threatened proceedings if it was not replaced, but was informed that 'if he will point out anything to justify his claim, it shall be forthwith considered'.

Walk Bridge

Ownership of Walk Bridge, and liability for its repair, was often a bone of contention for the Company. The road it carries, Whitminster Lane, from the end of Frampton Green to the Mill and on to the village, was private, and owned by the Cambridge family at the time the canal was built. Originally it was a hump-backed bridge, as evidenced by the steepness of the abutments on either side. When the Junction with the Gloucester & Berkeley was finalised in 1827 and the stretch of the Stroudwater between there and the lock at Whitminster was made 4ft higher, the bridge was heightened.

Charles Owen Cambridge claimed 5s in February 1845 for repairs he had made to the bridge. The Company was willing to pay him, but it transpired he was in arrears with ground rent of 1s per annum for five years. Later that year, Mr Martin, a Committee member, tried to ascertain liability of the Company to repair fences at the approaches to bridges at Whitminster and Saul, as accidents could occur and the public should have some security. Therefore, the iron railings on the approaches were erected, and are probably the same ones there at present.

Walk Bridge, looking towards Whitminster. This photograph was captioned by the Surveyor in 1948: 'If the canal is not navigable, the swing bridges could be eliminated, and the road widened.' It was then 9ft 6ins wide. (Courtesy of Gloucestershire Record Office)

At some time, possibly in the 1840s, Whitminster Lane, which had been stopped by a gate at Perry Way, was transferred to the Local Highways Board, largely thanks to the campaigning of John Goatman and others of Frampton. In the grass verge near Walk Bridge in the 1960s was a stone tablet with a carved inscription that Mr Cambridge had given a few feet for the re-alignment of the public highway.

In August 1855 a letter was received from Henry Hooper Wilton, of the noted Gloucester family, who had just bought the Whitminster Estate. He enclosed a proposition signed by several local residents in which they would substitute a swing bridge. The Committee deliberated and, ever cautious, pronounced that provided the Gloucester & Berkeley had no objection, and there would be no expense to the Company, the proposal could proceed. A concession was made whereby the parties undertaking the work could take the materials of the brick bridge to put against the expense of the new one. Then Mr Wilton announced at the General Meeting in October he would pay the whole amount and make good the road. It was arranged that the Company Surveyor would make the bridge and approaches, and keep a separate account for Mr Wilton. The only expense of the Company was incurred when the waterway needed to be reduced in width by 2ft, and this could be done only by building a wall, and the canal stopped for the work.

The Gloucester & Berkeley Company repaired the swing bridge in 1869. When a new one was needed in 1878, liability was questioned, as no definite understanding had been made. The Clerk went to see Mr Clegram, to ask if his Company could supply some materials. His reply is not recorded, but the question of the repair of highways over bridges in the dispute between the Company and Wheatenhurst Highway Board (another name for Whitminster) was referred to Counsel. The outcome was that in future the Company would keep them in repair.

This situation continued until GCC became concerned about the structure in the early 1950s. Three houseboats were moored just east of the bridge, which still had to be swung to give them access to the Sharpness Canal. It had a five-ton restriction on it, and buses and lorries were banned. Walk Bridge was one of two bridges which occasioned the application to abandon the canal and pass over road bridges to the County Highways. As soon as the Act was passed the swing bridge was replaced by concrete decking.

Whitminster Bridge

Sometimes in the Minutes, Whitminster Bridge, which carries a track over the canal close to the lock, is called the bridge near the paper mill at Whitminster. It is the only access to the low-lying fields to the south of the canal. As such it did not get very much wear and tear, and calls for maintenance were few. This swing bridge had a thorough overhaul in 1848 when it was replanked with oak and the carriageway and framework were repaired. Three years later strips were placed across the carriageway to make it more convenient for cattle crossing over it, they must have slipped on the oak planks, and when cows fall it is very difficult to get them up again. In 1864 the bridge was repaired again, at the same time as the adjacent lock.

A completely new bridge was made and put up in 1874, probably the same one as at present which has been topped with concrete and the bridge-hole filled in.

Lockham Bridge

Nothing can be seen of Lockham Bridge, except a modern footbridge more or less at the same site where the canal and river Frome now meet. It was a river bridge, and said to carry the track from the new village of Whitminster on the Bristol Road to the old part round the church and house. The way over the canal would have been over Stonepitts Bridge a few yards to the east. Whether another bridge carried the towpath over the river, which was actually the mill-leat for Whitminster Mill, is not known, because the 1884 Ordnance Survey map cuts off at precisely this point.

Lockham Bridge was mentioned in the Minutes in 1795 when some land was sold at auction to the solicitor Henry Burgh for £32. It was described as 'a piece of pasture land with a withy bed adjoining, on the west side of the canal at Lockham Bridge.' This pasture or land close to it is the subject of an indenture of 22 April 1843 when the Company bought back 'a small triangular bit' from C.O. Cambridge to make Lockham Aqueduct, and paid 10s. The only other record of the bridge in the Minutes was in August 1809 on the annual inspection when an examination and repair was ordered.

Stonepitts Bridge

Stonepitts Bridge is at the end of three tracks from Whitminster and gave access to meadows along the river Frome. Built as a hump-backed bridge, the arch was in bad order with the parapet all down on one side at the time of the inspection in 1953, giving cause for remedial work to be considered. By 1955 it had been removed and replaced by concrete tubes. Concrete decking was put across the bridge-hole, but is not wide enough for the farmer to get a combine harvester across. Some plans have been drawn up for a replacement bridge in keeping with the historic nature of the area, but future developments for the canal yet to be unveiled.

Occupation Bridge

Occupation Bridge is an almost perfect example of a Stroudwater Navigation brick hump-backed bridge, and as such is often used on postcards and calendars. As it served only for access to fields and had no track (there is none marked on the 1884 Ordnance Survey map) very little damage has been done to it. A few bricks have been replaced which do not quite match.

The Company do not own this bridge, although they built it in the first place. Locally it is known as Robinson's Bridge, presumably the name of a previous owner. An indenture of 17 June 1836 between Richard Martin (Jr) of Parklands Wheatenhurst and the Company, permits Martin to take down and remove the bridge, which has no name, but was built solely to give access to the fields known as Upper Mead, Middle Mead and Lower Mead, from the pasture known as the Oxleaze. Location of these fields is confirmed from the 1837 Whitminster Tithe Map when Richard Martin was the owner, and his son William the occupier. Indeed those fields are served by this bridge. He intended to use the materials of the brick bridge, and in lieu to erect a swing wooden bridge at his own cost. In consideration of permission to do so, and £20 paid to him by the Company, he thereby exonerates the Company and discharges them and their successors from all further and future liability to repair, maintain or keep the present brick bridge, the intended bridge, or any other bridge at the same place. Martin and his successors promised they would maintain and keep the bridge in a good substantial state so it would not prevent, obstruct or hinder free passage of boats, barges or other vessels passing along the canal. All this is rather strange, because the swing bridge was not built, and the owners of Parklands (latterly GCC) must still be responsible for the bridge.

Bristol Road Bridge

The entrance to the lock from the wharf was beneath Bristol Road Bridge, which is now completely obliterated by the roundabout on the A38 road. Although this was a very busy crossing, only one reference is in the Minutes for maintenance of it; in August 1835 the coping was ordered to be restored and repaired. The bridge was of brick with a stone arch and was widened several times by using concrete. Eventually,

Work in progress at Bristol Road Bridge. This is thought to be when Orchard & Peer constructed for the Company two hollow concrete block walls, 5ft apart at a height of 9ft, in 1961.
Above: Looking west, showing the choked-up canal, and the site of the wharf on the right.
Below: Looking east, the lock gates can be seen through the arch.
(Courtesy of the Cotswold Canals Trust)

after the 1954 Act, it was demolished by GCC, acting for the Ministry of Transport, the canal tubed and a solid embankment made. Bristol Road, built on a gravel embankment, dates from pre-Roman times. When it became a trunk road, maintenance of the bridge was taken over by the authorities.

Hyde's Bridge

Hyde's Bridge and the tracks leading to it from Fromebridge and Whitminster Court were eradicated by the M5 motorway and its approach road. It was a brick humpbacked bridge, probably named after a man called Hyde who had a square field in the vicinity marked on the 1837 Tithe Map for Whitminster. Later it was owned by the Trustees of the Bengough Estates. Henry Bengough owned lands in the parishes of Eastington and Whitminster; when he died in 1818, he left them in trust for the duration of two lives. This became ninety-nine years, through which the estate continued to expand.

Westfield Bridge

Westfield Bridge stands alone in a field, still in fairly good condition and challenging a new generation to bring its water back and give it life. It used to carry an old track bordered with hawthorn trees from Westend towards Eastington Church. The style of brick, the squarer arch and the date stone 1841 suggest this bridge was extensively rebuilt, or newly built at that time. Almost certainly it was a private bridge, with no records in the Company archives. However, the Trustees of the Bengough Estate held a right of way over the canal near Meadow Mill, so the bridge was not *their* property.

When the Ministry of Transport sold off land they did not need for the motorway, Mrs Hearsey, the local farmer, bought the bridge for farm use.

Pike Bridge

Formerly called Eastington (or Easton) Bridge, it acquired a new name after the Turnpike Trustees built a toll house on the corner. The road to Eastington was a major one, and circumstances called for bridge widenings at least twice, and on three bridges on the site. On 16 April 1823, Mr Hicks and other Trustees of the Cainscross District of Turnpike Roads attended the Company meeting to voice their opinions that the bridge near Chippenham Platt was 'inconvenient and dangerous because of its declivity'. They requested permission to take down part of the bridge and rebuild it at less elevation, by however many inches the Company would consider permissible without injury or inconvenience to the Navigation. The new part of the bridge should be wider, the Company to contribute 10,000 bricks and £50 towards the alteration. The meeting acceded to this request, provided the Company would not lose out on it. After a survey, the Committee agreed the bridge could not be lowered more than fifteen inches, and they preferred the alterations to be carried out by their own workmen under their own control. Therefore they needed to know how much

Pike Lock as seen through the arch, with the coal wharf on the offside, *c*.1927. (Courtesy of Peckhams of Stroud)

the Turnpike Commissioners would contribute towards the work of making the bridge lower without widening it; also the sum for lowering fifteen inches at the crown, and widening 3ft. The Company would see to the bridge only, and not the approaches to it. These arrangements must have been satisfactorily settled, because work was due to begin on 15 June.

After a fatality in February 1848, and probably at the behest of the coroner, a secure fence was ordered to be put up on the upper side of the bridge, i.e. over the lock. Accidents did not always prove fatal. William Beard, the lock-keeper, saved the life of Humphrey Hodges on the night of 13 June 1792 'by taking him out of the canal apparently dead and recovering him.' The Clerk was instructed to give Beard the customary reward of £2 12s 6d. Awards were occasionally noticed in the *Gloucester Journal*.

Again in October 1870 the Trustees of Turnpikes came to obtain permission to widen the bridge still further. The Company agreed, only if the work was done in a manner and at the right time as convenient to themselves, but in future, repairs to the added portions to the bridge should be borne by the Commissioners of Turnpikes. In the 1920s a new bridge with a wider carriageway was built by GCC, and this had stone balustrades.

Gloucestershire County Highways carried out some improvements at the approaches to the bridge to assist visibility in 1950. By 1953 they had built a new concrete bridge which was in good order. The Company received £100 in payment from them in 1977, for the bank and bed of the canal at Pike Bridge, but this is not recorded in the Minutes. In fact, the County Council own land beneath all bridges now in their jurisdiction.

Newtown Bridge

Newtown Bridge, also known as Roving Bridge, takes the towpath from the north back to the south side of the canal. It is an elegant brick bridge, recently repointed by the Bailey family, on behalf of the Cotswold Canals Trust. When James Stanton built the east lodge of Eastington Park, probably in 1884, he applied for nine inches to be added to the parapets of the bridge leading to his house, and he would pay half the cost. The Company were agreeable and the work would be done when other repairs to the bridge could be carried out at the same time. No provision for future repairs was apparently made, as a letter from the County Architect of 9 November 1972 draws the Company's attention to the disintegration of the brick parapet walls and state of the carriageway. He attributes the condition to uncontrolled growth of vegetation. An answer to this letter is not recorded but £376.05 was spent on repairs to the bridge in 1989.

Previously, repairs had been made in 1816, and after a mishap in 1863 when Thomas Hillman, captain of one of Mr Lewis' barges, had damaged the masonry through carelessness. He was brought before the Committee and reprimanded but was 'passed over' when he agreed to pay half the cost of repair of 15s.

Bond's Mill Bridge

Bond's Mill was one of the most important mill complexes on the river Frome, and the site still is, in a new role of industrial estate. Therefore the swing bridge has always carried a lot of traffic, some of it heavy. During the early years of the canal the Eycott family worked the woollen mill. They prospered and married into other local influential families. The mill was usually known as Mr Eycott's Mill, and is marked thus on maps, so the bridge became 'the bridge next Mr Eycott's Mill'.

Henry Eycott was working the mill by 1787, and started buying shares in the Stroudwater Navigation in 1800, acquiring six before his death ten years later. He was a prominent member of the Committee, and would often sit on a sub-committee when reports and site meetings were needed. In his will, after making provision for his second wife Mary, the shares were left in trust to his executors, William Stanton and Thomas Holbrow, for the benefit of four of his children 'to be divided between them share and share alike as tenants in common on their attaining twenty one years'. He stated that his eldest son, Henry Charles, would be amply provided for by his late father. H.C. Eycott bought shares in his own right, some after his marriage in 1818 to Ann Clutterbuck Fryer, whose mother was daughter of Ellis James. He had sold land at Eastington for building the canal, and then claimed for subsequent damage to his crops.

A new bridge at Bond's Mill was ordered in April 1806, in lieu of the one in a ruinous state, but by July the next year it still was not erected. Mr Eycott had said that the proposed new swivel bridge was higher than he expected and of an inconvenient material. So the Company ordered another to be constructed and erected immediately. Since then the bridge has been renewed many times. By 1953 the wooden bridge had been replaced by steel, and sometime after 1954 it was made fixed. In 1982 questions were asked about liability for strengthening and repairs, but this has never been resolved properly, as Messrs Sperry Gyroscope Co. Ltd, who owned the mill, contributed to the upkeep of the bridge, it being the only vehicular access to the site. Sperry's were engaged in important war work and asked in 1940 if the Company would provide guard-rails to the bridge. Employees leaving the factory in the black-out were having difficulties, and three of them had accidentally walked into the canal. The rails were fixed within a week.

Ocean Railway Bridge, Stonehouse

Work started on building the Bristol & Gloucester Railway in 1841, and by December that year Elisha Oldham, the contractor for the erection of the railway bridge over the canal at Stonehouse, had partly erected a temporary bridge there, and then applied for sanction for it. As power to make the bridge was given in their Railway Act of 1839, the Stroudwater Company had no objections to offer Oldham, unless some inconvenience to the Navigation was experienced. A penalty clause inserted in the Act insured that if the canal was closed for more than twenty-four hours at a time because of construction work, then a penalty of £50 was to be paid. Raymond Cripps attended a committee meeting in June 1842 at the behest of I.K. Brunel, Chief Engineer of the Bristol & Gloucester Railway, to persuade the Company to reduce this figure. It was decided the canal could not be stopped without damage to trade, and if lower terms were granted, it would be only with consent of *all* Proprietors.

Negotiations continued through the summer and autumn, concerning the towpath, a drain and the width of the bridge, which Brunel said could not be widened by 2ft as requested by the Company. Finally, at a Special Meeting on Christmas Eve 1842 agreement was reached. The railway at this point was carried on a steep embankment, the heaviest on the line, between Frocester and Stonehouse for a distance of two and quarter miles. The canal bridge was nearly at the northern end, with a width (span) of 30ft between piers and initially made of timber. The Railway Company would make a towpath under the bridge and the approaches to it by building a good substantial wall, coped with weather stone, no less than 2ft wide in parallel width and the surface no less than 1in thick. Approaches on either side of the bridge were to be at least twenty yards in length, and a compromise was made about the width of the towpath under the bridge: it would be 5ft. To settle proceedings, the Railway Company paid £125. This broad-gauge line was opened to the public from Temple Meads to Gloucester in July 1844.

In February 1967, a letter was received from British Railways, Western Region (successors to the Midland Railway who had taken over from Bristol & Gloucester), explaining that the bridge needed costly repairs, 'but in the light of the need to keep expenditure to a minimum', they intended substituting a solid embankment. This solution was actually in accordance with rights given under the 1954 Act. Since that Act, rights of way had been given to the towpath under the bridge, so the plan provided for two Armco tubes through the filled-in section of the embankment: one for flow of water, and one for the footpath. The Company had no power to object, so a site meeting was arranged. A representative from Messrs Hoffmans Ltd, who extracted water from the canal at a dam 100 yards west of the bridge, was also at the meeting, where it was agreed the towpath should remain 5ft wide. A piece of land was sold to the Railway Board for the ease of construction work, which took place one summer weekend in 1968. As no mention was made of demolition it is firmly believed the bridge and its abutments are still *in situ*.

Ocean Bridge

Ocean Bridge, at the eastern tip of Stonehouse Ocean, is a swing bridge, now fixed, which serves the lane running between Stonehouse Court, and Court Farm Mews, formerly the manor farm, to the fields in the valley below the canal.

Ocean Bridge, c.1910: a scene hardly changed today, apart from the absence of houseboats. Nutshell House and Cottage are in the distance on the right.

Apart from the normal maintenance of metal swing bridges, such as repainting and re-decking from time to time, the only problems attached to this bridge are those of access, which still continue. In response to a letter from Miss Harriet Mary Bradstock of Stonehouse Court in June 1844, regarding the swivel bridge, the Company lawyers were consulted. Whilst specific details were not disclosed, the lawyers recommended a sub-committee to make further enquiries, but in any case, all parties not legally authorised to use the road were to be stopped. The 1776 Act gave the Company, its representatives and servants, the right of access at all times to the canal for inspection on foot. Permission to use wheeled vehicles must be obtained from landowners. Likewise, the railway authorities have the right of access to their land. The lane which divides Stonehouse Court (now a hotel) from the former farm is on private land, although it is a public footpath leading ultimately to Beard's Mill and the houses near it alongside the river, through the railway viaduct.

By 1953 the bridge was already fixed, but a new structure was put in during September 1958, of concrete with oak planking. Plans for a new manually operated swing bridge are in hand, but pending.

Nutshell Bridge and Nutshell House

The aspect of the hump-backed bridge with the three-storeyed house with three sides to the east end, and Stonehouse Church viewed to the west, is well recognised as one of the beauties of the whole English canal system, and endearing to local people. Stonehouse adopted the image for its official sign when it achieved status as a town.

Nutshell Bridge was built by the Company about 1778 of local bricks, with ashlar keystones. It has a round keyed arch with curved parapet and retaining walls. The width of the canal under the bridge just above water level is 25ft 9ins, of which 5ft 6ins is taken by the towpath built up on the south side. A track from the church by Church Lane to Stonehouse Lower Mills crosses over the bridge, and is a public way. There is no permitted vehicular access, except for the owners of the two properties on either side of the southern abutments, with a weight limit of one ton.

Mr Hill's Bridge was how the bridge was designated in early Minutes and documents of the Company, and as marked on maps. Later it became Mr Davies' Bridge, but why it became 'Nutshell' is lost in the mists of time. William Hill, a wealthy clothier, was the owner of Lower Mills, having bought them from John Arundel in 1764. He is first mentioned in Minutes in 1780 when the Company wanted to charge him for a gate opening to the towpath. When Hill denied having anything to do with it, the matter was dropped. Edward Hill who was then under twenty-one, succeeded to the mill when his father died in February 1784, and was buried in Stonehouse Churchyard.

In April 1803 a Minute records:

Mr Edward Hill, having built a cottage on the Company's land on the lower side of the bridge at Stonehouse and being desirous of erecting a warehouse on the upper side,

Edward Hill held a share in the Company until 1812 when it was sold for £219.
Left: Sarah Hill (1765-1804). *Right:* Edward Hill (1765-1816)
They were married in 1786. (Courtesy of Jean Buchanan)

*the Company are empowered to grant him a lease of ground on both sides of the bridge
for ninety-nine years with a yearly rent of five guineas.*

A further proposal was made by Hill in October the next year when he offered to pay twenty guineas for six perches of ground on each side of Hill's Bridge on which the warehouse had been erected, and he would keep in repair that part of the bridge that was connected with the warehouse. The Committee accepted his proposal, and ordered their seal to be affixed to the Conveyance, which further stated that he could not rebuild the part of the bridge that immediately adjoined the two pieces of land. When Edward Hill bought a share in the Company in 1805 for £208 from Revd John Disney, a former Chairman, he became a prominent Committee member.

Edward and his wife Sarah (née Edwards) were involved in some financial agreements together. One of them dated 23 November 1789 was a security for £2,300 to William Cross, clothier of Worcester. In May 1798 he was released of an equity to William Merrick, his maternal uncle, of King's Stanley. Then he and his wife took up a mortgage from Sarah Cross of Clifton. Sarah Hill died in 1804, but her five children were already being looked after by her sister-in-law, Abiah Hill, at Laugharne in Carmarthenshire. Records there show them being inoculated in 1797, having whooping cough together the same year, and measles in 1799. William Hopkins Merrick died in 1812, leaving all his property which he had previously bought from his nephew, back to Edward Hill, who died himself, aged fifty-one in 1816. It is not known if Edward had already given up working the mill after his wife's death or if the property, including the buildings next to the bridge, were owned by his children under a trust. By 1823 the estate passed to the Davies family, who held it until at least 1912.

The warehouse was altered into a dwelling possibly in the 1820s as a datemark of 1827 has been found on the back of a chimney. The schedule for listed buildings describes it as a canal house, but it was never owned by the Company, and the only function for it mentioned in the records was as a warehouse. Of this there is no doubt: a hoist was shown on the canal side of the house in living memory, and warehouse-like openings were revealed inside when plaster was removed. A most distinguishing feature is a round-arched tunnel approached through a double arch down three well-worn steps from the kitchen of what is now Nutshell House, and may have been deeper. This is no ordinary cellar. It extends westwards into Nutshell Cottage next door, but the two parts are now separated by a dividing wall between the two houses, beneath the steep approach to the bridge from the south. The author suggests this tunnel was actually an internal dock or boathouse, constructed as an arm of the canal for unloading goods, or even passengers. We have seen how Edward Hill built the cottage without permission, and how he bought land at the southern approaches to the bridge, offering to keep it in repair without explaining to the Company why he needed it. If it was unofficial, the Committee would likely 'turn a blind eye' to the activities of a fellow member! A branch to the canal would have commanded a large rent.

Altogether, Nutshell House shows many interesting features, not all associated with it being only a warehouse. It is built in Flemish bond red local brick, with ashlar limestone dressings, and brick chimneys. The windows are large with twelve pane sashes and are half that size on the third storey. On the east is a tower-like structure with a hipped roof, and its three straight, narrow walls have alternating stone quoins and stone bands at floor levels. Some windows are blocked, as is a door to the towpath on the north. At the back, on the south, is a partially open-fronted lean-to which housed domestic offices. Inside, the rooms are spacious with pleasant outlooks, and all have a fireplace. The middle wall of the 'tower' shows signs in the interior of having been keyed-in at a later date. Either it was altered or had to be rebuilt. Normally dwelling houses display a certain pretension about communal areas, but here the staircases are plain, and the outer face of the doors leading off them are very simple, whereas the inside faces are moulded. It is possible this warehouse was converted into a boarding house, and rooms let out to passengers. In Ireland the Grand Trunk Canal built four hotels for the benefit of passengers on passage boats. Franklin's advertised a service to London from Gloucester, but vessels were not allowed to proceed on Sundays. The house was commodious for an ordinary family, and the kitchen was especially large.

By 1987 it became evident that major repair work was needed to the bridge. Some patching of brickwork had taken place as a result of vandalism. However, this time the centre portion of the arch ring was discovered to be so badly decayed to be beyond repair. The cause, according to Frederick William Rowbotham, the Company's Honorary Engineer, was poor-quality bricks, plus many years of water seepage, and (unstated) an old gas main crossing the bridge, causing the surface to break up. This gas main had damaged the crown of the arch in 1883 when the Gas Board laid pipes to supply the church. Mr Withey, the Board's Chairman, had

F.W. Rowbotham demonstrating the repair work on Nutshell Bridge in 1987. Note how the house abuts the bridge. (Courtesy of *Stroud News & Journal*)

promised to see to it. As the bridge was a listed structure, the Company was lawfully required to restore it. Long negotiations took place, fronted by Rowbotham, mainly with English Heritage who specified the type of mortar to be used, and how the work should be done. Particularly, they were adamant the elevations should not be altered. Help was given by the Cotswold Canals Trust, which provided a barge to sink beneath the bridge to anchor the centring, and GCC who lent temporary bridges to carry the right of way. Payments to both those bodies was included in the cost of the project which was about £15,000, grants being received from English Heritage and Stroud District Council of about £4,000 and £5,000 respectively. Messrs Moreton C. Cullimore Ltd were the contractors, and the bridge was re-opened by Miss Gwendoline Hooper, the longest-serving member of the Board, on a wet day in December 1988. She provided the plaque, which acknowledges the work done by F.W. Rowbotham and Cullimore's.

Bridgend Bridge

Variously known as Bridgend, Stonehouse, The Ship or Downton Road Bridge, all names are appropriate. It is situated in Stonehouse just south of The Ship (as was), in an area known as Bridgend from the bridge over the river, and on the road to Downton. This was the other bridge which caused great concern to GCC and prompted the application to Parliament to abandon the canal for navigation.

It was a brick-arched hump-back bridge, which afforded poor visibility and was close to a railway level crossing. Bridgend Estate, a high-density post-war development of houses, was planned on land immediately south of the canal, and Downton Road was the only access. Although it was in good order, the bridge was a potential danger spot. The 1954 Act gave powers for GCC to take responsibility for the bridge, replace it with a flat concrete structure, and install concrete culverts beneath to take the flow of water. Unfortunately engineers miscalculated the water flow, and silt continually built up around the culverts, allowed reeds to grow and choked up the course. F.W. Rowbotham, who was still working for Severn River Board at this time, said with hindsight in 1981, 'The choking of the canal is due to the type of bridge and would not have occurred if a clear span bridge had been built'. The silt was a constant trouble to the Company, and took up much of the Secretary's time, because water supply had to be constantly maintained to Messrs Hoffmans at Stonehouse. In fact in the drought of Summer 1962 the factory narrowly escaped having to be closed. Even ten years later, Alan Payne, the Secretary, was writing his 'bi-annual plea in accordance with the terms of the Stroudwater Navigation Act 1954 for you to remove obstructions in the culverts at Bridgend'. He was writing to the Divisional Surveyor of GCC, D.R. Martyn, and in 1974, a week after the reorganisation of local government, they were able to share a joke. Mr Gerald Critchley, in his new capacity as Environmental Officer for Stroud District Council asked the Company in no uncertain terms to clear the stagnant canal at Bridgend, and this was passed on to GCC with appropriate comment!

Maybe as a result of the ongoing harassment, GCC arranged to incorporate a new bridge suitable for navigation into the final stage of the A419 road improvements from the motorway interchange. Again, safety was the main issue: a statement by GCC declared their strategy 'to encourage local growth and increase accessibility to the Stroud Valleys area' and this included the canal. Work started in June 1999, and the opening ceremony for the bridge was at Easter 2000.

Bridgend Bridge, looking south, with the entrance to the canal/railway wharf on the right, 1948. This was regarded as highly dangerous for increased traffic, and was the main cause for Gloucestershire County Council taking over county bridges in 1954. (Courtesy of Gloucestershire Record Office)

Upper Mills Bridge

Alternatively this former swing bridge was known as Brush Works Bridge, from about 1914 when Messrs W.H. Vowles & Sons Ltd ran a brush factory, until 1968 when Stonehouse Investments Ltd took over the premises called Upper Mills and developed a trading estate. The bridge allows access to the estate over the canal and towpath, through gates between stone pillars. This is not the only entrance.

The firm of R.S. Davies, clothiers, had taken over Upper Mills as well as Lower Mills by 1838. At the Company half-yearly meeting in October 1838 Robert Davies complained about the passage of vessels through the bridge opposite his mill. He did not know whether there was some impediment in the canal or the bridge walls were too wide, but some of the barges were having difficulty getting through the bridge: the bridge was open for too long for his convenience, not to mention the mud. Some barges, particularly one belonging to James Nurse, were of unusual width. He made the same complaints at a site meeting with the Committee in August 1846, when he alleged the bridge was insecure and requested a new one. That was not agreed, but the Surveyor was ordered to widen the opening and to overhaul the bridge completely. Davies was still not satisfied a few months later and said the bridge needed two or three men to turn it. Also, 'a quantity of stone had been improperly removed from his premises'. Without comment, the Company arranged for four tons of stone to be sent in lieu of that taken by mistake. Inspections were made of both the gasworks' and Davies' bridges in April 1851, when it was discovered the former was wholly worn out, but the latter required only minor repairs. Mr Davies was to get his new bridge at last; the gasworks one was to be scrapped and the old Upper Mills one repaired and put in its place. By that expedient the stoppage of roads over the bridges would be avoided.

When Stonehouse Investments took over the Mills in 1969, having been refused permission to make a solid bridge with culverts, they straight away requested to widen the bridge by 6ft, introducing rolled-steel joists across the canal, with reinforced concrete infill and tarmac over the surface roadway. The Company agreed to this, and set out terms similar to those agreed over Gas Works Bridge. They were, that the applicants were to bear all costs, and take all responsibility for the bridge and rebuilding of it, the Company to be indemnified against all accidents arising from disrepair. The bridge was to remain the property of the Company. Stonehouse Investments remarked on the canal being in an awful state and an 'eyesore', intimating they would take over that stretch to keep it in reasonable condition in their vicinity. The Company chose to ignore these comments.

Midland Railway Bridge

In the Parliamentary Session of 1863, the Act for the Stonehouse & Nailsworth Railway was passed containing a section safeguarding the interests of 'the Stroudwater Canal Company' [sic]. There were six clauses to this, all concerned with the railway bridge over the canal, the arrangements for Stonehouse Wharf and the lay-by being a separate issue, made to placate the Company and engage their support.

Midland Railway Bridge, Stonehouse. Locomotive BR class 2-2-6-0 No.78004 is seen here crossing on her weekly run to Nailsworth, *c.*1960. (Courtesy of B.J. Ashworth)

The first clause stated that Stonehouse & Nailsworth could build a good and substantial bridge or viaduct over the canal and towpath to the satisfaction of the Engineer of the Company. There was to be a clear opening or span of arches between the walls or abutments of such width on the square sufficient to leave unobstructed the whole navigable width of the waterway, and space of not less than 8ft wide on the towpath. At the point of crossing the girders should commence at a point not less than 8ft above the present surface of the towpath, and the underside of the middle arch should be not less than 12ft above top water level. Extreme widths of the bridge between parapet walls were not to exceed 30ft. Other clauses stated that if a new bridge was built it was to be exactly the same; the canal was not to be altered in any way; if a boat could not pass because of obstruction the Company had to be paid £30 for every twenty-four hours it was out of action; all brooks, streams and springs were to be preserved by the Company. There was to be no interference with the powers and rights of the Company, as enacted.

A sub-committee made their own specifications in 1864. The width of the canal was to be 22ft wide and the towpath 6ft, but depth of water was of major importance. Under the bridge it was to be a uniform 6ft, also the same for 70ft on the east and west sides. A wall built between the towpath and the canal (perhaps meaning the bank) was to continue ten yards further towards Ryeford.

James Ferrabee, who founded Phoenix Ironworks at Thrupp in 1828, was the engineer and designer of the bridge. It was built on a complicated alignment, set at a very oblique angle, using a triangular cast-iron buttress on the north side, and of single-track width over the steel span. Difficulties were experienced by the contractors with subsidence of the supporting piers and with water supply. Railways had to be inspected by the Board of Trade before opening, and Colonel Yolland on their behalf was not satisfied at his inspection on 8 December 1866. Transoms and cross-ties were required between longitudinals that carried the rails, and some girders needed to be bolted down onto the cast-iron columns. By the end of the year criteria were met, and the line opened in February 1867, with no formal ceremony.

By that time the Company were already considering claiming for damages, and in June 1866 Charles Thornhill Harrison, an independent civil engineer of Frocester Court, was called to give an assessment of the bridge, and report if it was built in accordance with the Act. He was to take into account the modifications permitted by the sub-committee, and determine how far the bridge had tended to prevent boats carrying usual loads from passing freely along the canal. The Company wanted to know for how long navigation been impeded by the bridge so they could claim compensation. Parties claiming because of detention of their vessels at the bridge could be referred directly to the Stonehouse & Nailsworth Railway Co. under the forty-second clause of their Act. Mr Harrison produced his report in a month, resulting in the Company determining to take its stand and act through the solicitor. By how much the measurements were infringed is not known, but considering damages and costs, the total amount claimed was £1,060, which also included stoppage on 14 October when the railway company needed water to be let out to allow work to be done on the bridge. The money was not received until 1878 when the Midland Railway paid off debts incurred by the Stonehouse & Nailsworth Company, after the Midland Railway Incorporation Bill was passed.

A few months before the line finally closed in 1966 the timber span had been fired, so the track had to be shored up on 'military trestles.' These were eventually replaced by concrete plates, and the bridge is now a link in the cycle trail along the railway track to Nailsworth.

Haywards Bridge

Proposals had been made to construct a bypass for Ebley on the A419 for many years, when Mr Rowbotham received a plan from GCC for the canal crossing in August 1986. The new road was to go from the old station yard at Dudbridge on the Stonehouse & Nailsworth line to the Horsetrough Roundabout at Stonehouse, crossing the canal just south of the roundabout. The scheme also included approach roads at each end, with modifications to the Dudbridge canal bridge, and to the west the replacement of the Downton Road bridge.

The Board were given a chance to discuss the plans in March 1987 when they were introduced by Mr Boakes, who pointed out that the intended new bridge was to be a culvert for the canal. This was entirely contrary to the wishes of the Board and the Canals Trust who made strong representations against it as it would prohibit navigation. The Minute stated: 'The Directors were of the opinion that if they do not continue to fight this plan, there would be no point in the Company continuing'. They were concerned proper plans had not been submitted to them. GCC did amend the plan, widening the culvert, but it was not aesthetically pleasing.

All went quiet until 1990 when construction on the road started, and an amended plan showed that clearance for navigation was now possible, with an airspace of 8ft and a minimum width for the canal of 12½ft. When detailed plans were to hand in Autumn 1991, Director David Ashley discovered that a slight curve would not allow navigation by a tug with a barge in tow. The Company offered to negotiate terms if an alteration could be made. Fortunately GCC agreed to incorporate the design modifications at no cost to the Company. A deed of easement in favour of GCC was signed in June 1992, and subsequently the box-section culvert was constructed with a minimum width of 16ft and taking the towpath too. The name comes from this part of Stonehouse, called Haywardsfield.

Ryeford Bridge

Ryeford Bridge, listed Grade II, has two different fascias. The west side is mostly original in coursed stone up to the inclined stone band, with semi-circular keystone arch. Retaining walls are straight with plain pilasters. The east side, of 1833, is brick with a keystone to a semi-circular arch. Here the retaining walls are curved with stone coping, stepped at the north end. Obviously the bridge has been widened, not surprisingly as it was an old way from Stonehouse to King's Stanley and always very busy.

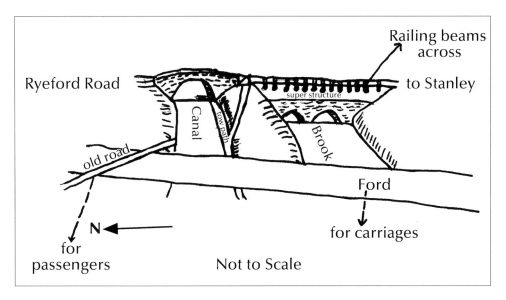

Ryeford Bridge. A diagram prepared for Counsel in 1817 for opinion in a case about repairing the canal and river bridges which are very close together.

From time immemorial there was a public highway across the brook at the Old River, called Stroudwater. At the time of constructing the canal, there was a stone bridge across the river for horses and foot passengers, but carriages crossed by a ford near the bridge (i.e. Rye ford). When the canal was built it was only fourteen yards from the brook and crossed the highway near the same place. The bottom of the canal was made one foot higher, and the surface of it about 7ft higher than the bottom of the brook, therefore the Company were bound to erect a bridge for public use across their canal. It was also presumed the Company were bound to make a proper way for the public to cross Old River with wagons and carriages instead of the ford.

In February 1817 an application was received from the parish of Stonehouse for the Company to repair the bridge over the river. Counsel opinion was sought. In order to fulfil their obligations, the Company resolved the new canal bridge should be made straight with the two arches of the 1727 stone bridge crossing the river. It was a county bridge by 1740, but the ford continued to be used. In order for the old bridge to be made passable for carriages, the Company raised it up by building a superstructure on the old arch, in brick, of several feet in height, and thus provided a proper descent from the top of the canal bridge. Further, they laid beams across the top of the superstructure which projected on each side, and laid wooden planks across them to make footpaths. Therefore the road was widened and made convenient for carriages and foot passengers at the same time.

By this means the Company had done all they were obliged to do, and at no time did Stonehouse parish complain. In fact they had constantly repaired the road over the old bridge and up to the wing walls of the canal bridge. The Company had repaired their own bridge and road, as well as the woodwork and railings they installed on the parish bridge, but they never repaired the masonry or the road over it. For seven years the pier of the old bridge had been sinking, although it had stood forty years with no such effect. The bridge and railings needed renewing and that is why the parish called on the Company, who refused because neither by prescription or tenure were they ever bound to repair it at all. In fact the parish had repaired the road, thus showing it to be their responsibility. Counsel was requested to give opinion on whether the Company should repair the old bridge, and were they liable for damages and costs of the parish?

Two Counsels replied. One stated that as the canal had prevented carriages driving through the ford, the Company were bound to keep alterations made to the bridge in lieu of it, in repair. The substratum of the bridge must have been weakened by the added superstructure and having carriages pass over it. He could not say which party was injured, but thought the Company may be indicted. Second Counsel said much the same, but was more precise. The best solution would be for the bridge to be rebuilt at the original height at the expense of those formerly liable, and the super-structure rebuilt at the Company's expense. This could only be achieved by compromise. If it could be proved the superstructure was the cause of the damage, it may be said the Company was instrumental in destroying the bridge, and would have to rebuild the whole of it.

Everything was then fine: the Company compromised. They repaired the masonry of the river bridge, superstructure, woodwork and rails, and made it more convenient for the public. And they repaired the surface of the road over both bridges, including the intermediate space. Then in September 1832 came a letter from Messrs Maclean, Stephens & Co. of Stanley Mill about the state of the Ryeford bridges. There had

Brunsdon's yard seen through the arch, facing west. Ryeford Bridge and the towpath were in need of repair in 1948. (Courtesy of Gloucestershire Record Office)

been an incident in which a stage wagon, loaded with wool for Maclean & Stephens, had overturned and which ended up in the river. The wagon belonged to Tanner & Baylis, well-known carriers of Rodborough. The whole process started over again.

It appeared that, notwithstanding alterations already made by the Company, the road over the river bridge was so steep it was necessary to tie or lock the wheels of laden carriages to descend from it. Roads were now wider than this bridge, which could not be made wider without a complete rebuild, or widening from the foundations. Besides which, the two bridges were not in a perfectly straight line. A small bend in the road as it passed over the bridges made for inconvenience and danger. The wagon had overturned between the two bridges and fell over the fence into the river below. Maclean & Stephens called on the Company, requiring them to make alterations for the improvement of the bridges and road. They pointed out that modern (i.e. 1830s) wagons were larger, wider and more heavily laden than when the canal was made. Modern refinements and attention to road construction and travelling seemed to necessitate road improvements here. The Company asked Counsel if they were bound to repair the bridge and road over the river. If so, were they bound to adapt it to conveniences of modern carriages and travelling even though this should require rebuilding the old river bridge and amending the descent?

As a corollary it was revealed that the Company paid an annual composition to Maclean & Stephens for keeping the road and bridges in repair on their behalf, being the most interested party concerned in the matter. The agreement was not in writing but a receipt for £3 3s 4d being payment for two years was produced, dated 3 December 1831. In which case was the accident a result of Maclean & Stephens' repairs to the road or because of the camber, which inclined towards the entrance of a field belonging to Maclean & Stephens, thus causing the wagon to swerve?

The wagon, piled very high with wool, had travelled from London with the same load, without incident. Possibly at the end of the journey the load, if not dangerous, was less firm and upright than at the beginning, and might have been overhanging or loose, causing it to overbalance. No evidence of this was produced. The wagon was broken and the wool a little damaged by water. The Company wanted to know if Maclean & Stephens could recover against Tanner & Baylis for damage to their wool? And could Tanner & Baylis, in turn, recover against the Company for damages to the wagon in consequence of the supposed defective state of the road? If so, would the mill-owners, as repairers of the road, be liable to repay damages to the Company?

Maclean & Stephens were entitled to complete indemnity from the carriers, because carriers are the insurers against loss by any accident. Answers to other questions are indeterminate, depending on whether it was daylight, and the wagoner had clear visibility, and proof would be needed whether the road and bridges were properly repaired. Counsel strongly advised the Company to do whatever was necessary to adapt the bridge and road to the convenience of modern carriages and way of travelling.

Consequently the Company was given powers in April 1833 to build a new bridge over the river Frome at Ryeford, to widen the canal bridge there, and to enter into contracts for the work. The following year they raised the road at Ryeford, at the request of Maclean & Stephens, who also applied to continue to repair the road as before, on payment of £20 per annum. Samuel Pinbury, Tanner & Baylis' agent, attended a committee meeting in October 1834, and agreed to accept £20 in compensation for the wagon. Stanley Mill was sold to Nathaniel Stephens Marling in 1842.

The bridge became a county road, but was terminated at the point where it met the Ebley bypass. The road to Stanley Mill and King's Stanley now turns at traffic lights on the same alignment, about 10ft lower than the former road, which indicates the steepness of the terrain there.

Ryeford Footbridge

This bridge at one time was allegedly the only way to the cottages on the offside which were associated with the canal, but not Company property, although they seem to date from the same time, late eighteenth/early nineteenth century. In August 1864 it was ordered to be repaired when the committee meeting was held onboard the Company boat, and they must have noticed the disrepair themselves. Only three years later a new bridge was requested.

Originally it was a wooden swing bridge, which needed replanking in 1959, when Geoffrey Workman of the adjacent Ryeford Saw Mill wrote to advise the Surveyor of this. His workmen would have used the bridge to get to work. In 1982 the Stroudwater, Thames & Severn Canal Trust (now Cotswold Canals Trust) made replacement of the bridge one of their main projects under the Manpower Services Commission Scheme, with contributions from the Company. The replacement is a low-level railway-type structure, which swings on a pivot. It is painted white, and is very attractive.

Oil Mills Bridge

Aptly named, because the bridge served the Oil Mills Estate exclusively, although sometimes it is called after The Bell inn, situated on the north-west side by a small wharf. All that, with some cottages, has been demolished, but the triangular piece of land it occupied is still owned by the Company. The bridge was the standard humpback, brick-arch, with a very steep angle to the singletrack roadway.

Oil Mill was built in 1721 to produce rape and linseed oils, and later became a fulling or cloth mill. It was sold to the Lewis family before 1820, who produced cloth until it was sold to John Biddle the miller. After the mill was offered for sale in 1892 it was owned by the Knight family, and was bought by the Smith family about 1910. Production switched to animal feeds after the Second World War.

A deed dated 1 October 1857 in the Marling papers deposited at Gloucestershire Records Office, concerns a strip of land, part of a pasture called Rack Hill. This strip is called Tram Road, and has been taken from the garden belonging to a messuage adjoining the Stroudwater Navigation, in the occupation of Joseph Eycott Lewis. For some time past the strip had been used as a tramway for the purposes of the mill, and

A photograph of Oil Mills Bridge taken from the top window of Holly Tree House, looking north-east over greenhouses towards The Bell inn and adjacent cottages. Ebley House is in the distance. (Courtesy of H. Beard)

Oil Mills Bridge looking back through the arch, 1948. (Courtesy of Gloucestershire Record Office)

Above: This photograph shows the position of the original swing bridge giving access to the New Mill (Greenaway's). The view looks west, with Oil Mills Bridge the in distance. (Courtesy of H. Beard)

Below: The replacement swing bridge for the previous one at the point leading into Ebley Mill. The area is now more elegant, as the building in front has been demolished. (Courtesy of M.A. Handford)

now it was agreed that a wall be built between the garden and the tramroad to separate them. William Lane was to have the use of the strip, but only as and for a tramway or roadway from the canal to the mills, for the purposes of the mill. There was a very small wharf by Holly Tree House which was for the use of the Oil Mills. Later, a siding called Lane's sidings was constructed across Ebley meadows to the Stonehouse & Nailsworth Railway and the wharf discontinued. Certainly it was not in use in the twentieth century.

Ebley Swing Bridges

Mr Warman of Ebley House complained in 1844 about damage done to his bridge at Ebley, occasioned by Mr Marling's bridge being so near his own. A margin note was added to the Minute, saying that Warman's bridge was ninety yards from the bridge to Bridge House. This suggests there was a private bridge from Ebley House to the meadow on the south of the canal which was part of the estate. Marling's bridge in question would have been the old one to the west of Ebley Mills, and the damage possibly due to wash from boats.

Stephen Clissold was the owner before the Marlings, and it was he, according to a Minute of 7 April 1806, who had built the swing bridge to give access to his land on the south side of the canal. There he built his New Mill in about 1816-20, and this bridge led to it from the turnpike down a trackway and into the millyard. By 1840 Messrs Marling were the owners, they demolished the old mill premises north of the canal, enlarged the New Mill and made a large reservoir to the east for supplying it.

In April 1840 Marling's wanted to move the swivel bridge from by the end of their premises to opposite the gates into their intended new millyard, 300ft to the east. They also wanted to use the towpath between the site of the intended bridge and the present one as a road for supplying building materials. Permission was granted, provided the work was done at their expense and using their own materials. It was to be done during the usual period of stopping the canal at Whitminster at Whitsuntide. A further stipulation was that the canal should be the same width at the new bridge site, and that the banks at the old site be restored to the general width of the canal. The new swing bridge was duly built, and gave entrance through stone pillars to the new millyard, and subsequently the other new mill building, but the old bridge remained. Nor were the banks altered, as indicated by a recently uncovered pinch-point. It was shown on the 1884 Ordnance Survey map by a swing bridge, and on a plan of the Ebley House Estate in 1894, although there was probably no way to it then. Sometime after that it was taken away.

The swing bridge to the east remained the property of the mill-owners, and in 1953 it was reported as a timber bridge with steel girders under, and not in good condition. As it was the only access to Ebley Mills, Messrs Marling & Evans applied in 1955 to construct a solid bridge in its place at the same spot. The Board agreed, subject to provision being made which would allow for free flow of water down the canal.

Hilly Orchard Bridge

In order to construct the original wooden swing footbridge across the canal to carry an ancient right of way across the valley, the Company bought up some south-facing orchard land. Hence the attractive name. Both the canal and footpath were very busy; Dudbridge wharf was a few yards to the east and vessels queued to use it. The right of way was the quickest means of getting on foot to Rodborough, Selsley and the Stanleys (nowadays to Sainsbury's). The bridge has continued to give problems since early days. To prevent horses and cattle crossing the bridge from the towpath side, in 1854 a turnstile was ordered to be erected by the swing bridge in place of the ordinary stile.

James Webb paid a £2 fine on behalf of his captain, William Meecham, in February 1865 because his vessel had run into the bridge before it was properly open. How much damage was done is not recorded, but only six months later a new bridge was ordered. More serious was the number of drownings at the spot, where children went bathing and fishing.

One such drowning, of two people, took place on the night of Monday 18 March 1833, and prompted a special sermon by Revd Benjamin Parsons, the legendary Pastor of the Countess of Huntingdon's Connexion Chapel at Ebley. A booklet was published to mark the occasion. Thirty-eight-year-old Joseph King of King's Stanley attended the chapel at least four times a week, and was Superintendent of the 200-strong Sunday School. The other victim was forty-year-old Mrs Mary Cosborne Pearse, wife of a solicitor of Minchinhampton. On the Sunday, Mr Pearse attended chapel, then went back to King's Stanley with Joseph King. They were old school friends, having been at Senckley (St Chloe) School together. Pearse happened to mention that he and his wife were to have tea next day with Joseph's brother Peter at Dudbridge. Mrs King suggested that Mrs Pearse should stay a few days with her at King's Stanley afterwards. On the Monday after evening prayer meeting, where 'he was penitential in prayer', Joseph duly called at his brother's to fetch Mary Pearse, and as he had a cold and was anxious to conduct family prayers at home, they were in a hurry.

It was an exceedingly dark night, so they decided to go via the wooden bridge at the bottom of Hilly Orchard, and then by the Turnpike Road. 'At the entrance to this passage over the canal both perished'. The approach to the bridge was awkward and dangerous to a stranger, especially a female, and since the accident the Proprietors made the place more secure. To avoid climbing a bad stile, it is supposed Mrs Pearse attempted to pass by a narrow space that was one foot wide, slipped, and fell into the canal. Joseph could swim and must have leaped in after her, but struck his head, as a mark on his forehead indicated, was stunned and sank. Mary's daughter was walking behind, heard a splash and someone said, 'Oh Dear'. She ran to the waterside, thought she saw her mother, and raised the alarm. When a light was brought, Joseph was found floating on his back, and could not be revived. In less than twenty minutes since he left it, his body was returned to his brother's house. By an unfortunate coincidence, a bargeman was close at hand, had heard them fall and ran down the hill to help. He was a tall athletic man who was a good swimmer, and could

Hilly Orchard Bridge was lowered in 1958, and subsequently replaced with concrete decking. It will be reconstructed in 2004. (Photograph by C.H.A. Townley, 1966: courtesy of J.A. Peden)

have waded into the water, but he fell, injuring his knee badly, and had 'to lie on the ground while they perished'. 'Their course was run – the last sand had dropped'. Mary had eight children, Joseph six.

In June 1884 A.J. Morton Ball was the coroner at an inquest on Henry Ashenford, aged nine, of the Laggar, Dudbridge, who was taken out of the canal by Hilly Orchard Bridge. His mother, Elizabeth, had gone out washing at the lock-keeper's house, and left Henry at home. Two little girls, Edith March and Maggie Clissold, saw him struggling and Mr Mattock and Mr Browning came to help, but it was too late. Henry was insured with Pearl Insurance Co. for £10.

Following this disaster, the Company started to investigate a safer, more convenient solution to the bridge. Mr Edwin Francis Gyde, the philanthropist of Ebley House, together with the Chairman and Clerk of the Company, went to see a footbridge over the railway near Bristol to consider if one like it could be adopted in lieu of the swing bridge. Mr Croome, owner and Trustee of land on the north side of the bridge approved, but Mr Barnard, owner on the south side, demurred. He wanted some concession from the Company for the right of road he had to his house on the upper side of Dudbridge Wharf. The Committee viewed the site, and agreed Mr Barnard should keep his right of road. Then Sir William Marling stepped in and suggested the substituted footbridge should skirt his land, and thus avoid the footpath. Mr Barnard was invited to the meeting on 21 July 1885, when his objections were shown to be more imaginary than otherwise. Therefore the high-level footbridge was to be installed.

In 1956 the boards on the footbridge were in a dangerous condition and needed replacing, so again the Company turned their thoughts to another solution. This presented itself in the summer of 1958, when the Severn River Board were on hand to adapt the canal to main river, as part of the flood relief scheme. Mr Rowbotham was in charge of the work. He agreed to lower the bridge, and they would supply the men and materials. However, the River Board would not cut the steel for the sub-structure, so Messrs Savage were engaged to do this, with a moiety of £33 17s 6d from Stroud Urban District Council. The decking was concrete slabs with a wooden handrail. Fifty-five years later the bridge is being reinstated, this time by housing developers.

Dudbridge Road Bridge

There is in the Company archives a ledger called the Commissioners' Order Book covering the years from 1777 to 1787. The Commissioners were eminent or leading citizens appointed to oversee the activities of the Company, and to ensure fair play. Most of their deliberations concerned arbitration on acquisition of lands, and of these is an entry:

> We do order that a substantial brick or stone bridge for horses, carts and carriages shall be erected over the canal on the Turnpike Road leading from Cainscross to Dudbridge. The bridge shall serve for communication to lands below the canal belonging to Daniel Chance and the executors of John Mosley, dec.

When William Franklin was engaged to build the Dudbridge Locks in 1778, he was already working on the stone bridge. His contract stated that the foundations were to be ragstone from Rodborough Hill. The remainder to be good weather stone from Hampton Common. The Company were to dig the foundations, and deliver the lime. Franklin was to receive £200, payable in instalments.

No references to maintenance on the bridge are made in the Minutes, which suggests the Turnpike Trust was responsible for it, then GCC. The carriageway was widened several times, once with brick and the last time with concrete when work was done as part of the A419 improvements, projected in 1987. The towpath passes beneath the bridge on the south side down a steep slope

Marling School Bridge

The field on the south side of the canal next to the former sewage works was taken as an extra playing field for Marling School about 1969, when the Bursar, James Coode, requested permission from the Company to construct a simple concrete bridge to connect with their playing field south of the canal. The Secretary, Alan Payne, gave his consent, but stressed that as the canal was now main river at that point, Severn River Board should be consulted too. The bridge has been barred as it is seldom used.

Gas Works Bridge

On 10 May 1833 the Company held a Special Meeting to discuss the request of William Morley Stears to buy a small piece of land near the canal bridge leading to Fromehall Mill as part of the site for an intended gasworks. In the chair was Henry Wyatt, a strong anti-slavery campaigner. He had just bought Farm Hill, above Paganhill. When the Abolition of Slavery Act took effect in 1834, Wyatt erected a stone arch as a memorial at the gateway to his new drive. He became a Board member of the gas company. The decision taken to sell the land was significant for Stroud and for the Company. The assured trade on the canal kept the waterway open for over 100 years.

A clause in the agreement had specific mention of the bridge. The gas company were to contribute half towards the expense of providing a new bridge, and doing repairs on the present or future bridge. It was a usual wooden swing bridge at the time. They were not called upon in August 1853 when Clarke, the master of the boat *Marzeppa*, carelessly ran against, and damaged, the bridge. The owners, Holmes & Co., had to pay £1, but were warned that if it happened again the full fine of £5 would be charged. Nor were the gas company required to contribute towards the 1854 restoration of the bridge on condition they would immediately stone and repair the road adjoining their works, although this proposal would not affect their future commitments. A new bridge was ordered to be put in at the gasworks as soon as possible, 'having regard to the convenience of traders', in July 1863.

That bridge was indeed paid for in half by the Stroud Gas Light & Coke Co., as it had become, after a new Act allowed them to raise capital up to £40,000. They had wanted to convert their original counterpart lease of 1833 into fee simple, but the Company pointed out that certain covenants had not been honoured, among them the business of the moiety on the bridge. Therefore if they paid rent arrears of £20 plus £44 7s 1d, half the cost of the new bridge, the Company would grant a new lease. The money was paid (less the 1d) in January 1864, and the lease for 1,000 years was sealed. The Gas Board are to pay half the repairs in perpetuity.

By 1877 a new bridge was wanting again, and this time the gas company installed it, sending the bill for half the cost, £68 11s 10d, to the Company. However, the Clerk said there had been other expenses not included in that sum which would balance out because of the half-value of the old bridge. The Clerk was instructed to send particulars of the expenses to the gas company, but not to alter the bill already sent in.

After supply of gas was nationalised and South Western Gas Board took over, a letter was sent in 1954 advising the Company that a lorry had damaged the bridge, which was in a dangerous condition. About that time a report described the bridge as fixed, rebuilt with rolled-steel joists and concreted deck. It was found the lorry belonged to Stroud Urban District Council, who would pay for the part of the handrail which had broken. The Company seemed to have the Board over a barrel. A resolve was made at a meeting in January 1959 that because a new bridge had been constructed in 1940 with a weight limit of eight tons, and unless the Board paid two-thirds of its repair, the bridge would be closed to traffic over four tons. In May the Board capitulated (there was no other access to the gasworks), agreeing to pay two-thirds towards the cost of the present bridge, and future maintenance would be on that basis. A fence was erected around the sides of the bridge. A new agreement with Ready Mixed Concrete (Western) Ltd, who had taken over most of the gasworks site, was signed in 1965, and they carried out repairs in 1978 after complaints from neighbours of noise and danger.

A rough census of traffic over the bridge from the south was taken on Monday 31 July 1939. There was a total of ninety-three crossings, the majority from the Gas-House [sic]. The number of crossings from the gasworks included sixteen private cars, eleven trade vans, thirty-four motor lorries, one motorcycle, and one pony and trap. From Fromehall Mill were seven movements, and from UDC (presumably this was the sewage site) there were twenty-three, including eleven lorries and one pony and trap.

Lodgemore Bridge

This heavily used bridge is one of four entrances to Lodgemore Mill, a close complex of mill buildings, offices, dyeworks and residential premises, the only mill in the Stroud Valleys still producing woollen cloth. Messrs Strachan & Co., when they took over the mill from Messrs Hunt & Co. (it is still called simply Strachan's locally) in 1866, renewed the arrangement made by their predecessors to pay the Company 2s 6d per annum as rent for the land between the southern end of the canal bridge and the gate to the mill. Difficulties over weight limits continue to the present day, likewise children playing nearby. Two boys, Edward Pritchard and Fred Gay of Stroud, came before the Committee and were severely reprimanded in July 1883 for leaving the swing bridge at Lodgemore partly open.

The swing bridge retains the cast-iron sub-structure and pivot as erected by Messrs Daniels in 1927, though it is now fixed. The area through which it would swing is still evident. The reason for its continued existence is indicated in a letter of 18 November 1975 in which F.W. Rowbotham explains that when the canal was made into main river, the Water Authority would have required a river bridge to meet the needs of the channel, therefore maybe the Authority should bear some cost of providing such a bridge, instead of a straight infill. He justifies this by suggesting (as he himself was the project engineer) that if the facility of using the canal had not been granted, then the Authority would have been involved in a vastly more expensive scheme.

Extensive remedial work was carried out on the bridge to strengthen it in 1976-77, but to a ceiling limit, as no contributions were received from any users or Stroud District Council. Weight limit notices of eight tons were posted at each end of the bridge, and prompted letters from Stroud District Council and the Fire Service. They claimed that refuse lorries and fire engines were in excess of that weight. The Secretary told the Council to find an alternative way, but fire engines not exceeding sixteen tons were allowed to cross in an emergency. The Secretary continued to stress that the Company's liability was to cater for weight limits as held in the eighteenth

Lodgemore Bridge in the 1930s, showing details of the structure erected by T.H. & J. Daniels Ltd of Lightpill Iron Works in 1927, looking towards Wallbridge. (Courtesy of Peckhams of Stroud)

century, and if vehicles damaged the bridge because they ignored the limit, then they would have to pay damages. Later the limit was fixed at ten tons, but a safe working load is believed to be in the region of thirty tons.

5

The Working Canal

Towpath

When the Company was negotiating with landowners to set up the canal, the conveyances which still exist all specify the land is required for the Navigation and towing path. Boat propulsion was by teams of men 'bow-hauling' so it was not necessary for the ground to be absolutely level, or the path very wide or fenced. Stiles were used to separate each enclosure. It was a long job, which would take all day to bring a vessel from the Severn to Stroud, with the prevailing wind behind. Trows could hoist a sail in a favourable westerly breeze, but were not allowed to pass through locks with sails up, therefore the tackle was usually left at Framilode until needed for the journey on the Severn again.

As the towing path was on private land, the Company charged for the use of it for purposes other than hauling, like access across or along it. To establish their rights, the Company would close off parts of the towing path at yearly intervals for one day. This practice still continues where any footpath is only a permissive right of way, not a statutory one. In January 1784 five sections of towing path were to be stopped, one each day between Thursday 1 January and Tuesday the 6th, except Sunday. The respective sections were looked after by the nearest Company servant: George Lodge, from Wallbridge to Dudbridge; William Beard, Dudbridge to Ryeford; Thomas Lewis, Ryeford to Mr Eycott's Mill; James Barns, from there to Bristol Road; and an unknown person from Bristol Road to Framilode. In fact they would help each other at the various points.

Three men – John Lawrence, Joseph Davis and Samuel Golding – were brought before two magistrates in the spring of 1809 for cutting 'five apertures' in the towpath at the lower level of the canal and were fined £20. Whether they did it for mischief, as a means of draining land, obtaining water from the canal, or any other reason is not apparent, but the Committee finally settled for £10 each.

A Minute of 21 February 1810 states, 'Mr Cambridge having very handsomely given up his claim to the towing path from Lockham Bridge to Whitminster Lock, it was ordered that the towing path be gravelled 3ft wide, and first raising the low places to prevent water from flowing over'. This difficulty would have arisen through lack of fences, then as now. A cryptic marginal note in pencil in the Index Book reads, 'He has given up that which was not his!' A similar situation arose with Mr Clissold at Ebley Mill in 1817, when the towpath had been damaged. Clissold had previously damaged the towpath by cutting it through to take water to wash his wool, so the Company was not well disposed to him although he had mended the bank. This time a sub-committee was to ascertain the boundaries.

Mr Price of the Foundry at Dudbridge beside the canal signed an agreement about the towpath in 1822. He acknowledged:

> that the use of the road which I exercise and use from the stone bridge [Dudbridge] to my foundry and premises near there and of which road leads over the towing path belonging to the Company of Proprietors of the Stroudwater Navigation is used and exercised by me at the Company's permission only, and with their lease and licence and not as a right in me. And I agree to relinquish such road at any time on receiving notice from the Company or their Clerk, and in the meantime I agree to pay the Company the annual sum of one shilling on the first of January every year if demanded.

Over thirty years later there were repercussions on this agreement.

The footpath over the present Nutshell Bridge has no natural connection with the towpath, and a Minute of 16 April 1823 throws some light on this. Robert Davis of the Lower Mills was to be informed by the Clerk that the Company refused to allow the footpath running from Stanley to Stonehouse, through the yard of the mill, to be diverted along the towpath as he had done. If Davis did not turn the road back again, then the Clerk would obstruct the towpath. Today there are stiff penalties for barring public footpaths.

Owing to pressure from the Thames & Severn Company, the Stroudwater finally agreed to installing a horse towing path in 1825. Mr Harford, the agent to the Thames & Severn, had tried to no avail in 1812; the Stroudwater Company had said it would cost too much and be of little advantage. Now their Chairman, John Disney, pointed out that when the Gloucester & Berkeley Canal was completed, it would mean that navigation below Brimscombe would be the only part of the canal system unusable by horses in the communication between the north, Midlands and the east. The Company reluctantly resolved that a horse towing path would be expedient when the ship canal was completed. Two years later they were still having cold feet. They knew it would be necessary to purchase land to widen the road, and a considerable number of adjacent landowners would require fences. Messrs Davis, however, would not. Therefore the total amount of fencing required would be about five miles. To put up a ragstone wall 4ft 6ins high, stopped with road drift, put in gates and adapt bridgeways for horses would cost in the region of £3,000. The decision was put off until the General Meeting in April 1827.

Because of assurances that trade and tolls would improve, it was agreed to adapt the present towpath for horses or other beasts as a temporary experiment for twelve months, on the understanding 'it would not be made permanent unless its success should justify its continuance'. The present towpath was to be repaired, and bargemen were to use only one horse or other beast, not lower than thirteen hands – subject to a £2 fine; horses were to be muzzled, and not allowed to trespass –

subject to a £5 fine. The success or otherwise seems not to have been discussed, one important development was that flyboats could now be employed.

However, it did mean the banks had to be strengthened at regular intervals to keep up the towpath. This sometimes involved piling. In 1833 it was decided to make four labourers employed on canal maintenance redundant, and advertise for tenders for contracting the work instead. George Basham came forward as Contractor for £110 per annum which would include two labourers to assist in piling 'which requires to be done by the Engine called a pile-driver' for a week, at any continuous job, and he would supervise the whole of the other back piling himself if the piles were brought to the spot for him. He would supply labourers for any purpose on request for 2s 6d a day. Basham did work for the Company for a long time.

Charles Harrison proposed in 1836 to dig out and put in a weather stone wall 2ft wide at the Broadwater (the Ocean) to support the towpath, to put down flagging, and to reset the present flagging. His estimate was accepted and it is believed the work can still be seen. A few months earlier Mr Halsey of Whitminster had complained of damage to his fence near Bristol Road Bridge by towing horses passing through the bridge, because it was difficult for them to manoeuvre. He proposed the Company should put a gate in his fence to facilitate the horses passing from one side of the bridge to the other. His offer was to be accepted if the Clerk thought it expedient.

Gates punctuated the towpath at strategic points They were functional and robust, and later painted white for improved visibility, with probably a weight allowing them to self-shut. Mr Driver the Surveyor was called on to install a gate at the request of Mr Harper of Ryeford in 1851, and another near Ryeford Mill soon afterwards.

John Battershall of the Dudbridge Iron Foundry was told in 1853 not to use the towpath between his premises and the gasworks as he had been doing without permission, because the path was being damaged by it. Two years later he applied to take trucks through the gate at Dudbridge Lock and along the canal path to his foundry. That was all right as a temporary arrangement if he would keep the path in repair. After all, there was a precedent.

Although the towpath was continuous from Framilode to Wallbridge, there was not a path through the two main wharves, Dudbridge and Wallbridge, which were shut off by doors for security. In 1884 Revd Palmer, a non-conformist minister, was given a key to open the doors on Sundays to enable him to walk along the towpath from Cainscross to Thrupp to take services. When asked the next year if he wished to renew, he did not reply. Writing in 2000 about Strachan's of Lodgemore Mill, Charles Early mentions Ken Neale, the mill caretaker, part of whose duties was to lock the gate at the end of the footpath at least once a year, and also the gate at Wallbridge. The practice has now lapsed.

At the time of the following incident in 1901 it was the practice to close the towpath triennially, and to advertise it beforehand. On 13 February the towpath was stopped between the Midland Railway bridge back to the swing bridge at Stonehouse when along came George William Sibley of Wycliffe College with a score of his assistant masters and pupils. They violently forced their way past the

Company's men, A. Bassett, W. Bullock and Edward Hill; the last named was pushed into the canal and his leg was broken. The Company left this matter to a sub-committee of Sir William Marling and Messrs Ball, Little and Mills with power to institute legal proceedings against Sibley or take another course. They applied to Counsel, who said the Company had good cause of action, but that he had written to Sibley, and advised him to give an undertaking that he would not trespass on the towpath again. Therefore the Company said if Sibley would sign accordingly and pay five guineas costs, they would abandon the action. Hill was given two weeks' wages, and offered a loan until the insurance materialised. They wanted Sibley to sign the undertaking and have it publicly advertised. To his credit he did it thus:

> *To Stroudwater Navigation Company. I find that I was misinformed as to the public having right of way over the Company's towpath at Stonehouse and regret that I attempted in the interest of the public to assert a supposed right to use the path on February 13th last, on which day it was stopped by your orders. I hereby undertake not to make any such future attempt and I consent to your publishing this undertaking. Signed GW Sibley, 7.5.1901*

Sibley also paid the legal expenses and the cost of the advertisement, besides giving £5 to Hill.

The towpath is now a right of way more or less for all of its length, but still with the exception of Dudbridge and Wallbridge Wharves.

Dredging

One of the chief problems in running a navigation is the question of mud and silt, the removal of which is a time-consuming and costly operation. On navigable rivers it is a constant occupation, but on canals, being narrower, the waterway needs to be closed, thus losing revenue, and even today it is not easy to get plant to the right spot. In theory, canals should not need dredging, being static and not prone to flooding, but in fact the natural streams which feed them, plus erosion of the banks from constant wash from the boats, leads to build-up in certain places. This was the case with the Stroudwater Navigation, particularly where it shared a bed with the Frome at Whitminster and connected with the Severn at Framilode. Other streams like the Badbrook, Painswick Stream and Cuckold's Brook, although culverted in the early days, would ultimately have emptied into the canal to a degree.

In February 1815 the Company realised that navigation was being hampered by the accumulation of mud in various parts, which required immediate attention. They were advised their best course would be to buy a steam machine. Mr Upton of Gloucester had one which was supposed to be the most economical and eligible. When the Committee saw it they were not convinced of its competence and asked an independent engineer, Mr Price, to give his 'opinion of the Power of goodness of the said machine'. It was resolved to pay £546 for the machine, in spite of Mr Upton having misled them as to the height at and the distance from which it ought to throw the mud on to the banks. Also the boat on which the machine was mounted was not satisfactory. Therefore Mr Upton was not paid the full amount until he supplied a windlass and other necessary furnishings. The machine was probably a variation of the original scoop dredgers worked by hand, but with an excavator-type bucket with treadmill-operated windlasses to move and lift it.

A tarpaulin was bought to cover the steam dredger in winter. The Company were very proud of the machine, especially as the Gloucester & Berkeley Company did not turn to steam until 1849. In May 1817 the Company contracted with Mr Miller to do the mudding and they embarked on the Company's barge at 8.00 a.m. on Wednesday 11 June to go down the canal and inspect the work. However, it was found the boat on which the machine was fixed was not in a fit state to complete the mudding. Mr Miller offered to take the old boat, furnish a good one, and fit it up for £25. For a further £25 he would complete the mudding. By 1821 George Basham had taken on the contract.

Basham was still working in 1836 when he signed a contract to remove mud and silt from Framilode Basin for £15. Then a sub-committee identified many other places where mud should be removed, but it should be done by the 'bag and spoon' method, without letting water out of the canal, and a proper vessel for raising and removing the mud be provided. This suggests that the older method of dredging by hand was more efficient as it could get into nooks and crannies more easily. The machine would have a scoop or bag on the end of a pole, which had a cutting edge about eighteen inches long. Two men would do the work, one man would push the scoop into the water, while the other winched it out. The contents were then dumped into the boat, each rope bag would hold about half a hundredweight. Basham won the tender, the specification being to raise about 5cwt at a time. Mud could sometimes be sold for ballast for vessels, but on this occasion it was to be distributed at convenient places.

Negotiations would have to be made with local farmers and landowners to dump the mud on their fields, but to achieve this was always a major worry. Ultimately, later in the nineteenth century the Company bought a mud tip next to the Bristol & Gloucester Railway line where the spoil could be wheelbarrowed from the boat and tipped down the steep bank towards the river. Today a licence is necessary for such work.

A new boat was specially built in 1850 for clearing mud. In one week in December 1857, a gang of seven men spent five out of six working days on mudding in the Stroud length, the other day clearing paths, for a wage of 2s 6d per day, the leader earning 6d more than the others. At Christmas 1857 a gang of three labourers spent Christmas Eve mudding, and were back at it on Boxing Day, having had just Christmas Day off. When extra jobs needed doing, such as dredging the Whitminster level in 1853 because of complaints from Samuel Sims, Mr Driver had to employ two more hands, and four for mudding when Saul Bridge was being erected by the ordinary labourers in 1854.

Mr Driver was very busy that year, because the Committee on their annual inspection by barge in August decided that Framilode Basin was in such a bad state as to need urgent attention. He was to flush it as soon as possible through the lock into the Severn, and if that did not work, then report back to the Committee. Flushing was not considered good practice, it might damage the puddling and at best could transfer the problem elsewhere. It was important to keep the river entrance at Framilode free of silt. The outcome of this operation is not recorded.

The Committee was asked to look at the mud boat at Eastington in January 1875 to determine whether it should be repaired or broken up. The verdict was to break it up, so at the next meeting it was decided to ask the Staffordshire & Worcestershire Canal Co. what they would charge for hiring their steam dredger. They were a much larger enterprise than the Stroudwater, being over forty-six miles long.

Mud and silt contributed to the demise of the Thames & Severn Canal. A file of correspondence between G.A. Evans of Marling & Evans Ltd on behalf of the Company, and James Smart the carrier of Chalford, dated 1922-23, illustrates this point. Smart complained that one of his boats, the *Trial* carrying 38 tons of coal, had taken four and a half hours to travel the single mile from Bowbridge to Brimscombe. On that occasion he was blaming the lock-keepers who were not doing their job. They were not always present, and were not closing the gates properly, nor moving obstructions from the gates. Loss of water was the main drawback, necessitating drawing from the pounds above, as far as Brimscombe Station Lock. Mr Evans reported to the Company Chairman, Jack Margetson, that the Stroudwater was in fairly good condition but was losing revenue because of the bad state of the other canal.

Further correspondence in 1923 between Margetson and Edward Gardom, Clerk to GCC, further exacerbates the problem. GCC were entirely responsible for the Thames & Severn at this time, but were reluctant to do anything about it. On 22 February 1923, Margetson wrote in response to traders complaining about the silted condition of the Thames & Severn. He cited the experience of Smart's barge *Perseverance*, a new vessel of the same name as an earlier barge, but capable of carrying 50 tons.

[She] *was to take a full load of coal to the Brimscombe Mills on 4th January last. The barge left Stroud about 1.05 p.m., and arrived at the Mills about 4.45 p.m. – a distance of about two miles. The barge was hauled by two donkeys, but at times several men assisted on the line.*

He goes on to say that in former times goods were conveyed to all parts of the canal, but now, 'in consequence of the waterway being narrowed by accumulation of mud, there is now only width enough left in many parts for these barges to pass along with so shallow a draft of water, and consequently with so light a cargo, as to make it impossible to work them to commercial advantage'.

No definite answer was received to that letter until 27 March, when Gardom sent to the Company for £150 as the contribution of the Stroudwater to the deficit of the Thames & Severn! In a lengthy correspondence, the Chairman reminded Gardom that the Stroudwater had been out of action for ten weeks, with no income, because of a serious accident at Bristol Road Lock. If GCC would dredge their canal, trade would improve all round. The Council debated the issue, which was reported in *The Citizen* of 29 May 1923. The statement issued said that as the canal was sufficient to accommodate the barges which mostly used it, that is, those carrying about 30 tons, they could not undertake the work necessary to take larger barges, as the cost was prohibitive. The traffic return for the previous half year was £57 3s 2d, and the cost of dredging would be between £1,200 and £1,500. However, GCC did call for a report, which resulted in closure of the Thames & Severn east of Whitehall Bridge in 1927, and full closure for navigation in 1933.

The Company successfully brought an action against GCC in 1950 for discharging water brought down by the Slad stream into the Stroudwater Navigation and causing mud and silt to build up, contrary to regulations.

Ice-breaking was an important job in the winter, and the Company kept their own boat. Labourers normally engaged in mudding were switched to ice-breaking when necessary, and earned more money. It was hard work, taking at least six men: one to lead the horse, one to steer, and two each side of a central bar mounted on a platform to rock the boat. The boat was narrow, and about 30ft long, and had either a double thickness of planking or iron plates fixed below the gunwales, because ice was so sharp it would cut into the wood. It could not be used if ice was more than 4ins thick, so in very bad winters trade would stop, sometimes for many weeks. Ice in the locks was broken manually with a 'pounder', doing just that. A horse was hired for this work for five days in December 1860 at 6s per day.

Tenders were put out for a new ice boat in July 1878 and the one selected was from Evans, the boatbuilder of Saul. He was to build it ready for 1 December for £70, to exclude all extras, and the old boat to be taken in exchange.

Withies (Osiers)

Withies provided a subsidiary source of income for the Company. There were many withy beds by the canal which were acquired when the land for making the Cut was first bought. Some were fenced off and sold back to landowners but several were kept, and the crop sold each year. A Mr Hawker applied to buy the crops of withies in June 1786, and the Clerk was empowered to make him an offer of all the beds at £8 per annum for the next eight years. This offer included carriage up the canal, free of toll. Alternatively, Mr Hawker could buy the crop annually at the market price. Presumably the buyer would harvest the withies himself.

Baskets were an important commodity, right up to modern times, and were made by itinerant basket-makers. Withies were grown in small fields or waste corners, and at Eastington where they grew smaller than in the Severnside beds, they were valued for their superior toughness. Before the days of plastic, baskets were used not only in the home and farm, but in the woollen mills of the Stroud Valleys, where two women would carry baskets of bobbins between them. Coal merchants too would deliver coal in baskets strengthened with iron round the rim.

There were numerous withy beds in this area: one just west of the Junction; two at Lockham Bridge, one owned by the Company, the other by Richard Martin; one

Trow *Gertrude* at Hilly Orchard Bridge, *c.*1907. It was against regulations to sail on the canal fully rigged. (Courtesy of M.A. Handford)

near Double Lock (called Dubble in the Wages Book of 1874). At Dudbridge Messrs Sandling had basket-making premises from 1865 to 1965 very close to the canal and very likely they obtained withies from the two osier beds at Friggs Mill on the Nailsworth Stream.

Boats, Boatbuilders and Carriers

Two types of vessels most commonly associated with the Stroudwater Navigation are the trow (rhymes with crow) and the Stroudwater barge. Both were derived from craft which plied the river Severn for centuries, and were flat-bottomed (i.e. with no fixed keel), to withstand being stranded on sandbanks at low tide. An article in the *Gentleman's Magazine* of 1758 describes the trow as being generally 16ft to 20ft wide, and 60ft in length, of 40 to 80 tons burthen. They had a main and a top mast about 18ft high with square sails, and some had a mizzen mast. When new and completely fitted out, they would be worth at that time £300. Three or four men were needed to navigate them. Graham Farr in his seminal work, 'The Severn Navigation and the Trow', published in the *Mariners' Mirror* of April 1946, adds that early trows were double-ended, but later developed a square flat stern, and true trows were open-holded. The movable keel was 28ft long, 2ft deep and ⅓ins thick, with brackets on the upper side at either end so it could be slung over the side when the vessel was light. When in narrow waters it was normal to unship the main booms and sail with the mainsail loose-footed to avoid damage to bridges. Sometimes there was a tow-boat, and the rope for hauling was fastened to the masthead.

Stroud barges worked at the same time as trows, but were used increasingly after the Gloucester & Berkeley was opened, possibly because the Severn was then bypassed. They were also double-ended, but not with the characteristic D-shaped transom of the trow; it was flat-bottomed too, but had a massive keelson (a keel constructed inside the boat). Edward Paget-Tomlinson calls it a hard chine sailing barge, in a different family from the trow.

The Company briefly owned a fleet of vessels, unlike the Thames & Severn Company, but relied on carriers: the Grazebrook family, and later the Nurse family. However, they did need boats for maintenance work, and the first ice-boat was a large tow-boat bought at Bristol in 1785. It was sent to Board Oak, near Newnham-on-Severn in 1794 for graving. Also that year, Mr Powell of Broad Oak was asked to build a strong flat-bottomed boat of 12 or 15 tons for use as a dredger boat at a cost of £45. The same year they bought a lighter for £30, but two years later it was worn out and another was bought from William Bird. It would have been used to transport materials, like stone, and took a lot of heavy wear. Company carpenters were able to build one themselves in 1799.

Other vessels mentioned in the Minutes are a ketch and a schooner. In January 1804 it was reported that the new schooner was now finished, and the builder was

A Stroud barge rotting in the canal, west of Junction Lock, 1948. (Courtesy of Gloucestershire Record Office)

John Peacey (b.1844) with his sister Ellen at Hillslie, Houndscroft, Amberley, *c*.1900-1910. (Courtesy of R. Chidlaw)

to be paid £400 on account if it was found to be built to specifications of the contract. Further investigation may reveal what it was used for. A Stourport firm enquired after the Company's ketch in 1807, and were offered it for 500 guineas. That was too much, so the price was dropped to £500, which seems a good price for a vessel which had been laid up for twelve months and had previously been employed in the coal trade.

A pleasure barge, as they called it, was always available for Company use and replacements of it were called *Stroud*. An inventory in the archive dated 13 January 1777 details the rigging and contents of Mr Hall's barge when the 'Company took to her'. It all sounds very second-hand, so perhaps this was a stop-gap until a bespoke new barge was commissioned in 1779 from Mr Hillhouse for £98. It was similar in design, but smaller and not so flamboyant as the barges owned by the Merchant Taylor's Company on the Thames. *Stroud* was fitted out for the Committee to make inspections of the waterway, and hold meetings. Carpets were on the floor, and flying pennants were a gift from Mr Bigland of Frocester Court. Messrs Hillhouse were a firm of shipbuilders in Bristol, well-known for the epithet 'Shipshape and Bristol Fashion', who had started building prestige ships and naval vessels in 1761. Samuel Bird of the boatyard at the Bourne, Brimscombe, was given three months in 1807 to build a new barge for the Company to his estimate of sixty guineas. In later years the Company would hire a boat from Edwin Clark of Brimscombe for their inspections.

Boatbuilding at the Bourne continued into the twentieth century by the Gardiner family, the business being started about 1845 by Ezra, who was succeeded by his son Matthew Henry. Another son, Benjamin, set up a boatyard on the bank of the Severn at Framilode, near the Passage. He employed John Peacey of Oakridge Lynch. John would walk to work on Monday morning, arriving at 8.00 a.m. During the week he lodged at a public house by the canal, probably at Eastington, where he was given special treatment by the landlady, as he was teetotal. He gave up boat-building in 1869 to get married and start a family. One of Ben Gardiner's trows was *Queen Ann*, built in 1860 and named after his wife. Captain O. Dangerfield of Arlingham wrote of his memories of *Queen Ann* in *Gloucestershire Countryside* in 1951. She had a long life and was over fifty years old when he was master. He was the last to sail in her before she was turned into a lighter.

Fred Evans was the boatbuilder at Saul Junction and used the dry dock there for repairs. He contracted in 1878 to build for the Company a replacement houseboat for workmen to use when doing repairs on the canal, and deliver it furnished and fit for use in all respects by 30 November for £70. The contract had been made at the end of August. Other places along the canal and recorded for boatbuilding are Cainscross, Dudbridge, Eastington, Stonehouse, Whitminster and Stroud. The latter saw a spec-tacular launch of a trow from Wallbridge wharf on 8 February 1854, when upwards of 1,000 people gathered to watch as Captain Longney named the boat after himself. The *Stroud Free Press* reported the event: '*Longney* is a vessel of about seventy tons burthen and universally acknowledged to be a beautiful model, combining great carrying capacity with fast sailing qualities and extraordinary strength, and it is not saying too much to pronounce her the best built vessel trading on a canal.' She was built by Henry Lewis of King's Stanley for John Biddle, miller, of Stratford Mills, and her dimensions were 65ft long, 15½ft wide and 5ft deep. As *Longney* set off down the canal with 200 people aboard, a salute was fired from Rodborough Fort, and Ebley Brass Band who went with her played *I am Afloat*, followed by *A Life on the Ocean Wave*. It was a fine day, and celebrations went on the whole afternoon.

Second-hand trows were usually sold by private treaty or auction. The Clerk, Edward Hains, advertised two trows for sale in the *Gloucester Journal* in November 1807, but their names were not given. They may have been ex-Company, for they could be inspected, with rigging and other necessary appurtenances, at Wallbridge Wharf. The Company kept small boats for getting about, and in June 1875, two naughty boys, James Bassett of Paganhill and Walter Twinning of Ebley, knocked the lock off one boat lying at Dudbridge, and set it adrift. She was found below the bottom gates at Dudbridge Lock half-full of water. The boys were admonished.

The Nurse family of Framilode and Dudbridge were associated with the canal for many years in the nineteenth century as wharfmen and carriers. They worked for other boat owners, and navigated their own boats. Sometimes they were in trouble for minor offences, as when in 1854 George Nurse and John Butt made a false decla-ration of cargoes carried in the *Ellen and John*. They were sent letters informing them proceedings could be taken. More serious frauds occurred in the 1820s when James Nurse was master of John George's barge at Brimscombe. Accounts exist for journeys they made from Bullo with coal, and to Radcot on the Thames, and back with corn. The frauds amounted to a sizeable percentage, and a court case took place. One of the Eastington Five Locks was damaged by George Nurse's boat *Fanny* in 1856 and he was asked to pay for the repair.

After working in conjunction with each other for many years, the Company and the Nurses seemed to part in 1868 when an advertisement inserted in the *Stroud*

Trade card of James & Fred Nurse. An advertisement was placed in the *Stroud Free Press* on 3 January 1851 announcing the acquisition of the new trow *Emperor*. The 'rough and boisterous weather' refers to the passage of the Severn, not the canal!

WATER CONVEYANCE.

Trows Emperor and Royal William,

TO AND FROM

STROUD AND BRISTOL.

JAMES NURSE,

In thanking his friends and patrons for all favors hitherto received, begs to inform them that induced by their very liberal support since plying the

EMPEROR,

In the Stroud & Bristol Trade, he has during the past year placed the

ROYAL WILLIAM,

In the above line, to ply alternately with the Emperor, thereby enabling him to pay greater attention to the safe and punctual delivery of all goods committed to his charge.

JAMES NURSE would call the attention of his supporters and the public at large to this fact, that no other two Vessels on this station will be able to keep their Cargoes dry, and perform their passages with punctuality in rough and boisterous weather, one leaving the Welsh Back Bristol, and the other, Dudbridge Wharf, near Stroud, every saturday.

For particulars of freight &c. apply to James Nurse, Framilode, or Dudbridge Wharf, near Stroud; or his agent, C. Bawn, 3, Butts, Bristol.

Journal for 1 February 1868 gave notice that George Nurse & Co. had removed their old established trade from Dudbridge Wharf to the Dudbridge Railway Station, where they would 'render the following coals at much lower rates than they were in a position to do so at the wharf'. The coals were from the Forest of Dean and the Midlands. Dudbridge Station had only been open a few months. Other carriers who advertised included the Stroud Galley Co., whose vessel *Galley* left Bristol every Saturday and delivered goods at Framilode, Eastington, Ryeford, Dudbridge and Wallbridge on Mondays.

James Smart of Chalford was fourteen when his father, also James, drowned while drunk and he had to take over the canal carrying business in about 1853. The coroner advised him never to touch intoxicating liquor, and he never did, attending France Lynch Church for the rest of his life. By 'thrift and perseverance' he became the principal carrier on the canals, mostly carrying timber to the Midlands and coal in return in the five trows and fourteen longboats which he eventually owned. Besides *Perseverance*, he owned *Temperance* and perhaps there was also a *Thrift*. The business was taken over by his youngest son, and is still in existence today, but by road.

Various bye-laws were introduced from time to time for the better management of the canal, and booklets printed, namely *Rules, Orders and Regulations to be Observed by Bargemen, Watermen, Boatmen and other persons using the Stroudwater Navigation*. That one contained fourteen pages, but whether those who were meant to read it could do so is doubtful. The most important law was: 'All vessels passing shall have the owner's name, with the steersman or master on some conspicuous part of the vessel.' It was also an offence subject to a 5s fine to have two donkeys abreast hauling a boat.

Boatmen were regarded as 'bad lots', not notorious criminals, and this notion has gone down in folklore. Cecil Sharp's *Collection of English Folk Songs* includes one sung by Mrs Elizabeth Smitherd of Tewkesbury in 1908. *Jack Williams* had the refrain, 'I am a boatman by my trade/And a waterman also,/Through keeping of such company/ I bought myself to woe/ … I went a-robbing night and day'.

Above: The barge was abandoned in the field next to The Anchor inn, Ryeford. She was registered No.16 at Stroud. Her dimensions were 68ft 4ins by 12ft 6ins. The hold when open was 3ft 11ins.

Below: Perseverance facing aft. Marling coal pen can be seen on the other side of the canal. Both photographs were taken on 22 September 1935. (Copyright National Maritime Museum Picture Library; courtesy of National Waterways Museum)

Boatmen were accused of covering up loads of high-toll goods with low ones, conniving with lockmen, and fiddling the 'truck system', although the Stroudwater did not adopt that system, as the Thames & Severn Company did. Punishment was harsh: for stealing ten yards of rope at Eastington in 1836 William Harper, waterman of Stroud, was sentenced to seven years in Van Dieman's Land. Thomas Pitt, a waterman aged twenty-two, from Minchinhampton, was committed to fourteen years in the same place in 1822 for stealing rope at Whitminster, the property of William Pugh, barge owner.

During the latter part of the nineteenth century the Company gained a significant income from the boatbuilding firm of Edwin Clark of Hope Mill, Brimscombe. Clark was only thirty-one when he died in 1896 but by then he had gained a reputation for steamboats all over the world. Most of the engines were supplied by Messrs Sissons of Gloucester, but as there was no crane in the vicinity of the boatyard, Clark used the facilities at Dudbridge Wharf, which had good road and rail access. The boats were towed there by horses or men. The *Gordon*, the first boat launched by Clark in 1885, was tested on the Stroudwater with Clark at the helm and subsequently many other boats were tested there, Clark paying an average of 10*s* a time. Boats which were too large for shipment in one piece were dismantled into parts and shipped in barges on the Stroudwater Navigation for re-assembling elsewhere. When the business was wound up in 1901, it was acquired by the firm which became Abdela-Mitchell and continued until forced to close when GCC could not keep the Thames & Severn Canal open.

Pleasure boat *Meran* entering Stroudwater Navigation from the Thames & Severn in 1910 en route to Dudbridge Wharf, seen with the grounds of Far Hill on the offside. She was 40ft long with a steel hull, built by Abdela-Mitchell, and was destined for Brazil.

Longboat *Pioneer* approaching a railway bridge at the Ocean, returning empty after delivering coal, *c.*1920. Her owner was Charles Brayston of Gloucester. Note the coal shute on the embankment. (Courtesy of M.A. Handford)

The Company were not keen on steamboats as a regular thing, and did not encourage Ford Brother's *Queen Esther* which was too large to manoeuvre in some locks, as the wash tended to damage the banks. The Severn & Canal Carrying Co. used motor barges in the twentieth century, and their *Kathleen* did regular trips to Butler's Tar Works at the Severn Parting from Stroud Gas Works. One of their boats was the last one to use the canal in May 1941, carrying coal from Shelton in Cannock.

TRADERS

Ford Bros.

Certain traders became important customers of the Company in the second half of the nineteenth century. They were Messrs Ford Bros. of Ryeford Mill, who had a fleet of vessels; Messrs Marling of Stanley and Ebley Mills; John Biddle of Stratford Mills and the gas company. Each of them were continually asking for concessions, such as drawbacks on tonnage, or permission to construct culverts. More often than not, the Company conceded because it was expedient to do so.

There was a love/hate relationship with Ford Bros. in particular. They were meal men, initially from Millbottom Mill, Nailsworth, but by 1853 were in partnership at Ryeford Mill with Mr Joseph King, a corn miller. In June of that year the premises were put up for auction and Ford Bros. purchased the freehold. The accompanying plan shows the mill to the south of the canal, with mill leat and millpond, and the main house, a smaller mill, cottages, stables, orchard and gardens to the north, linked by the footbridge over the canal.

George Ford was senior partner of the family firm of five brothers. He applied to the Company in December 1853 for an agreement whereby he could rent his tonnage on coal and flour, and was informed that within the powers of the Act, it was not permissible to make such an arrangement. Ford persisted in such requests, and gained an agreement for wheat coming up and flour going down the canal to be offset against each other, and a credit account was activated. In 1855 Ford was thinking of installing a steam engine at Bristol instead of Ryeford, and wanted a reduction on the excess of flour, possibly to make him change his mind, but the Committee were adamant the excess should be paid. When Ford's diversified into saw milling in 1857, they proposed that in case timber should be carried up the canal for conversion they should be allowed to carry down converted timber free of charge. After being told the total carried would be not less than 500 tons per annum, the Committee agreed that when timber was carried up to any sawmill or works, an allowance of half tonnage would be made on a similar number of tons of converted (sawn?) timber carried down from the same mill in the same half year. But Ford was to pay up his rent already due. A question arose in 1858 with HM Customs; Ford's

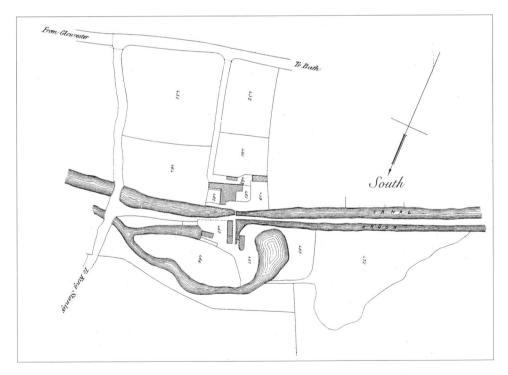

Plan and particulars of Ryeford Mill for auction in 1853 when it was bought by the Ford Brothers.

wanted to know if vessels from foreign parts could be brought up the canal to discharge their cargoes on the banks. The answer was no; permission would only be given to unload at a particular sufferance port. Supposedly the nearest were Gloucester and Sharpness; a Customs Officer did live at Purton.

Ford Bros. owned at least four trows: *Caroline*, built by Henry Lewis of Stonehouse in 1855; *Emily*, named after George's daughter; *George*, built at Stonehouse in 1873 and *Florence*, a later addition which carried in 1862 59 tons of flour to Newport, Mon. and 40 tons of coal on return. *Queen Esther* was the steam vessel for which Ford's wanted to excavate and rebuild Blunder and Pike Locks in 1859 at their own expense, under supervision of the Company, guaranteeing the canal would not be closed for more than three days. The Committee eventually conceded to this, but it is unlikely the work did take place, because the vessel was reported being fast in Framilode Lock in July. A letter was sent warning Ford he had to move it or pay for the canal stoppage.

The most significant concession given to Ford's was the building of their own wharf at Ryeford, on the eastern side of the bridge from the Company's wharf. A sub-committee looked into their application in 1855 and concluded there was not enough room for unloading barges on the south side, but if a wall were built there to carry the weight of the bank, the water deepened near the towpath, and a cutting made on the north side of the bank from their own land, there would be ample provision. Ford's could then build a warehouse as they proposed. By an agreement dated 7 May 1856, the Company were to do the work on the south side at their expense, and pay half of the north side. A clear waterway of at least 33ft was to be left at 27ft to the west of the mill, increasing in a regular line to the west for the entire length of the work. Ford's were to provide beech piles and slabs to support the north bank. All the new walls were to be considered the property of the Company. Only a week later Ford's asked if they could have a lay-by into the warehouse to give more space in the actual canal. Naturally no more expense could be spared, except if Ford's paid for it themselves, and there is no record to indicate the work took place. However, part of the north wall collapsed into the canal and carried soil and piles with it. The Company Surveyor had to remove the obstruction, which was caused by Ford's placing earth on the bank. A worse misfortune occurred in February 1870 when a wing of the mill, constructed about four years before, collapsed into the canal, stopping it for a day. Down came bricks and timber as well as 700 bushels of corn. Water forced upwards dashed against the wall of the Fords' house opposite, and smashed windows.

Another bone of contention was the state of the millpond, which often flooded the towpath. In 1859 George Ford was told he was responsible for any accident which may occur on the towpath. He was to remove the wooden railing encroaching on it as well as sundry old iron and timber. Also the quoin of the mill next to the towpath should be cut away six inches as agreed when the lay-by was made. By 1865 the situation was no better; the Surveyor reported that by raising the water above the weir at the mills the towpath was being flooded, and it was ordered to be remade the next year. Still the problem went on, and Ford's were told either to lower their boards, or raise them and make good the towpath by piling at their expense. In 1867 the situation was still the same. Again in 1882, not having drawn up the floodgates in the autumn floods, the towpath had been flooded by the brook. Ford's were informed in future they would be responsible for any damage by neglecting to draw the floodgates to the fullest extent when required.

A series of other misdemeanours upset the Committee. None of the brothers were Proprietors, so 'a quiet word' was not possible. *Emily* carried bricks (possibly for the new building) from the railway bridge at the Ocean to Ryeford without giving an account, and removed a quantity of dirt from the railway wharf likewise. They were sent bills in 1866. Mr Fallows, the Company Foreman, reported he had received very abusive language from George Long, one of Ford's captains. A solicitor's letter was sent. One of their barges was moored in the way of traffic and some coping stones were dragged into the canal. Ford's had to replace them.

When the proposal for a railway over the Thames & Severn Canal was heard before a Parliamentary Committee in 1866, George Ford was called as witness, and admitted to being a Director of the Stonehouse & Nailsworth Railway (fifty shares) and the Severn Junction Railway. By that time he was dealing in grain, timber and coal, receiving 20,000 tons in and the same out of Ryeford Mills per annum. Most of the grain came from the Lechlade area, down the canal. He was asked whether it was ever delayed for want of water, and replied yes, once it was in a warehouse for six weeks, referring to the Thames & Severn. He claimed the new railway would save the mill-owners, most of whom were using steam as well as water power, about 2s per ton, the current cost at Stroud being half a guinea per ton.

A lengthy case was brought to the High Court in 1878 between George and Aaron Ford against the other brothers, and the partnership dissolved acrimoniously. Just before this their assets over liabilities were estimated at £36,400. The Haywardsfield Estate was sold in 1881 to Wycliffe College, who later took over the little tin Methodist chapel the brothers had endowed for their families and workers at Ryeford (opposite the present-day garden centre), and then conveyed to the Wesleyan Conference. Ryeford Mill became a sawmill.

Marling Family

From about the early 1830s, when John Marling bought Ebley Mill, the dealings the Company had with the firm mainly concerned the feeder to the canal at Ebley. Business with them was not with wool, either in the raw or finished state which would go by road, but with coal after steam engines were installed in their mills. Descendants of John Marling bought up many Stroudwater shares, starting with Nathaniel Samuel of Stonehouse Court in 1844. The family continued to support the canal and were major shareholders right through until the 1954 reconstitution of the Company.

There was a coffer dam on the Frome near Ebley millpond for regulating supply of water to the canal, and in 1834 it was resolved that paddles or stop gates should be provided. A mark was made on the wing wall at Dudbridge canal bridge on a level with the sill of the coffer dam to enable the Dudbridge lock-keeper to monitor supply. Thomas and Samuel Stephens Marling sent a letter in 1840 suggesting they should take charge of the feeder. Their reason was that either water comes down suddenly, or their wheels are stopped so unexpectantly, that regulation would best be done by a person connected with the mill. They added that 'in making the experiment it would of course be understood that rights of neither party would be altered or conceded'. So Marling's were given a key to the paddles of the weir which fed the canal, and were permitted to assist in supplying it with water which otherwise would run to waste, or when superfluous water would not normally pass into the canal. The Company resumed control of the feeder in 1843 because they needed to establish whether there would be any practical difficulty in keeping up supply to the Navigation, or whether further measures should be taken.

Circumstances regarding supply of water to Ebley Mill were defined in the Company's Act of 1776, but at that time it was a different mill. The building on the north side had been demolished in favour of the New Mill on the same side as the reservoir. Therefore the Company was concerned that a much larger amount of water was now needed to supply the new mill, and supply to the canal was in jeopardy. Samuel Marling was concerned about the amount of time taken to fill the reservoir or millpond, and agreed to do it at a time satisfactory to the Company.

Mr S.S. Marling attended the committee meeting on 4 June 1849 and outlined his proposal to build a large grist mill at Dudbridge, with a steam engine. First he wanted assurance of access for bringing boats from the canal into his millstream and reservoir. The Committee had a site meeting and asked for detailed plans for the next meeting two weeks later. There were four options, of which number four was chosen. Marling persuaded the Company to pay for the connection between the waterways if he gave up the land and paid £200 towards the work, half to be paid in instalments of six months, the rest to be set against tonnage passing through the works. He undertook to keep the works in repair for three years. Stipulations in the agreement were that the waterway was not to be used for any other purpose than the passage of boats, and particularly not used as to interfere with the works for supplying water to the Navigation. Big heavy gates shut off the entrance to this unique branch opposite a winding hole near what is now Frome Gardens. A new weir was constructed between the existing one and Ebley Mill. The grist mill became known as Kimmins Mill, built in stone in 1849, prominent at the entrance to Sainsbury's and now a repository for archives of the construction industry. The small dock next to it at the end of the navigable mill leat is about to be excavated.

Ebley Mill relied on water power long after other mills in the neighbourhood had turned to steam. Even the beam engine installed about 1862 was coupled to the drive from a waterwheel. However, the Marlings did have coal pens, perhaps hot water was needed for the dyeing process. N.S. Marling in 1836 asked for an enclosed space set apart for his coals on Wallbridge Wharf and the Clerk arranged this. Stanley Mill had steam engines, which had been delivered in parts from the Midlands via the Stroudwater. They took a lot of coal which was landed at the Company's wharf at Ryeford, from trows probably owned by A. Field. In 1858 Messrs Marling &

Above: The towpath over Ebley Connecting Weir between the canal (on the left) and the Frome (on the right). It was constructed as part of an agreement made by the Company with S.S. Marling for a side opening to a navigable waterway to Kimmin's Mill.

Below: The river Frome side of the weir, showing culverts, now blocked. The weir is built in a recess of the riverbank and could be very close to the point where vessels made the detour. (Photographs taken by F.W. Rowbotham on 26 October 1956: courtesy of the Environment Agency)

Marling coal pen, Ryeford. (Photograph by C.H.A. Townley, 1966: courtesy of J.A. Peden)

Strachan & Co. complained the coal pens there were not adequate, and then occupied some land on the east side of Ryeford Bridge next to Ford's mill.

Ford's decided they wanted to build a warehouse on that site, and applied to the Company for it in 1863, but were turned down because it was important to the Marlings. The next year Ford's renewed the application and the Company set up a sub-committee to deal with the matter, summoning S.S. Marling to a meeting on 24 February 1864. Mr Marling agreed to give up the lease on condition that the canal company would erect for him another coal pen on his own land below the bridge, making it accessible by a good road and diverting the present road into his land beyond that point. It was resolved that Ford's request should be acceded to and a sixty-year lease be granted at a nominal rent of 10s on condition they put in a dock wall in continuation of the present one up to the bridge. Also they were to pay a moiety of making the new pen and road for Mr Marling.

Ford's agreed to the arrangements with provisos: they would pay half of the cost of building the coal pen if they could have rebate from the Company if their own annual account exceeded £600 or they would build the pen and road themselves. The Company affixed their seal to the agreement with the first of the propositions, and it was arranged for Messrs Marling to do the work. When the pen was completed in September 1864 the Company resolved that:

Marling & Co. be allowed the right of road for horses, carts and carriages at all reasonable times over the towing path from the turnpike road [Ryeford Lane] to the new pen situated on the west side of the bridge over the canal and to a piece of land on the west side of the pen at the east corner thereof, paying annually to the Company rent of 1/- and keeping the said path in good repair. Such right of road nevertheless to cease when and so soon as the new coal pen shall not be used as a place of deposit or landing for coal or merchandise carried on the canal.

The Company Treasurer, J.C. Hallewell, paid a cheque to Messrs Marling for £158 11s 4d on 30 November 1864. The Ford's half, £79 5s 8d, had been paid in cash on 1 October to the Company. This was the total cost of making the pen which amounted to £143 11s 5d as per estimate, plus the cost of making the road and the floor of the pen. It is enclosed by a very fine limestone wall, mostly coursed and dressed work and some ashlar, and is in good condition. It was built to a high standard, probably using stone from their own quarry on Selsley Common nearby. A consignment of 26 tons of stone was brought to Ryeford pen on 24 June 1864 from Chalford, free of conveyance charge, and this was probably used for the flooring of the pen. Walls have a height of approximately 6ft. The corners are curved to allow for easy access for carts, and two shutes in the wall alongside the towpath once had hinged timber boards which let down to allow planks to be put across to the ledge. Wheelbarrows were wheeled along the planks, and the coal then tipped over into the pen. The chamfered gateway is set at an angle, with an iron gate, possibly not the original one. This coal pen is the only survivor on the Stroudwater Navigation.

John Biddle

John Biddle was a flour miller, owner of Stratford Mill, the lowest on the Painswick stream, and lived at Stratford Abbey next to it (now the Tesco complex).By a lease dated 5 January 1834 between him and Joseph Grazebrook of Far Hill, he acquired a strip of land on the east of the brook, as a towpath beside the navigation of the Painswick stream. He had already erected a wooden fence to separate the path from Far Hill meadow. Grazebrook also gave him power to navigate the brook with boats, for the length within his power. Biddle could enter the meadow from any part of the demised brook and could pass under the turnpike bridge and along the brook to the west of Far Hill garden. He could not use any other roadway or passage at Far Hill. The lease was for ninety-nine years at £5 per annum. In return, Biddle was to preserve and keep the banks in good repair to prevent water from flooding the meadow, except by Act of God. The fence was to be kept in repair and of the same colour and appearance. If Biddle should be hindered at any time by neighbours, John Snowden (Lodgemore Mill) or James Withey (Gannicox), then Biddle could end his lease by giving six months' notice.

In 1839 Biddle wanted to make an excavation in the canal bank at the east end of the wing wall of the Lodgemore feeder for mooring barges unloading corn for his mill. He would then have smaller boats bow-hauled up the stream to his mill, with a flash-lock midway. Permission was granted, provided he would extend the wall and pile it into the mouth of the stream, and not build it further than 7ft from the square of the canal at present. Work was to take place during the normal Whitsun stoppage. Five years later Biddle and his partner Bishop applied to extend the lay-by at the Company's expense for increasing their trade. The cost would be £6 10s which was considered worthwhile if it meant extra tonnage.

The annual stoppage for repairs was an inconvenience to Biddle, who owned other mills and a large new warehouse at Gloucester Docks. In 1844 he managed, by canvassing members of the Committee, to get the stoppage cancelled by pointing out he would be obliged to pay £5 per day demurrage. In 1846 he got it shortened from two weeks to one.

When Biddle bought Messrs Watts mill at Wallbridge in 1849, he asked if he may vary the line of fence between the Company's garden and the millyard. So the Company said yes, if he would build a good wall instead, the same as the one at present from the corner of the stable to the end of the Company land adjoining the late Mr Watts' garden, and Biddle agreed. Furthermore, if any trees were in the way, they could be removed. The next year Biddle wanted a warehouse to be built for him at the Company's cost. This was agreed, provided the total amount was not more than £400, and would be repaid to him in half-yearly instalments and he started building as soon as the agreement was signed.

A controversy blew up in 1849 appertaining to a resolution of the previous year that Biddle & Bishop should be charged tonnage on the amount of flour exported beyond that of wheat imported. When challenged, Biddle said his original agreement enabled him to export as much flour as he had imported wheat, without reference to the half-year balances. The Clerk's view was that the firm had imported more than 2,000 tons of wheat beyond the amount of flour exported. The Committee resolved that the half-year balancing be postponed until Biddle had caught up the amounts.

John Biddle also acted as campaigner for charitable causes in Stroud. He requested a donation be given by the Company towards paying off the debt of the Stroud National Schools Building Committee and £5 was sent in 1849. In the bad winter of 1854/5 he petitioned the Company to give coal to the poor and tonnage already paid for it should be returned if proof that the coal had indeed been given to the poor was produced. After his death in 1863, his firm became Stratford Flour Mills Co. Ltd, later Townsend's, then Rank Hovis. The navigable stream was superseded by a private railway siding at a higher level.

6

The Canal and
Other Undertakings

Thames & Severn Canal

From at least the seventeenth century, thinkers had been advocating the union of Thames with Severn but promoters of the Stroudwater Acts were not ambitious in that respect. However, they were not oblivious to the fact that it could be achieved by Proprietors more entrepreneurial than themselves, and were prepared from the beginning to be co-operative with such a body, as it could bring only further prosperity to their own canal. Naturally they considered it vital that the connecting canal should start from Stroud, and to this end commissioned a survey of the route through the Golden Valley and on to Cricklade in April 1781. The inaugural meeting of Proprietors of the Thames & Severn Canal took place in September that year, with the majority being London-based businessmen. Only five Stroudwater Proprietors held shares in both canals.

There was a disagreement about the Badbrook (i.e. Slad Brook) discharging into the Thames & Severn at Wallbridge and bringing mud through their first lock into the Stroudwater, causing considerable expense in clearing it. Negotiations started in 1805, and were still not settled when legal measures were threatened in 1807. Thames & Severn at first said they would pay half the cost of a culvert, but then reneged, and would not pay expenses incurred by the Stroudwater because they preferred an aqueduct. The same problems occurred a century later.

Relations between the two companies were amicable. They concerned themseleves with changes in tonnage, the differing zones for tonnage, drawbacks, and evidences of fraud on the part of boat owners regarding cargo carried. Generally they co-operated over opposition to proposed railways, until in 1866 an application was made to Parliament to make part of the Thames & Severn Canal into a railway. The Company of Proprietors drafted a petition and along with other canal companies opposed the Bill, largely because of loss of trade, and particularly of water down the valley. An interesting Minute of May 1845 notes that Mr Willson, on behalf of the Thames & Severn, had attended a committee meeting to submit his views on amalgamation of the two canal companies. Nothing more was heard of this.

The report by the Royal Commission on the Canals and Inland Navigations of the United Kingdom (1906) is invaluable for the deposition made by the Rt Hon. Sir John Edward Dorington of Lypiatt Park, Chairman of GCC, on the Thames & Severn Canal. From it we learn that following the failure of the Great Western Railway (GWR) to profit from that canal, an Allied Navigation Trust took over, and included representatives from the Stroudwater. Another trust was set up in 1895 to administer the Thames & Severn after an Act of Parliament, still including Stroudwater, until GCC became owners in 1901, when Stroudwater was to make contributions towards deficits. W.J. Snape was secretary/manager of both canals, operating from Wallbridge headquarters.

Gloucester & Berkeley Canal

Need for a bypass of the difficult circuitous part of the Severn between King's Road at Bristol and Gloucester was recognised for a long time before any plans were made. Then an advertisement in the *Gloucester Journal* of 8 January 1784 announced an application was to be made to Parliament for an Act to construct a canal from the Severn at Gloucester to the Stroudwater Navigation. The Company worried it would take away their trade, particularly at the westernmost part of the navigation. They concluded the announcement was premature, the scheme was not necessary, but even so they put aside £1,000 to spend on maintaining interests of the Company. This sum was increased in April to £2,000 when they heard that Whitworth was actually making the survey and a sub–committee of five was appointed to determine no infringements of Company rights and lands would take place. The agents engaged to do this were Lane & Jepson, solicitors of Gloucester. They sent in a bill of expenses, first for attending a meeting at Gloucester to hear proposals from the new canal people. This took all afternoon on 29 November, costing 13s 4d. Mr Grazebrook was

Bill Spiers the bridge-keeper letting a trip boat through the Junction, c.1966. The extension to Junction House was added in 1869.

The dry dock at the Junction with *NB Sarah* in August 1963.

then informed of the particulars. On 16 December a journey to Stroud to meet the Gloucester Canal Committee meant staying the night, costing £1 11s 6d, and hire of a horse; sundry expenses were 6s 6d.

Most of that meeting was concerned with tolls the Gloucester & Berkeley Company were intending to charge. As there was no indication Stroudwater were to get compensation, nor would it be of benefit to the public, the Company said they could not accede to the proposal, *but* when the Thames & Severn was completed no doubt they would be able to agree. The matter was dropped until 1793 when new proposals were made to build a canal right through to Berkeley, passing the Stroudwater. This time the promoters intended to insert a clause into their Act regarding safeguards for the Stroudwater. However, nothing was done until a new plan was produced in 1817 which showed an altered line, ending at Sharpness, not Berkeley Pill, and the Stroudwater was to be passed not above Whitminster Lock, but below it. Levels were to be altered so the two canals passed on the same level.

Difficult negotiations were held over many years about culverts, stop gates, taking water, and the best way to build the Junction without damaging the interests of the Stroudwater. Inevitably there were unforeseen delays, and a few times the Gloucester & Berkeley were accused of starting work without due consultation. At last the Junction was finished, at first by using the existing bed of the Stroudwater, and in 1820 the new canal was open for traffic from Gloucester to the Junction. Robert Miles, who had been carpenter of the works, was appointed lock-keeper there, to oversee passage of vessels from the wide canal into the Stroudwater. The Company refused to pay all his salary but contributed 'four shillings a week as remuneration for his trouble'. In 1838 his wage was increased by 1*s*. Miles must have been satisfied with the amount Gloucester & Berkeley paid him. Matthew Peyton who worked for the Company at Framilode was moved to the Junction in 1869 when the house there was enlarged and the small office on the east side was added for him. He was to work for both companies, and be paid accordingly.

The same year the dry dock was built across the south side of the Junction to provide not only repair facilities, but to give access to the half-mile stretch of the Stroudwater for which Gloucester & Berkeley were responsible as it served as a feeder for them. Because their steam dredger could not negotiate the sharp turn into the Stroudwater, the dry dock had gates at both ends, an ingenious solution to a tricky situation.

RAILWAYS

Stroud & Severn Tramroad

In 1824 there arose the most serious threat to the Stroudwater Navigation throughout the whole length of its existence. This was called the Stroud & Severn Railroad, although it was really more of a tramroad. A meeting was held in Stroud on 24 September for manufacturers and others interested in reduction of charges for carriage of coals and goods from the Severn to Stroud. A railroad was to be built from Frampton-on-Severn, where it would connect with the Gloucester & Berkeley Canal when it was finished, to Wallbridge and Brimscombe, with a branch to Nailsworth. Reference was made to exorbitant tolls charged by the Company of Proprietors and a resolution was passed unanimously that negotiations should be entered into with them to lower the tonnage. The Company held a meeting on 20 October, the very same month that Joseph Sandars, a Liverpool corn merchant and underwriter, sent a letter to Parliament outlining his proposals for the first public railway between Liverpool and Manchester. The General Meeting conferred the fullest power on their Committee to negotiate or not with the Proprietors of the tramroad. If they thought fit, the Committee could petition Parliament, employ counsel, engage engineers, commission surveyors and liase with landowners to oppose the scheme.

Negotiations with the tramroad company were held in writing to avoid misunderstanding and misconstruction by either party. The Company asked what specific amount of tonnage reduction was expected, the answer was 2½*d* a ton, in total. As Stroudwater was empowered to charge 3*s* 6*d* for all the way to Brimscombe, with 1*s* 3*d* paid back to Thames & Severn, this was very unreasonable. Nevertheless they did reduce tonnage by 3½*d*.

The Bill was presented in Parliament, and some gentlemen attended on behalf of the Company. A paper was prepared giving assertions of the promoters, and corresponding answers of the opposers. The Company stated it was at first a losing concern, and during its forty years had averaged a return on capital of only £5 17*s* 6*d*, the last five years being the most productive. Following the recent reduction, average charges were less than 2*d* per mile on the Stroudwater. Trade was small, averaging below 77,000 tons over the same period. The Bill was lost at the second reading by 101 votes in May 1825. The Liverpool & Manchester Bill was thrown out as well. Their promoters had also been campaigning against high canal tolls, and, like the Stroudwater and Thames & Severn, tried to win support by promising the equivalent of their motto 'Celerity, Regularity and Economy'. Members had failed to be impressed by the rhetoric of Sandars (quoted by Simon Garfield in *The Last Journey of William Huskisson*):

> *Are the powers of the human mind to be controlled – are its efforts to be restrained by a small body of men, for the protection of their own comparatively insignificant interest? Are their pools of water to form the boundary beyond which science and art shall not be applied…?*

Sandars and his body of supporters put forward a revised Bill, which was passed and the Liverpool & Manchester Railway was opened in September 1830. The Stroud Railroad project died, to the gratification of the Board, who presented John Snowden, the Chairman of the Committee, with a piece of plate valued at more than 100 guineas. Hindsight tells us both rejections happened not so much because of faith in canals, but the money panic which occurred in 1825 as a result of over-speculation. This was checked allegedly by Government printing money at a fast rate.

Railway mania

Railway mania soon set in as the advantages of using locomotive steam engines on fixed rails were plain to see. The Company opposed every Bill which was presented to them for Gloucestershire as a matter of course. The Bill to promote the Forest of Dean Railway in 1843 had failed before the Commons Committee, who advocated meeting with the Stroudwater, Thames & Severn and other opposers to obtain their views. In 1846 the South Wales Railway Co. proposed to take over the Forest of Dean as a branch, but as they intended to cross the Stroudwater at Saul, the Company opposed them. The canal had been receiving coal from the Forest via the Severn and Wye and the Forest of Dean Railway, and the Company considered they could not compete with the larger body. They managed to get a clause inserted in the Bill regarding charges on tonnage. Dissent was given to the Wilts & Gloucester Junction Railway, who wished to cross the canal and coal wharf, and to the Monmouth & Hereford Company, who may have poached some freight. It happened that the Board of Admiralty refused consent to any bridge erected over the Severn, so the South Wales and Monmouth & Hereford railways were unable to proceed.

In 1842 the Company were negotiating with the Bristol & Gloucester Railway about the bridge at the Ocean, where the position of a drain was causing concern. There were some advantages to the Company as a vast amount of materials, timber and stone were to be brought up the canal to erect bridges at Dudbridge and Wallbridge, besides Stonehouse. Drawbacks were requested on the tolls, but this could be accommodated. When first mooted in 1836, plans for the Bristol & Gloucester had included a branch to Stonehouse and Stroud. The main line appeared to be nearer Bond's Mill than when eventually built, and the branch was to lead off from there, over the main street of Stonehouse, then run alongside the GWR from Haywardsfield to Stroud. Hence the other bridges mentioned. It was reported in 1843 that James Smith of Cirencester had brought up more than 2,000 tons of iron and timber for this extension, which was the minimum amount he was allowed drawback for. As the branch was not built, it would be interesting to know what happened to those materials.

A significant Minute of 12 May 1852 indicates there was a railway/canal transshipment point at the Ocean. Mr Dykes of the Midland Railway Co. applied to cut an opening to form a loading place for barges on the upper north side of the present platform and shoot from the railway. This was approved provided it was constructed to prevent water escaping from the canal. The Midland Railway explained that this new route would help them to establish a considerable trade in coal for manufacturing purposes, which they needed to sell at very reduced prices. Therefore the Company were forced to reduce tolls to them, to 6d a ton carried beyond Stonehouse and 1s from Double Lock to Lodgemore.

The Company benefited from transit of materials carried up for the GWR Cirencester & Swindon Railway in 1841, so for the next two half-years they paid dividends of £10, but it could not last. By 1852 it was reported that coal was delivered at Cirencester by rail at 1s per ton less than by canal. This was counteracted by allowing a drawback of 6d a ton on coals from Framilode or the Gloucester & Berkeley to Wallbridge, thence to the Thames & Severn. Owners of vessels would need a special certificate signed by the Clerk to present to the Thames & Severn.

Messrs Warman & Kearsey, solicitors, went to London on the Company's behalf in July 1865 to petition against the Severn Junction Railway Bill. They procured agreement to insertion of clauses to protect interests of the Company, particularly for the interchange of traffic between the railway and canal at Framilode where the railway was to cross the canal. So opposition was withdrawn, and a peppercorn rent was agreed on land required by the Company for accommodation of traffic with the railway. This too was abortive.

Papers addressed to Walter Prideaux of the Goldsmiths' Company in 1866 concern the Thames & Severn presenting a Bill to change their name to the Thames & Severn Railway & Canal Co., which would allow them to abandon parts of their canal and raise money to build a railway. The Parliamentary agents were J. Dorington & Co. There were to be 1,150 new shares, most of which would be held by Thomas Salt, Chairman, and John Charles Salt, Treasurer of the Thames & Severn Company. Existing agreements and arrangements with the Stroudwater Company were to be honoured with regard to the parts of the canal left, but could be modified or annulled from time to time. The main opposers were GWR and the Stroudwater Company. The promoters thought they could win over the Company by offering them the western end of the Thames & Severn. The Bill did not get enough support and was dropped.

Some local clothiers and businessmen obtained an Act in 1863 to construct a railway from the Midland line at Stonehouse to Nailsworth, its main purpose being to benefit the cloth industry in the Nailsworth valley, although a branch to Stroud was constructed later. The Company opposed the Bill, because the railway ran parallel with the canal and threatened its trade. They withdrew opposition when offered a free siding at Stonehouse Wharf. Some factories were to have their own sidings. The Company claimed damages for interruption of traffic as per clauses in the Bill, which helped to make the business unviable and Midland Railway took over the private company in 1867. Thereafter there were good relations between the canal company and the railway. Towards the end of its life brushes from Vowles Brush Works would be taken by road to the wharf for shipment by rail and one trainload of coal went to Nailsworth each week. The line closed in June 1966.

UTILITIES

Canals, being fairly straight and level, have proved a useful vehicle for providing public utilities, and an important source of income for the canal companies. Starting with gas pipes in the mid-nineteenth century, telegraph and telephone lines followed at the end of that century, then sewage, mains water and postal services. Electricity supplies utilised towpaths in the twentieth century, along with cable television, radio and oil pipelines. Mobile-phone masts, back-pumping for water supply, fibre optics and as yet unknown other modern technologies will make use of the convenient line of communication the canals offer in the twenty-first century.

Gas

'Illuminating gas' started to be produced commercially at the beginning of the nine-teenth century, and by 1816 it was fairly common in London, but not for domestic use. From then on the industry became widespread in England and William Morley Stears, a gas engineer from Leeds, proposed to set up a gas company in Stroud in 1833. At first he approached the Company in March because he intended leasing a piece of land at Wallbridge, and needed to cover over the brook next to Company land to build on. Soon Stears was back at the Company asking instead to buy a strip of land close to the road and bridge leading to Fromehall Mill. The rest of the site was bought from other landowners, notably Mr Halliday.

A clause in the agreement specifically refers to permission granted to the gas company to lay pipes along and under the towpath or bank of the canal from the gasworks through Wallbridge Wharf to the turnpike there and westwards to the bridge at Chippenham Platt. They could also connect branches to the same main. Richard Wyatt, as representative of Stears and the gas company, agreed to pay £5 for the land and to pay £1 per mile of gas pipe per annum (and proportionately) as rent. As a large amount of coal would be brought up the canal, a special agreement was made for tonnage: £5 per mile per annum for a burthen of 700 tons per annum. A proviso stated that the right to lay down pipes was determinable on the cessation of use of the gasworks. The Company was not to be caused expense or trouble over the works or the land. The seal to the agreement was affixed on 19 December 1833. The Company understood, although it is not minuted, that because they had granted permission for the Stroud Gas Light & Coke Co. to use the towpath, it meant they were given an exclusive right to it and future utilities therefore had to obtain agreement from them as well as the Company. This eventuality was not envisaged in 1833.

Apparently the gas company did not do so well at first. In 1839 they requested an allowance for their full amount to be reduced to their counter-claim for lights on the wharf (probably Wallbridge) from the Company to that date. This was mutually agreed. The gas company's original capital was £5,000, of which Stears subscribed £2,000. Of the other main subscribers, at least three – Henry Wyatt, William Cosham of Cainscross, and Paul Hawkins Fisher, attorney-at-law of Stroud – were also Proprietors of the Stroudwater Navigation.

By-products of coal gas are coke and tar, and both were carried back down the canal. In 1863 Mr Withey attended a committee meeting on behalf of the gas company to explain they now had a facility for disposing of coke, which would lead to increased consumption of coal in the neighbourhood. The circumstances were not explained, but as the amount of coke was going to be inconsiderable, no tonnage would be charged on it. Problems with tar falling into the canal were dealt with by an edict of 1864 which stated that the gas company had to take measures to prevent tar being dropped or spilt into the canal at their works.

The wharf or lay-by at Downfield by the gasworks was built sometime between 1858, when a site meeting took place between the Company and the gas company near the bridge to determine the spot and the expense, and 1865, when Joseph Cottle, the lock-keeper at Dudbridge, was charged with supervision of the Downfield Wharf. At some point Cottle applied for, and was given, money to buy a mackintosh for himself.

Perhaps the original agreement had not been absolutely clear that damage to the towpath by the gas company had to be repaired by them. By excavating the towpath west of their works in 1858 to supply gas to Nailsworth the gas company had damaged it, and ignored requests to reinstate it. Eventually Mr Driver, the Company Surveyor, had done it for £3 2s and applied for reimbursement. Neither did the agreement allow for pipes under Gas Works Bridge, so Mr Withey asked in 1867 if they could lay a pipe under the canal there. Reluctantly the Company agreed at 2s per annum as an acknowledgement that it was there only on sufferance and would be removed when required.

Preparatory to obtaining a new Act in 1864 authorising them to raise capital up to £40,000, the gas company made a new agreement with the Stroudwater Navigation. The indenture confirmed the original agreements, only extending them to include pipes leading from a gasometer or other works situated on the banks of the canal between Wallbridge and Chippenham Platt, and now they could take up the pipes for renewal or repair. The rent per annum was to be £5 for not more than seven miles. By 1881 when the gas company had added more pipes, the Company asked for the full amount of rent due because not so much tonnage was being received from them. For thirty-one years only £4 per mile had been charged and paid, and Mr Payne attended a committee meeting in 1896 to say his Directors thought £5 per mile for five and a half miles was too much. The Company adhered to their resolution inasmuch as they asked for a rent of £29 per annum without prejudice to their right at any time to require full rent under provisions of the 1864 Act.

When Gas House Lane, connecting the works with Cainscross Road, had to be widened in 1899 for better access, a strip of land about 100 square yards was taken from Company property at the corner on the north-west side of the bridge. It was bought by Stroud Urban District Council on condition the walls and pillars would be rebuilt. Also, the gradient of the lane as it approached the bridge down the slope had to be eased and improved. The Stroud gas company were to keep the roadway between the works and the towpath in good repair in perpetuity.

Two important facts regarding the gasworks came to light in the Parliamentary Debate for the 1954 Act of Abandonment. In his speech in favour of closing the canal, Sir Robert Perkins MP said the last barge to use the canal had brought 10 tons of coal to the gasworks on 27 May 1941. (It had taken nearly two days to journey the six and a half miles to there from the Junction.) Before that no barge had got through for about three years. (Coal supplies were getting to the gasworks by the LMS branch line to Stroud from Dudbridge from which they had a siding and gantry straight into the Works.) Sir Robert had tried to persuade South Western Gas Board to import coal again by canal. Their reply was 'it is the Board's intention to close down Stroud's gas production as soon as arrangements can be made for delivery of necessary pipes to integrate Stroud with Gloucester'. As the mainstay for the opposition to the Bill was that the canal could be used again commercially, this statement must have struck the death-knell for them.

Sewage

By 1863 the Local Board of Health had built sewage works on the low-lying land west of the gasworks. This meant that pipes going to it would often have to be carried over the canal. The Board applied to the Company in 1867 to lay sewer pipes from Paganhill to the tanks at Lodgemore to cross the canal just above Gas Works Bridge. It was to be a twelve-inch iron pipe laid below the bottom of the canal to avoid obstruction to navigation. As usual the Company agreed, providing it was done to satisfaction, and payment would be £1 per annum. Back came a reply from the Board saying they had power to lay down pipes in perpetuity, and only payment for any damage done could be made. Therefore the Company had to comply, and waived the rent in consideration of benefits the public would derive from sewerage being treated! Meanwhile they sent a bill for £5 9s 6d, being the cost of their Surveyor overseeing work done by the Board. Ultimately new works were built at Stanley Downton and pipes still cross the canal, notably near the Ocean.

Postal Services

Postmen used to cycle along the towpath to make deliveries, and probably still do. Some postboxes are on or close to canal property. Mr E.T. Ward, coal merchant and canal carrier of Dudbridge Wharf, asked if he could have a postbox put in the wall of the Company's house there in 1875. He was told he could, but must give written acknowledgement that in case he leaves the house, and the box is removed, he will make good the wall. The firm had started in 1855, and continued until 1970, although by that time they were at the GWR yard at Stroud.

Within living memory Mrs Pockett, wife of Leonard Pockett, lock-keeper at Framilode, ran a post office from the little office at the side of Lock House, and the postbox is still in the garden wall. The Company paid her a pension for some years after her husband's death; he had been the last employee.

Telephone

Sharpness Docks had a telephone system installed by the National Telephone Company, a successor to the private telegraph line they had in 1858. The Gloucester & Berkeley Company also had a private link with their bridge-keepers. Mr Fredericks of the Junction, who worked for the Stroudwater jointly, mentioned in 1894 how impressed he was with the system, which benefited the working of the canal and traders. He suggested the Stroudwater would find it invaluable, but it was some years before the Company took heed.

Stroud had its first telephone exchange in 1895 in Palace Chambers, London Road and in 1896 there were only thirty-four subscribers in the National Telephone Directory for the town. However, the next year two of the canal's main Proprietors, Charles Hooper & Co. and Marling & Co. Ltd, both had business telephones at Stonehouse.

In 1966 the Post Office built Stroud's first automatic telephone exchange close to the canal at Lodgemore, and the present-day BT pay way leaves for several lines crossing. The towpath is punctuated with poles and stays.

Water

The Stroudwater Navigation's involvement with water in the district is threefold: conveyance of mains water; a receptacle for storm drains; as main river for purposes of flood alleviation.

Easements (one-off payments) have been accepted from time to time by the Company when water authorities required to connect properties with mains water. With increased housing development in recent years this is a major issue. Likewise with storm drains, where an agreement is usually with the developer, who finds a ready-made channel in the form of the canal a cheaper option than newly constructed drains.

After the passing of the Abandonment for Navigation Act, the Company was left with a waterway which was a part of the landscape, and had almost become a river in its own right. It could easily have become a liability and public nuisance. When the Severn River Board came to negotiate to change one section into main river as part of a flood alleviation scheme, it was like pennies from heaven, although no money changed hands. By the agreement signed in 1956 the Board was to *utilise* a length of canal from a point 450ft east of the swing bridge at Ebley Mill to The Point at Wallbridge, a distance of 1,727 yards. The Board were to assume all obligations and liabilities of the Company with respect to the waterway in that stretch, but the Company were still to own it, having the right to dispose of it should they so wish. All responsibilities for towpath, bridges, culverts and drains should remain with the Company. As part of the scheme the canal between the diversion at the side of Ebley Mill and Double Lock was filled in. The stretch was dredged, and then instead of culverts, the three streams (Slad Brook, Painswick Stream and Randwick Stream) were allowed to drain into the canal, thence returned to the Frome at the weir by Ebley Mill, which would be lowered by 3ft 4ins. It is not certain whether the works were carried out exactly to the above plan, as survey plans are not in Company archives. A letter from the River Board of 29 July 1958 assures the Company they still own the bed of the canal, its banks and fishing rights.

Electricity

Electricity undertakers pay easements for utilising the towpath.

Dudbridge channel is seen here completed and in water, as part of a scheme to change the canal into the main river. (Photograph by F.W. Rowbotham, 21 June 1957: courtesy of the Environment Agency)

Bond's Mill: the pill box was manned by the Home Guard when Queen Mary visited Sperry's Gyroscope Ltd in 1941. (Courtesy of Peckhams of Stroud)

The Second World War

The Stroudwater Navigation played a small part in the war effort which is worth recording. When war was imminent, an Air Raid Precautions unit was formed at Dudbridge with Mr S.H. Sandling as chief warden. Their first exercise was on 9 August 1939, less than a month before war started on. Two other exercises were recorded: one of them on 13 December 1943, when a fictitious bomb had fallen on Dudbridge canal bridge, which was demolished and four houses destroyed.

As a preparation for war in 1938, shadow factories were being set up for key industries in 'safe areas'. One of them was Stonehouse, so Sperry Gyroscope came to Bond's Mill and a large factory was built for Hoffmans' ball and roller-bearing Company, both very close to the canal. Sperry's formed their own Home Guard unit. The governors of Wycliffe College decided to move the school to Lampeter in Wales when their campus was requisitioned for the Meteorological Branch of the Air Ministry, four days after the outbreak of war. Actually Stonehouse was not hit, but evidence has come to light recently that it was earmarked, when a German aerial photograph was found showing the two factories and the canal.

After the evacuation of Dunkirk, the Home Defence Executive decided a defence plan should be set up with a line of pill boxes (concrete blockhouses) called the GHQ line. Obstructions were built along natural and artificial waterways to make an anti-tank obstacle, with pill-boxes for rifle, machine-gun and anti-tank fire, manned by the Home Guard. 'Stop Line Green' was from Highbridge in Somerset to Stroud, ninety-one miles. Three pill boxes were between Framilode and the A38, one can still be seen from that road beside the canal. Another was at Eastington, and possibly four or five others elsewhere beside the canal or river Frome. Messrs Sperry, being of national importance, had a two-storey box right by the bridge over the canal, and this was an exceptional structure.

In the middle of the war, for about eighteen months, the RAF had a maintenance unit for air-sea rescue launches and other small craft, based at Wycliffe Boathouse on the Gloucester & Berkeley Canal. They had to be kept in tip-top condition ready for immediate service when needed. The stretch of the Stroudwater between the Junction and Walk Bridge was an ideal mooring place for the craft, and the bridge itself was used when an engine was changed. The boat would be placed in the bridge-hole, and a mobile crane parked on the bridge above would lift the engine out and put another in. If pedestrians happened to want to cross, a small boat was at hand to ferry them over.

7

The Canal and Leisure

Canals, although built primarily for commercial interests, have, over the past 200 years or more, become part of the natural landscape, and as such are used for leisure pursuits, especially as in the case of the Stroudwater, where they have a flow of water.

Fishing

Fishing is the most obvious and oldest of the non-commercial activities. The last clause of the 1730 Act deals with the aspect of riparian rights of Lords of Manors or other owners of fishing or fowling in the Stroudwater Navigation. Their rights and privileges were to be reserved to them. As the navigation was not built under this Act, and the 1776 Act was not clear, it became necessary to amend that clause, and Counsel opinion was sought. The preamble given to him in 1782 states:

> *In this new navigable cut is a variety of very fine and large quantities of fish which are taken by any persons who think proper by net angling and other methods and particularly by the owners of land through which the canal is cut who insist that they have a right to the fish therein. The Company of Proprietors on the contrary insist that they alone under the words of the last Act of Parliament are entitled to the fish in this canal and that no other person has any right to fish therein.*

Counsel opined the Company alone was entitled to fish, and the 1730 clause merely meant to preserve old rights, and not to give new ones. As the canal was made by the Proprietors on their own ground, the Lords and other owners had 'no more right to the fish than they would have to those in any private fish pond made by the Owner of an Estate in his own ground.' He thought it reasonable the Proprietors should give notice by advertisement of their intention to prosecute all persons fishing.

Following this decision in 1783, the Company saw an opportunity to cash-in on their fishery, but as the value of it was not ascertained, they would issue tickets at 10*s* per annum. This was not wholly successful because some people were abusing the privileges given by the ticket. In 1785 a warrant was taken out against Samuel Hodges for taking fish, and a Minute ordered that 'no person taking out a ticket for angling in the canal be permitted to take more than one friend with them at one time, and that person must not be an inhabitant of the neighbourhood.' Hodges was fined 5s, but some other people were found fishing in the Company's fish pond near Saul Bridge and prosecuted the next year.

A purchase of fishing nets in October 1781 suggests the Company were harvesting their own fish. A Minute was passed in 1790 that their labourers were to catch fish and dispose of them for the benefit of the Company, and report their produce to the next meeting. Five years later new fishing tackle was bought for the use of the canal as the old lot was worn out.

William Chance, a landowner of Ebley, came near to prosecution in 1790 when he was seen fishing near his own house and he declared he had a right to do so, and would exercise that right whenever he thought proper. The solicitor was instructed to disabuse him, a concession was given by Chance and proceedings to prosecute were dropped. Similarly Mr Hawker, whose family were Proprietors, was also apprehended and acquainted with the Company rights.

The recurrent problem of poisoned fish occurred in 1794 when large quantities were found in several levels below Bristol Road. An advert for a reward of £20 was placed in the *Gloucester Journal* for persons to give evidence sufficient to convict offenders, but it was not taken up. Unfair means of angling by people with tickets was reported, so tickets should in future be issued with the proviso that fishing was to be rod and line only. Even so, destruction of fish continued by trawling and other unauthorised means, the order of 14 October 1783 was rescinded, and tickets discontinued in 1798.

Unlawful fishing continued to take place, both with casting nets and rod and line with occasional prosecutions, until in 1868 it was decided to re-introduce fishing tickets at 2s 6d per annum. They were printed with the words 'Netting not allowed' at the bottom. In 1884 'Not Sundays' was added. Police Sergeant F. Scriven of Stonehouse caught Charles Lewis of Ryeford netting in September 1882 and asked the Company what they wanted to happen. They asked him to take out a summons if he considered it a clear case. The likelihood is that Lewis was let off.

During the period after the canal was closed to navigation, the Company sought to encourage fishing by licence and were at pains to keep stretches in water and clear of vegetation. The Stroud newspaper reported in April 1958 that the Stonehouse & District Angling Club had obtained fishing, boating and bathing rights over nearly three miles of canal waters. They had been stocked with 350 trout by the President, and sixty from Stonehouse Secondary Modern School. The canal company had provided 12,500 rudd and were thanked for help in providing a boat, tools for weeding and a hut. The club committee had worked to clear weeds and build a dam. Local Angling Clubs still rent various stretches at a certain amount per peg per annum. A massive 22lb pike was fished from the canal at Ryeford in September 2002 and was said to be about twenty years old. Fowling has not been known on this canal.

Ballooning

Ballooning seems an unlikely pastime to be associated with canals, but in fact Wallbridge Wharf was the scene of one of the earliest ascents in England. The

Montgolfier brothers sent up the first balloon in public in June 1783 near Lyons, in France. The first manned flight in England was in London in November of that year. James Sadler (1753-1828) of Oxford advertised his ascent to take place in Stroud on 17 October 1785. Crowds gathered, and according to Paul Hawkins Fisher in his *Notes and Recollections of Stroud* too many people turned up to witness the event in the wharf. As a six-year-old he was able to sit on a man's shoulders and watch from a point where later the entrance lodge to Far Hill, the residence of Benjamin Grazebrook, was built. This gave a good view of the wharf below. Other people climbed on houses, but preparations took nearly all day, as Sadler had to make his own gas.

Eventually the balloon went up in the evening and travelled three miles in a quarter of an hour to descend near Stanley Park, the seat of Thomas Pettat Esq. An eloquent report appeared in the *Stroud Journal*. 'The hospitality which has ever marked the character of the environs of Stroud was fully displayed upon this occasion. Handsome cold collations were spread on every board to regale their numerous visitors'. It is believed Sadler retired from ballooning shortly after this for several years, until he made a flight from near Birmingham to Heckington, Lincolnshire, in October 1811, 120 miles in eighty minutes.

Bathing

Swimming, or bathing, is an ancient pastime, but in 1801, Joseph Strutt, author of *The Sports and Pastimes of the People of England*, wrote 'that swimming is by no means so generally practised with us in the present day as it used to be in former times'. Gradually it came back into fashion with the young, and what better place to practise than canals? No undercurrents, weed-free, accessible to all and fairly clean, the Stroudwater was all of these. In August 1806, a Minute, written by an elderly Clerk, states: 'many disorderly persons were seen bathing to the great annoyance of passengers passing along the towing path'. Bills were to be posted on bridges informing such people in future they would be prosecuted. Thomas Watkins was detected bathing one day a year later, and warned he would be prosecuted unless he made a confession. This he duly did and the signed acknowledgement was to be inserted in the *Gloucester Journal* in September 1807.

By 1848 bathing was becoming a public nuisance. (The first public swimming baths were opened in Liverpool in 1828.) Notices were fixed on boards: 'All persons found bathing will be deemed trespassers and punished accordingly'. Such notices were still to be seen well into the twentieth century in places. It was understood to have very little to do with the law. However, the Company did not give up. Before Magistrates W. Capel, R. Winterbotham and R. Wyatt on 6 June 1851, as reported in the *Stroud Free Press*, came William Browne, Henry Chandler, Alfred Wheeler, Charles Stone, Joseph Smith and Augustus Millington, all charged with bathing in the Stroudwater Navigation. They were each fined 7s 6d (a nice little earner for the Company) and warned that in default of payment they would be committed to the Horsley House of Correction for fourteen days.

George William Sibley founded a private school on the Haywardsfield Estate in Stonehouse, which he had bought from the National Provincial Bank, which held it after the bankruptcy of George Ford in 1882. He named the school Wycliffe College, and it soon became renowned for sports activities. After a few months Sibley asked if he could use a portion of the canal on the east side of the Stonehouse & Nailsworth Railway as a bathing place for his pupils. The Company asked a rent of 1s per week, with a special agreement to be drawn up and paid for by Sibley. The spot chosen was just west of the Midland branch line bridge, where the canal was deeper, and formed a suitable pool. Rowing was added to the curriculum soon afterwards.

Elsewhere bathers continued to be a nuisance. Mr Lydeard of Dudbridge complained of boys bathing at Hilly Orchard Bridge on a Sunday evening. This was a favourite place for many years. The Clerk was to seek out a boy named Cook, and caution him. In 1885 a Mr Buckler asked permission for his boys to bathe, the Chairman declined, but the Committee agreed. In the 1890s mention was made of the Stonehouse Polo Club, who were using the canal, and were given a licence for bathing.

No background information has been found concerning a Company who erected bathing huts by the canal in the 1890s. One was by Hilly Orchard Bridge, and had its entrance in full view of passengers on the bridge. This had not been in the agreement, so their solicitor was contacted. In no time the shelter was moved to a less exposed position. Probably as part of that agreement regulations were made about times of bathing. The *Stroud News* and *Gloucestershire County Advertiser* carried

Hilly Orchard, a favourite place for bathing, 1948. (Courtesy of Gloucestershire Record Office)

a case on 22 July 1898 which had been brought before Mr Jenner Davies. Police Sergeant Smith had caught lads bathing on a Sunday morning, out of the appointed hours, and he suggested they were outsiders. His solution was that a charge of one penny should be made on non-residents. Mr Davies said the Chairman of the Company should have power to appoint and pay a man during bathing hours, and the Committee should make a bye-law accordingly.

W.A. Sibley, who had taken over as headmaster of Wycliffe College in 1912, wrote in 1920 to ask if he could build a swimming pool on the west of the boathouse for a small rent. He said the canal was getting muddier, and the enclosure could be concreted or gravelled. It was required for boys learning to swim and easier for them indoors. A gas-engine pump would be used to pump out the water for cleaning. The Company agreed, but the pool was not built. George Loosley, a subsequent head-master who was a pupil in the 1920s, maintained he spent many hours excavating it then, and many more filling it in during the next decade. Canal bathing is strictly forbidden in the twenty-first century on health and safety grounds.

Pleasure Boating

Richard Owen Cambridge, of Whitminster House, a dilettante and friend of Horace Walpole, first introduced pleasure boating to the Stroudwater before the navigation was built. After his marriage in 1741 he settled on his inherited estate, and set about beautifying it. The stream which ran through his grounds, a branch of the Stroudwater, was made navigable for three miles from the river Severn and he used it for conveying building materials. One of his many pursuits was boat designing, and he owned several vessels which were adapted to the Severn. The largest was similar to a Venetian State barge, with a cabin for thirty people decorated with pictures of different types of boats by the marine artist Samuel Scott (c.1710-1772), another friend of Walpole. His domestic servants, not watermen, were deployed to row a twelve-oared barge, but the *pièce de résistance* was a double boat, what we would call a catamaran.

Excursions by canal were undertaken from the end of the eighteenth century onwards, sometimes in fiction, as in C.S. Forester's *Hornblower and the Atropus*. Tales of voyages based on fact include Thomas Love Peacock's *Crochet Castle*, commemo-rating a trip up the Thames with Percy Bysshe Shelley; the *Torrington Diaries* of 1787 by the Hon. John Byny; Sir Richard Colt Hoare's *Journeys Through England & Wales, 1793-1810*; Temple Thurston's *The Flower of Gloster*. All of the writers entered the Thames & Severn Canal at Inglesham, and, with the exception of Shelley who turned back, passed through the Sapperton Tunnel eventually to join the Stroudwater. But *not one* mentions the Stroudwater. The very name Thames & Severn conjures up beauty and romance at a leisurely pace through the Cotswolds, but the Stroudwater, equally picturesque, suggests 'backwater' and was ignored.

Being a commercial waterway, the Stroudwater had very few pleasure boats, and was closed on Sundays anyway. Some local adjacent landowners applied to erect a boathouse. Mr S. Stephens successfully applied for one in 1868, subject to the Surveyor's approval. In 1890 Mr Kimmins connected his boathouse at Ebley with the

A church outing, sailing west near Occupation Bridge, Whitminster, *c*.1916. (Courtesy of H. Beard)

canal without permission, and was informed the charge would be 5*s* per annum. A charge was made for pleasure boats, possibly for the first time, in 1872 of 2*s*, provided they were not powered by steam.

Jerome K. Jerome's *Three Men in a Boat* published in 1889, sparked off a lot of interest in inland waterways for pleasure, and punt or canoe journeys in particular. One honeymoon couple in 1907 travelled around for five weeks by punt, calling at the office in Stroud for a Thames & Severn ticket after spending the previous night at the Junction. Did they buy a Stroudwater ticket at all? Spending the long hot summers living on a houseboat was idyllic for a young girl called Molly Hill Round of Gloucester. She was about twelve years old in 1894 when her family bought the *Nautilus*, which for most of the time was moored on the Gloucester & Berkeley Canal. In her book *This Generous Earth* (1968), written under the name of Hill Field, she recalls not only the *Wave* and the *Lapwing*, but a longboat called *The Girl Pat*, which would call at the Junction and give Molly and her brother a lift up to the next bridge, towed by a donkey. The family who lived and worked on the boat had three children and a black cat.

Sometimes the family would move *Nautilus* to a quiet lay-by on the Stroudwater near Walk Bridge (exactly opposite the spot where this author lived sixty years later). There only an occasional passing donkey-drawn barge would disturb them. Growing on the banks were kingcups, yellow iris, meadow sweet, wild mint and forget-me-nots. Nearby was a withy bed, a damp and swampy haven for water voles and otters. A heron would steal moorhen's eggs, and once there were a dozen bullfinches on the

withy sticks just above the water. They were able to watch dragonflies hatch out, and the swan's three cygnets grow up. Later, as Mrs Fielding, Molly was able to hand on her love of nature and her artistic talent, nurtured by her canal holidays, to her grand-daughter.

In 1953 when the Company was preparing for the Act of Abandonment, an inventory of the boats moored between the Junction and Whitminster Lock was made. There were fourteen cabin cruisers, four in poor condition; eight motor boats, three very bad; six narrowboats; two canoes; two sailing dinghies; two pontoon conversions; two auxiliary yachts; three open boats, one part submerged; one passenger-carrying pleasure boat in poor condition; three houseboats, one of which was the *Glossor* which the Tuckers bought for £250 in 1961 and renamed *Sarah*. She was a butty narrowboat, built on the Grand Union in 1938. Because there was no engine fitted she was difficult to sell, and went for £100 in 1967.

The only boat to use the canal regularly at present is the *Perseverance* used by the Cotswold Canals Trust to run trips between Blunder Lock and Bond's Mill and back. In anticipation of more users when the canal is reinstated, the Company has recently increased the licence fee to £50 per annum.

Above: Molly Round, aged sixteen, is seen here with family and friends on the houseboat *Nautilus*, moored on the Gloucester & Berkeley near Peghouse Bridge when the photograph was taken in c.1897. (Courtesy of D. Bruton)

Opposite: A boathouse at Ebley, perhaps Mr Kimmins', near the site of the old swing bridge, c.1912. (Courtesy of M.A. Handford)

Rowing and Canoeing

In August 1867 a Mr F. Howard applied for and was given permission to use the canal with his canoe. As he was not to draw water by passing through locks, there was no charge. This was early days for the sport of canoeing, which was sparked off by the books of John MacGregor who travelled the waterways in his canoe *Rob Roy*, built to his own design. His Baltic journey was published in 1866. The Royal Canoe Club was established in the same year, and British canoes were shown at the Paris Exhibition in 1867.

Wycliffe College was given permission to use their rowing boat *Maggie* on the canal in 1884. She was very steady, but light, and could carry three persons. Rowing and canoeing were popular pastimes, judging from the number of picture postcards which feature them. In 1887 two and a half acres of land adjacent to the canal opposite the school were leased at £25 per annum and a boathouse erected. The land was then bought for £631 in 1903. By that time the first boathouse had been demolished and replaced by one which would store the boats on dry land. It was built of wood and corrugated iron, with a changing room above. By some miracle this building still stands, although it has suffered some vandalism.

Sculling was introduced as a water sport, but the Stroudwater Navigation became silted up because of decreasing traffic. The school helped by forming the Water Buffaloes, a sort of Boy Scout group who devised ways of dredging and clearing weeds, but they were fighting a losing battle. A new boathouse was built at the Junction on the Gloucester & Sharpness Canal in 1936 and boat activities were transferred. Plans are now afoot for using the Stroudwater site as well.

Wycliffe College boathouse at Stonehouse, *c*.1916. (Courtesy of H. Beard)

The late J.H.A. Anderson, in his book *Stonehouse – A Pot-Pourri*, has an illustration of the Stonehouse Brass Band at Stonehouse Regatta in July 1898. He states that it took place at the Wharf near The Ship inn. That was the Railway Wharf, but what the event entailed or what took place is not known. Mr Tony Pugh of Stonehouse has in his keeping a metal trophy inscribed 'Stonehouse Regatta July 3rd 1897', and on the reverse 'From Ally Slopers Half Holiday'. Mr Pugh found a reference in a newspaper to 'a large concourse of people gathered on the banks of the canal'.

Cycling

Cycling is included in this section, although strictly speaking it is not permitted along the towpath. For many years 'No Cycling' notices were posted, a bye-law almost impossible to enforce. The towpath was, and still is, a quick way to get to work and causes little inconvenience to other users, except on Sunday afternoons when the traditional family walks are disrupted by cyclists who fail to dismount. This situation will be solved when the SECTA (Stonehouse–Eastington Cycle Trail Association) trail, which at present uses the former track of the Stonehouse–Nailsworth Railway, is extended.

By 1895 the pedal-bicycle was being mass-produced in huge numbers, and was very popular with both men and women alike. The Company found it necessary in 1901 to prohibit bicycles on the wharves and towpath. This upset the postmen, to whom this quick method of travel was invaluable. Postmasters from Stonehouse and Stroud asked for special permission for their staff to ride on the towpath, but the Committee put off making a decision. They were in a cleft stick because permission had already been given to two people who wanted to get from Sparrow's Nest Cottage to Ryeford Bridge, and were charged 1*s* per annum. Mr Sibley of Wycliffe College and two ladies were seen riding bicycles in April 1902 between Ebley Mill Bridge and Hilly Orchard. It was resolved to take no action, except to send a letter to the culprits.

Public Houses

The canal did not pass through the main parts of any villages, or Stroud, and as the majority of vessels were day boats and did not have living accommodation or facilities, inns and beerhouses were gradually set up at convenient mooring places on the banks. The Company owned only one such inn, The Ship at Wallbridge Wharf, on their own land. Similarly the Thames & Severn Canal Co. owned The Bell inn at Wallbridge next to their own wharf. The 1884 Ordnance Survey map indicates this was demolished and rebuilt when the Midland Railway connected Stroud with Dudbridge, and access to a station was at that point.

Most of the inns or beerhouses began as private houses, two of them were associated with wharf houses – Bristol Road and Dudbridge – where wives of canal workers would also sell beer or cider for consumption off the premises. The Company permitted this within reason, and often a brewhouse would be included in the rent. Some inns provided shelter for horses, or more usually donkeys, and a

The Victoria Tap at Dudbridge, taken in 1966 just before demolition. (Photograph by C.H.A. Townley: courtesy of J.A. Peden)

small building to the rear of the New Inn at Newtown, on the roadside, is likely to have been a stable. Often, landlords had a day job: William Knee who was a coal merchant at Wallbridge, and had a fleet of boats, worked for the Company as well. Others were coal merchants, smallholders or watermen.

The Ship inn at Framilode was first noticed in a Directory for 1856, when G. Williams was the landlord. It was owned by Stroud Brewery Co. and steps in the bank still give easy access to the canal. Next door was the Bell owned by the Purnell family until it was taken over by Cordwell & Biggs of Hamwell Leaze Brewery, Cainscross about 1900. The Junction inn, better known to locals as The Drum & Monkey, was isolated in the area between Saul Bridge and the Junction, with only a rutty lane connecting it with the village, and was on the offside of the canal. In 1882 the publican, John Clark, applied to have a small boat to take beer to his house and bring empty casks back. Stroud Brewery was to pay 5s per annum for this facility, but if locks were used, the price would be 1s 8d each time.

Another Ship inn was at Stonehouse Cross, a few yards from the bank, with its front to the road, as we remember it. The licensing register of 1891 lists it as a beerhouse, owned by Stroud Brewery. It was demolished in 1997 for road improvements. The Anchor was a beerhouse on Ryeford Wharf, at the end of a row which housed a bakery and cabinet-maker's workshop. Arthur William Brunsdon was the licensee in 1903 when it was a house of Godsell & Sons Brewery of Salmon Springs, Stroud. The Brunsdon family ran a haulage business from the premises well into the twentieth century, and there were substantial pig-sties in the garden. At Newtown, the New Inn was a house, built in a vernacular style very similar to those at Lower Framilode in local brick with dentilation below the eaves. They are about the same date, but not built by the Company. Godsell's were also running the New Inn by 1903, when the landlord was Charles Smith. The Bell was a small, simple beerhouse at Ebley Wharf, owned by Clissold's Brewery of Nailsworth.

Perhaps the best-known pub was the Victoria Tap, a tall brick building beside Foundry Lock at Dudbridge. It kept open until 11.00 p.m., but another good attraction was the daughter of publican James Clarke, Annie, who was born in the house in 1893. It was the haunt of canal workers and boatmen, and men from the gasworks nearby, and at lunchtimes by Marling schoolboys, who would sneak out to the 'Trap' after hiding their blazers and ties in the shrubbery. Tony Jones describes their exploits in the *Trow* (Issue No.60). When one day he noticed the old men grinning and nudging each other, and asked why, they told him Annie had been 'a fine handsome wench' and all the young men 'were round her like wasps round a jam-pot'. They said it was a 'Trap' all right and 'wasn't she lovely bait?' Annie took this with a faint smile and twinkle in her eyes. She never married, but took over the pub by 1939, when it was known as 'Annie's Place'. In 1957 she wrote a letter to the Company asking who owned the road leading to her pub from Gas House Lane. She and her parents had lived in the Victoria for over eighty years and never found out. (It was the only access for deliveries.) The premises were demolished in the 1960s.

For two and a quarter centuries the Stroudwater Navigation has played a vital part in the life of the Stroud valley. Indeed it is a prominent component of the landscape between the river Severn and Stroud, and has become almost a river in its own right. Nevertheless, the role it has played for the last fifty years has been somnambulant.

Now the Company of Proprietors of the Stroudwater Navigation, who have guided the canal through historic times, are to enter a lease with British Waterways Board. The canal will be fully restored between the Junction and Brimscombe Port on the Thames & Severn Canal, where a marina will be constructed. The result will be regeneration for the area, with the emphasis on leisure, although the possibility of commercial use will not be overlooked.

Inevitably, there are opponents; expense is a major factor, but the Company still owns most of the canal land. The main concern is damage to the natural environment. In this respect the Waterways Trust, the body who will administer the project, is overwhelmingly concerned about natural habitats for wildlife.

Suffice to say that when we were taking photographs of the closed-up weir at Ebley in September 2003, on the opposite bank of the river a few yards away a water rail, one of the shyest of birds was quietly feeding, unnoticed by Sunday morning strollers. Only the previous week the location was the scene of intense activity when the canal was being dug out and refilled with water.

Selected Bibliography

Ashworth, Ben. *The Last Days of Steam in Gloucestershire* (Alan Sutton: 1990)

Conway-Jones, Hugh. *The Gloucester & Sharpness Canal: An Illustrated History* (Tempus Publishing: 2003)

Cuss, Edwin and Gardiner, Stanley. *The Stroudwater and Thames & Severn Canals in Old Photographs* (Alan Sutton: 1988)

Cuss, Edwin and Gardiner, Stanley. *The Stroudwater and Thames & Severn Canals: A Second Selection in Old Photographs* (Alan Sutton: 1993)

Fisher, Paul Hawkins. *Notes and Recollections of Stroud* (Alan Sutton: 1986 paperback reprint of 1891 edition)

Gotch, Christopher. *The Gloucester & Sharpness Canal and Robert Mylne* (Privately published: 1993)

Gurney, Ivor. *Poems of Ivor Gurney* (Introduction by Edmund Blunden) (Chatto & Windus: 1973)

Handford, Michael. *The Stroudwater Canal* (Alan Sutton: 1979)

Handford, Michael and Viner, David. *Stroudwater and Thames and Severn Canals: Towpath Guide*. 1st ed. (Alan Sutton: 1984)

Harrison, Crystal (compiler). *Ebley Village: Notes and Poems* (Privately published: 1989)

Household, Humphrey. *The Thames & Severn Canal* (David & Charles: 1969)

Hurd, Michael. *The Ordeal of Ivor Gurney* (OUP: 1990)

Loosley, S.G.H. *Wycliffe College: The First Hundred Years* (Wycliffe College: 1982)

Maggs, Colin G. *The Bristol and Gloucester Railway*. 2nd ed. (Oakwood Press: 1992)

Maggs, Colin G. *The Nailsworth and Stroud Branch* (Oakwood Press: 2000)

McGrath, Patrick. *The Merchant Venturers of Bristol* (The Society of Merchant Venturers, Bristol: 1975)

Mills, Stephen and Riemer, Pierce. *The Mills of Gloucestershire* (Barracuda Books: 1989)

Tann, Jennifer. *Gloucestershire Woollen Mills* (David & Charles: 1967)

Tucker, Joan. *Stroudwater Canal: Heritage Trail*. Series of seven booklets. (originally published by Stroud Civic Society: 1999; republished by Stroud District Council: 2001)

Urdank, Albion M. *Religion and Society in a Cotswold Vale. Nailsworth, Gloucestershire, 1780-1865* (University of California Press: 1990)

Victoria History of the County of Gloucester, Vol. XI: Bisley Hundred (OUP: 1976)

Victoria History of the County of Gloucester, Vol. X: Whitstone Hundred (OUP: 1972)

Viner, David. *The Thames & Severn Canal: History & Guide* (Tempus Publishing: 2002)

Index

Numbers in *italics* indicate illustrations

Selected Waterways Titles
by Tempus Publishing